J. R. R. TOLKIEN:
This Far Land

J. R. R. TOLKIEN:
This Far Land

edited by
Robert Giddings

VISION
and
BARNES & NOBLE

Vision Press Limited
Fulham Wharf
Townmead Road
London SW6 2SB

and

Barnes & Noble Books
81 Adams Drive
Totowa, NJ 07512

ISBN (UK) 0 85478 355 0
ISBN (US) 0 389 20374 2

Printed and bound in Great Britain by
Unwin Brothers Ltd.,
Old Woking, Surrey.
Phototypeset by Galleon Photosetting,
Ipswich, Suffolk.
MCMLXXXIII

Contents

Introduction

by ROBERT GIDDINGS

It is strange, but true, that *The Lord of the Rings* has been very seriously neglected by literary criticism in Britain. Although it has a tremendous cult following here and has been subject to critical exegesis in America, Middle-earth is almost an un-discover'd country through whose bourn few British academics or critics have travelled. The snobbism is curious. On the one hand we have a text read by thousands and thousands of readers, and an author with a cult following; a book perceived as a 'good' book—that is to say, one held to be emphatically the opposite of corrupting, willingly handed over by librarians to young and old and bought by doting aunts for younger relatives; a work broadcast on Radio Four twice recently more or less in its entirety, and turned into a popular animated cartoon film. On the other hand we have the fact that serious literary evaluation of *The Lord of the Rings* has hardly begun here. It has not even been taken up in the school curriculum—it has not been prescribed as a G.C.E. text.

Yet the book must mean something to millions of people. But what does it mean? As Claud Cockburn wrote in *Bestseller: The Books that Everyone Read 1900–72*:

> . . . you cannot deny that if book X was what a huge majority of book-buyers and book-borrowers wanted to buy or borrow in a given year, or over a period of years, then Book X satisfied a need, and expressed and realized emotions and attitudes to life which the buyers and borrowers did not find expressed or realized elsewhere . . . of all indices to moods, and, above all, aspirations, the best-seller list is one of the most reliable.

There is no way of fudging it. What must be asked is what are these needs, emotions and attitudes which *The Lord of the Rings* satisfied, and what is the nature of the moods and the aspirations which this reveals?

*   *   *

An understanding of the need *The Lord of the Rings* was seen to supply may help us to an awareness of the book's real qualities. One thing which it seems clearly to satisfy is the need for a complete, whole and entire world—an environment, which although complex and vast, does make whole, complete and entire sense. The world which Tolkien offers readers is one which they can comprehend within the context of its own laws. Problems are proposed, and difficulties are encountered, but there are, ultimately, answers. Tolkien's world offers the same kind of security as that offered by institutions, say, public schools, colleges, the armed forces, hospitals—self-contained worlds which may exact the cost of certain losses of freedom and individuality, but in which it is possible to negotiate the establishment of identity, gradations, obedience, authority, power. Deeply buried in the structure of *The Lord of the Rings*, it might be argued, is the image of the British traditional school—Gandalf as headmaster, Aragorn as head-boy, with the obviously identifiable prefects, Upper and Lower Shell, fags, and all the ceremony and ritual which holds such a performance together. There are heroes, and there are bounders and cads. *The Lord of the Rings* may be viewed as a discourse through which fundamental categories and relations which constitute the contextual culture we all recognize are denoted and demonstrably manipulated.[1] This is particularly true in Tolkien's portrayal of the power structure, of class relations and the construction of maleness and femaleness.[2] It is here that the verbal texture of the book is so significant.

Although it offers itself to the reader as something which approximates to high literature (it has the length and the trappings of an epic), its syntax and its vocabulary bespeak an antique quality. Several of its characters strain towards assertion of the archetypal—yet it is not actually difficult to read, provided the reader has the staying power required of its many pages. Reading *The Lord of the Rings* can give the illusion of handling 'great literature'—yet it is easy, compared, say, with effort required to accomplish a reading of Henry James, George Eliot, Joseph Conrad or even D. H. Lawrence. *The Lord of the Rings* is like climbing Mount Olympus by escalator. It is a vast province, a colony, an empire, which is easily claimed, explored and conquered. You can *possess* it easily. This is an important element in the Fashion for Tolkien. The fraternity are very possessive. Anyone who has ever written or broadcast anything about the master's work will know that the slightest slip of name, incident or geographical nomenclature will result in massive and often strenuously corrective mail. You have trespassed on the domain. It is very much to the point that the B.B.C.'s *Mastermind* final was won in 1981 by a competitor who had all the information on Middle-earth in his mental retrieval system.

Here lies one of the importances of the style of *The Lord of the Rings*. Its differences from the work of Michael Moorcock, Douglas Hill, David Lindsay, or other masters of fantasy writing, are deeply significant. The fact that it tells its story in that compulsively archaic mode literally makes it more telling. Because the tone of voice is partly scriptural and partly that of a chronicler, the world view gradually assembled in *The Lord of the Rings* seems God-willed, long matured by human experience and the lessons of history. There is a useful analogy to be made here between the way texts operate on the imagination, and the use of images in advertising and publicity. John Berger in *Ways of Seeing* (1972) talks about the effective use publicity images make of classical images which they echo. Does the language of publicity, he asks, have anything in common with that of oil painting, which, until the advent of photography, dominated the European way of seeing for so many centuries? There is a direct continuity, he claims:

> Only interests of cultural prestige have obscured it. At the same time, despite of continuity, there is a profound difference. . . . There are many direct references in publicity to works of art from the past. Sometimes a whole image is a frank pastiche of a well-known painting. Publicity images often use sculptures or paintings to lend allure or authority to their own messages. . . . A work of art 'quoted' by publicity serves two purposes. Art is a sign of affluence; it belongs to the good life; it is part of the furnishing which the world gives to the rich and the beautiful.
>
> But a work of art also suggests a cultural authority, a form of dignity, even of wisdom. . . . The continuity, however, between oil painting and publicity goes far deeper than the 'quoting' of specific paintings. Publicity relies to a very large extent on the

9

language of oil painting. It speaks in the same voice about the same things. . . .

The parallels with the art of Tolkien are fascinating and assist in qualifying the real nature of Tolkien's achievement. [3]

This frequently undervalued aspect of Tolkien's art manifested in *The Lord of the Rings* is his immensely professional ability to provoke very deep echoes in the reader's consciousness which lie immediately beneath the glittering surface structure of his narrative. At its lowest level this is rightly perceived as cheap (if slick) legerdemain, a kind of quality-by-association technique, analogous to the skill used in composing film and T.V. scores which subconsciously remind one of various moments in music by the classical masters and work on the imagination by exploiting these associations. Much of the success of Annigoni portrait-painting was the result of a masterful ability to draw on a massive collection of half-forgotten visual memories of the work of other painters and visually to orchestrate these memories, so as to create a patina or surface quality of Old Masterlyness through which to perceive modern portraits of the world's leading figures. It strikes me that much of Tolkien's success in moving and pleasing and satisfying so many readers is the result of his capacity to manipulate our memories of the classics. This is especially true of those moments in *The Lord of the Rings* where something of an epic kind is required. The battle scenes draw upon memories of Shakespeare and medieval romances. [4] The Edwardian-nostalgic-Georgian qualities of the idyllic landscape of the Shire are to a considerable extent conjured up by association with memories of *The Wind in the Willows* and Matthew Arnold's *The Scholar Gipsy*, vaguely recalled from school English lessons. Rural nostalgia is a powerful magnetic pull in the British suburbanite ideology and links up with yearnings for unspoiled romantic innocence with an almost universal appeal. [5] In Tolkien's case the feelings were personal and very deep, as the Thames and the county landscape he loved so much became by a curious accident of industrial development one of the centres of British motor manufacturing. It is usually the case in advanced capitalism that the life enjoyed by the privileged élite and the means of production needed to produce the wealth to support it are kept separate and discrete. In Tolkien's experience the two collided. Oxford meant not only the Thames valley, dreaming spires, college life, but also Cowley, Morris motors and all that mass production industry involves. In Tolkien the situation was at once personal, but with a huge general appeal. The conclusion of Frodo's epic endeavours certainly affects readers, because Tolkien is able to remind you at all sorts of levels of translations of Greek heroic myths read in childhood and of the more rhapsodic sections of Tennyson's version of the passing of Arthur. In his cosy insularity and undying enthusiasm for the cult of the past—not the immediate past, but a past well beyond the Renaissance—Tolkien tuned in to a very powerful frequency in British ideology. It is claimed that urban dislocation has created a passion for local history and archaeology which may be evidenced by enrolment at evening classes all over the country. Figures show that more people want to study archaeology and local history in adult education courses than want to study English literature, politics, economics and sociology. Professor W. G. Hoskins's two television series on the history of the English landscape were followed by an average audience for each programme of 1,000,000 viewers in 1976 and 1978. For those who do not share much of an affinity with the Middle-earth cult it is all too easy to dismiss the wearing of the home-made armour and the Queen Guinevere outfits, the half-jokey half-sincere adoption of Middle-earth names, the various 'moots', etc. as so much silly display behaviour, but these are all significant pieces of evidence of very deeply held beliefs about the nation and its history which have surfaced at a period of great uncertainty and anxiety.

The Lord of the Rings persistently strikes chords in its readers, which set up very powerful sympathetic resonances which Tolkien harmonizes and develops, often using themes from very well-known sources, familiar to us all. This is basic professionalism in the skill of mass communication. The obvious parallel is the successful politician, who is able to detect what the public is thinking, what it fears, what it aspires to, and is able to articulate views and opinions already widely in circulation. The politician then proceeds to tell the public what it wants to hear.

This is one important aspect of Tolkien's art, which is amply demonstrated in *The Lord of the Rings*. It is the art of the demagogue transferred to authorship and developed to the height of genius. It is impressive that Tolkien's imagination functions simultaneously at several levels, operating on the readers' deep need for consolation and assurance that the world need not change, exploiting nationalist paranoia and in a world of complex and baffling materialistic problems, political and economic, supplying spiritual and 'other worldly' answers to intractable mundane questions. It is characteristic of *The Lord of the Rings* that the surface quality of its medievalism, its consciously harking back to the chivalrous past, its 'Northerness' and all the accoutrements of its cult, should be little more than skin deep, and its real subject matter should be modern.

It is essentially a modern phenomenon. As a commodity it is a product of the age of mass publication. *The Lord of the Rings* became a massive best-seller in an age of the mass production of books. Two thirds of all the books ever published were published after 1950.[6] It was written at the direct request of its publisher, rather than at the promptings of the relentless pressures of its author's own inspiration.[7] It was hyped by all the methods of advertising and public relations possible at the time. A very large proportion of its success is obviously the result of its author's ability to reach into deeper recesses of the collective minds of its readership. For all its talk of the 'ominous and disquieting' Evil Powers released upon the world, being driven out by the White Council, all the references to Mordor and the Dark Tower 'from where the power was spreading far and wide', in the face of all the dwarfs, knights, hidden kings, turrets, battles, banners, funeral pyres, wizards and orcs—the anxieties and tensions are modern ones and beneath the top dressing of its self-conscious medievalism its world is our world, or, rather, it is the world as perceived by Tolkien's readers. In *The Lord of the Rings* the evil striven against seems to have been disembodied and then to have gone on and infected other people and other creatures. Some creatures are damned beyond recall, nothing whatever could be done to save them. The orcs, for example, are totally irredeemable. The evil in the world as portrayed by Tolkien has nothing whatever to do with social or economic causes. It is evil, pure and simple. Consequently there is no need for change of socio-economic conditions, the environmental conditions of life, relations between different classes, etc., etc.—all these things which make up the very fabric of a society, of *any* society, are perceived by Tolkien as totally beyond any need or possibility of change. As Bob Dixon comments:

> The effect of this kind of literature, as with tract literature, is to divert people from the here and now and persuade them that it's not possible to do anything about the problems of the world. Of course, some people find this a very comforting thought. . . . *The Lord of the Rings* isn't an allegory but of course it does have a meaning. It says something. It says a lot of things about power and hierarchy. [8]

Class relationships are vividly portrayed in *The Lord of the Rings*. Tolkien's lower orders are fairly efficient in being deferential to their betters. The strong implication is always present that this is all part of an immutable plan for the world.

Another deep chord which *The Lord of the Rings* struck in its readers which set up long sounding sympathetic resonances was the conspiracy theory. It is interesting that the great success of Tolkien's epic has been coincidental with the cult of James Bond, [9] the fashion for Len Deighton and John le Carré, which collectively form such a revealing aspect of Cold War ideology. The author of *The Lord of the Rings* believed that its success was without explanation. It was just a matter of personal taste. W. H. Auden claimed that 'Nobody seems to have a moderate opinion, either people find it a masterpiece of its genre, or they cannot abide it.' The word genre is a useful clue. Tolkien created a work which locates itself in a long tradition which has always had a great pull for English readers—the conspiracy story. A foreign power is plotting to invade/ overthrow/destroy this green and pleasant land. . . . As Roland Barthes put forward, a book may often mean something to its readers which was not deliberately intended by its author, and there is a close analogy between fashion and literature which may both be seen as homeostatic systems:

> . . . that is to say, systems whose function is not to communicate an objective, external meaning which exists prior to the system

but only to create a functioning equilibrium, a movement of signification.[10]

Stories which detail the intentions of a wicked power to take over the world, or to invade the island homeland of the British, or to work for the overthrow of democracy as we know it, etc. have continually exerted a deep fascination for English readers since industrial and colonial rivalries created the tensions in international relations which found expression in Bismarck's foreign policy and the whole network of secret diplomacy which laid the foundations of the First World War and the apparently never ending international unease which is the legacy enjoyed by succeeding generations.

Robert Erskine Childers published *The Riddle of the Sands* in 1903 after a yachting expedition to the German coast. It purported to portray the fiendish cunning of the Germans in secretly planning for war. German ambitions he wrote, were perverted by two principles,

> perfect organization: perfect secrecy. . . . Germany is pre-eminently fitted to undertake an invasion of Great Britain. She has a great army . . . in a state of high efficiency, but a useless weapon, as against us, unless transported over seas. She has a peculiar genius for organization. . . . She has a small navy, but very effective for its purpose. . . . She has little to lose and much to gain. . . .[11]

The hero of *The Riddle of the Sands* actually sees with his own eyes an experimental rehearsal of a great scene:

> to be enacted, perhaps, in the near future—a scene when multitudes of sea-going lighters, carrying full loads of soldiers . . . should issue simultaneously, in seven ordered fleets, from seven shallow outlets, and, under escort of the Imperial Navy, traverse the North Sea and throw themselves bodily upon English shores. . . . recent as are the events I am describing, it is only since they happened that the possibility of an invasion by Germany has become a topic of public discussion.[12]

In 1909 the play *An Englishman's Castle* was performed at Wyndham's Theatre. It was written by Guy du Maurier, brother of the actor, Sir Gerald du Maurier. In substance it is a piece of national paranoia which portrays the homeland a victim to foreign invaders. Joseph Conrad's *The Secret Agent* had only recently bodied forth the idea that the enemy was already amongst us and had projected the vision of 'an anarchist haunted London', in Terry Eagleton's phrase.[13] 'Criminal aliens'—'anarchists', etc.—provided ideal news-copy for the sensational press during the Tottenham Affair of 1910 and the panic caused by the Siege of Sidney Street in 1911. Some desperadoes, described by the police as 'anarchists', shot their way out of a house in Houndsditch. Three police-men were killed. A police raid at another house revealed the body of an armed man as well as guns and ammunition, some oil paints and a painting signed 'Peter'. Such were the origins of the saga of 'Peter the Painter'—which ended in Sidney Street, Stepney, in January 1911 and involved 750 police, a detachment of Scots Guards, two field guns, machine guns and the personal appearance of Mr. Winston Churchill, the then Home Secretary. A bill was put before Parliament in favour of new expatriation orders aimed at foreigners. H. H. Munro's pro-war fantasy *When William Came* was published in the year the First World War started, and portrayed Britain conquered and occupied by the armies of Kaiser Wilhelm II.[14]

The second year of the war saw the U-boat blockade of Britain, the attack on the Dardanelles, the first use of Chlorine gas by the Germans at the Battle of Ypres, the sinking of the *Lusitania*, the execution of Edith Cavell, the collapse of the Russian war effort and the publication of John Buchan's *The Thirty-Nine Steps*. Buchan captured exactly the mood of the readers of the day. In his autobiography Claud Cockburn describes how middle-class families of the time actually expected the German conspiracy to come to fruition any day and that they would see German troops in the street: 'Guests came to lunch and talked about the coming German invasion', he says.

> On Sundays, when my sister and I lunched in the dining room instead of the nursery, we heard about it. It spoiled afternoon walks on the hills with Nanny. . . . I thought Uhlans with lances and flat-topped helmets might come charging over the hill any afternoon. . . . It was frightening, and a harrassing responsibility, since Nanny and my sister had no notion of the danger.[15]

The essential delusion of this invasion paranoia is supported by the fact that if there were plans for war and invasion, it might well seem that Germany was the beleaguered nation. In 1910 British defence estimates reached £68,000,000, France's reached £52,000,000 and Russia's £7,000,000. Germany's was £64,000,000 and Austria's £17,000,000. Great Britain had fifty-six battleships in commission and under construction, Germany had thirty-three. By 1914 defence estimates in Britain had reached £76,800,000 and France's topped £57,400,000. Germany's reached £110,800,000. Britain had nineteen Dreadnoughts and thirty-nine pre-Dreadnoughts. Germany had thirteen Dreadnoughts and twenty-two pre-Dreadnoughts. The naval expenditure of Germany's potential foes exceeded her own expenditure and that of Austria in the decade prior to the outbreak of war by £461,986,392. Taking military and naval expenditure together, Russia and France had between them spent £229,868,853 more than Germany and her ally on armaments in the period 1905–14.

John Buchan wrote in the dedication to his classic novel of German espionage in these days: 'The wildest fictions are so much less improbable than the facts.' The facts would seem to suggest that it was Germany who was threatened. At the end of the Second World War, when German Foreign Office and military archives were captured and sorted and analysed it was revealed that as late as 1914 there were no plans for an invasion of Britain. In 1914 Bertrand Russell wrote of the 'universal reign of fear' which had caused the system of alliances, 'believed to be a guarantee of peace', which was proving to be a cause of world wide disaster,[16] despite the undisputed fact that with the single exception of a guerrilla war against a Hottentot tribe in South West Africa, Germany had been at peace since the Franco-Prussian War.

Nevertheless, the strength and the fascination of the conspiracy myth continued. From the early days of the 1914 War, right up to 1939, spy stories proved successful mass entertainment provided by the film industry—*I Was a Spy*, *The Man Who Knew Too Much*, *The Thirty-Nine Steps*, *Lancer Spy*, *The Spy in Black*, *Dark Journey*, *British Agent*, *Secret Agent*, *The Lady Vanishes*, *Espionage Agent*, *Confessions of a Nazi Spy*—all seemed to play to a powerful public demand. Hitchcock's version of Buchan's yarn (1935) is a fine example of the genre. It seems he had not even read the original[17] and played to the fears of the time by having baddies talk with upper-class Mosleyite accents. He even wished to insert a whole new sequence showing the underground hangars in the Highlands of Scotland built by the cunning Huns for our destruction.[18]

During the Second World War espionage drama boomed and included *Foreign Correspondent, Night Train to Munich, Casablanca, The Conspirators, They Came to Blow Up America, Berlin Correspondent, Across the Pacific, Escape to Danger, Ministry of Fear, Continental Agent, Sherlock Holmes and the Secret Weapon, Hotel Reserve.* To reveal that the villains were really enemy agents was an oft repeated trick in films of this kind, especially in comedy thrillers.[19]

In the immediate post-war years two new fashions in spy films became noticeable.[20] With the introduction of the new leading figure, downbeat, neurotic, guilt-torn, often seedy heroes made their appearances for the first time—*Orders to Kill, Hotel Berlin*—while there also appeared the now-it-can-be-told story—*The Man Who Never Was, Diplomatic Courier.* In the opening decade of the Cold War Nazis and Japs were dethroned in favour of 'Reds'—*I Married a Communist, I Was A Communist for the F.B.I.* The mania for spy films spilled over into comedies and gave the world *Gasbags* (with the Crazy Gang), *To Be or Not to Be* (with Jack Benny), *Top Secret* (with George Cole), and, ultimately, *Carry on Spying.* The romantic spy figure re-emerges in the late '50s and reaches his box-office apotheosis in the James Bond films, beginning with *Dr. No* in 1963. The film version of Richard Condon's assassination-conspiracy thriller, *The Manchurian Candidate*, was released the previous year, but Fleming's novels fully exploited the world conspiracy theory. Bond clearly owed a great deal to Bulldog Drummond and the Fu Manchu stories, but their avid consumerism, sexism and technological obsession mark them unmistakably a product of their moment.[21] Imitations of Bond were legion and all the leading male stars attempted the genre—Cary Grant in *Charade*, Paul Newman in *Torn Curtain*, Frank Sinatra in *The Naked Runner*, Yul Brynner in *The Double Man* and Robert Vaughn starred in a James Bond-derived American television series, *The Man From U.N.C.L.E.* which lasted from 1964 to 1967. British television series such as *The Avengers* and *The Professionals* further testify to the tenacity of the genre.

17

Star Wars (1977) was a science fantasy revamp of the same old yarn. Invariably the leading ingredients of these narratives feature a plot by a sinister gang who work for a 'power'—another nation/galaxy/aliens, etc.—an informer on the good side tells the hero, whose integrity is tested and whose task is therefore defined. Post-war fears of Soviet Russia gave *The Lord of the Rings* an amazingly powerful resonance as Tolkien's epic cued itself so smoothly into a long loved archetypal pattern.

The world-view constructed in current Reagànite foreign policy involved a re-awakening to the Soviet 'threat' and the spread of the belief in the Soviet world conspiracy. In Ronald Reagan's own words about the Vietnam War:

> I think we were right to be involved. The problems in South Vietnam weren't just internal affairs, and we weren't there because we were imperialistic, as the communists claimed, or altruistic, as we tried to appear. The plain truth of the matter is that we were there to counter the master plan of the communists for world conquest, and it's a lot easier and safer to counter it 8,000 miles away than to wait until they land in Long Beach.[22]

The view through this transatlantic refraction recently prompted E. P. Thompson to say that it was based on infantile perceptions of political realities:

> derived, I suppose, from too much early reading of *The Lord of the Rings*. The evil kingdom of Mordor lies there . . . while on our side lies the nice republic of Eriador, inhabited by confused liberal hobbits who are rescued from time to time by the genial white wizardry of Gandalf figures such as Henry Kissinger, Zbigniew Brzezinski, or, maybe, Richard Allen.

Now although a devout Tolkien fanatic would attempt to pick holes in Thompson's comment by indicating his poor Middle-earth scholarship—Eriador is hardly a republic, it was at one time ruled by the Kings of Arnor; the Hobbits' Shire is but one small region of Eriador and is to some extent a self-governing democratic republic of sorts; Mordor is not a kingdom, etc., etc.—the fact remains that he does seem to be describing a world view in which one kind of Manichaeism invokes another. This is the essential nature of the struggles which convulse Middle-earth.[23]

All texts signify, but not all texts are significant. It seems to me that insofar as *The Lord of the Rings* shapes, textures and conditions the nature of our perceptions of the world we live in, insofar as it is used in negotiating the construction of our realities, then it is extremely significant. It is frankly an impossibility to regard it simply and purely as a fine piece of writing, devoid of political, economic or ideological significance. It cannot be regarded simply as an arrangement of sounds, in spite of some of its advocates who seem anxious so to describe it.[24] It is in the nature of Tolkien's genius that he took an old war-horse like the conspiracy yarn and threw over it a certain medieval charm, decorated lavishly with the trappings of chivalric romance, decked it out with his unique wit and sent it charging out armed with an unmistakable theological force which seemed to identify itself with quite respectable blazonry. This again demonstrates Tolkien's skill in drawing on deep reservoirs of experience which we seldom recognize while reading the words on the page. Yet it is those unconscious hardly identified textual echoes which reinforce the seeming inevitability and God-willed plan for the world which is at the heart of *The Lord of the Rings*, and renders the 'common sense' world of Tolkien (in Gramsci's phrase) in terms of scriptural authority.[25] Tolkien seems to share a world-view with Evelyn Waugh, a writer he is not usually linked with, but, as David Lodge has pointed out, Waugh accepts the doctrine of original sin and with it the sense of mankind as exiled from a lost Paradise. The Faith is perceived as a haven, an institution under providential guidance in a world where civilization has fallen into decline. These ideas constantly recur in Waugh,[26] even if satirically: *A Handful of Dust* takes its title from Eliot's *The Waste Land* and accepts Eliot's view of modern times, but the basis of the narrative is sexual betrayal, which is basic in the raw kind of Christian mythology Waugh adopted. The New Jerusalem appears to Tony Last during the hallucinations of his fever. Sexual betrayal, the decadence of modern times, and the operation of divine grace are likewise the basis of *Brideshead Revisited*. In a review of Graham Greene's *The Lawless Roads* in the *Spectator* of 10 March 1939 Evelyn Waugh wrote:

> Mr. Greene is, I think, an Augustinian Christian, a believer of the dark age of Mediterranean decadence when the barbarians

were passing along the frontiers and the City of God seemed yearly more remote and unattainable.

In the *Sunday Times* of 16 July 1961 he wrote that for P. G. Wodehouse 'there has been no fall of man. . . . the gardens of Blandings Castle are that original garden from which we are all exiled.' The description of Tony Last's deranged vision in the Brazilian jungle is worth careful regard:

> Looking up from the card table, Tony saw beyond the trees the ramparts and battlements of the City; it was quite near him. From the turret of the gatehouse a heraldic banner floated in the tropic breeze . . . the sound of music rose from the glittering walls; some procession or pageant was passing along them. . . . The gates were before him and trumpets were sounding along the walls, saluting his arrival; from bastion to bastion the message ran to the four points of the compass; petals of almond and apple blossom were in the air; they carpeted the way, as, after a summer storm, they lay in the orchards at Hetton. Gilded cupolas and spires of alabaster shone in the sunlight.[27]

Of course Waugh writes as a satiric ironist, and the imitation of Bunyan and *Revelations* are almost carried to the level of parody.[28]

In *The Lord of the Rings* it is all played straight, played for all it is worth, and is spread over several pages of highly wrought prose.[29] *The Return of the King* moves slowly to its climax:

> And so they stood on the walls of the City of Gondor, and a great wind rose and blew, and their hair, raven and golden, streamed out mingling in the air. And the Shadow departed, and the Sun was unveiled, and light leaped forth; and the waters of Anduin shone like silver, and in all the houses of the City men sang for the joy that welled up in their hearts from what source they could not tell. . . .

After the appearance of the great Eagle bearing tidings from the Lords of the West which cause the people to sing in all ways of the City, it begins to grow and build up in the manner of a Rossini crescendo:

> The days that followed were golden, and Spring and Summer joined and made revel together in the fields of Gondor. And tidings now came by swift riders from Cair Andros of all that was done, and the City made ready for the coming of the King. . . .

The prose now takes on a rather self-conscious antique glint and moves with stilted syntax reminiscent of the King James Bible:

> All things were now made ready in the City; and there was great concourse of people, for the tidings had gone out into all parts of Gondor, from Min-Rimmon even to Pinnath Gelin and the far coasts of the sea; and all that could come to the City made haste to come. And the City was filled again with women and fair children that returned to their homes laden with flowers; and from Dol Amroth came the harpers that harped most skilfully in all the land; and there were players upon viols and upon flutes and upon horns of silver, and clear-voiced singers from the vales of Lebennin.
>
> At last an evening came when from the walls the pavilion could be seen upon the field, and all night lights were burning as men watched for the dawn. And when the sun rose in the clear morning above the mountains in the East, upon which shadows lay no more, then all the bells rang, and all the banners broke and flowed in the wind. . . .

The great moment arrives and Aragorn shows himself:

> But when Aragorn arose all that beheld him gazed in silence, for it seemed to them that he was revealed to them now for the first time. Tall as the sea-kings of old, he stood above all that were near; ancient of days he seemed and yet in the flower of manhood; and wisdom sat upon his brow, and strength and healing were in his hands, and a light was about him.

As Faramir cries 'Behold the King!', at that moment

> all the trumpets were blown, and the King Elessar went forth and came to the barrier . . . and amid the music of harp and of viol and of flute and the singing of clear voices the King passed through the flower-laden streets, and came to the Citadel, and entered in; and the banner of the Tree and the Stars was unfurled upon the topmost tower. . . .

What is important here is the effect of applying the imprimatur of almost divine revelation upon a set of values and social assumptions implicit if not explicit throughout *The Lord of the Rings* which are well worth exploring and deserve properly to be questioned.

J. R. R. Tolkien: This Far Land

NOTES

1. Cf. Paul Bouissac, 'The Meaning of Nonsense', in Ino Rossi (ed.), *The Logic of Culture: Advances in Structural Theory and Methods* (London: Tavistock, 1982), pp. 202–3, for an hypothesis similar to the meta-cultural phenomena I am trying to identify in *The Lord of the Rings*. See also Janet Wolff, *Aesthetics and the Sociology of Art* (London: Allen & Unwin, 1983), pp. 49 and following.
2. See Lucy Bland, Trisha McCabe and Frank Mort, 'Sexuality and Reproduction: Three "Official" Instances', in Michele Barrett, Philip Corrigan, Annette Kuhn and Janet Wolff (eds.), *Ideology and Cultural Production* (London: Croom Helm, 1979), pp. 78 and following; and cf. Naomi Weisstein, 'Psychology Constructs the Female', in *The Norton Reader: An Anthology of Expository Prose*, edited by Arthur M. Eastman (New York: Norton & Co., 1973), pp. 1010 and following. See Kenneth Plummer, *Sexual Stigma: An Interactionist Account* (London, 1975), pp. 5–8 and 23 and following, and P. L. Berger, *Invitation to Sociology: A Humanist Perspective* (London: Penguin, 1966), pp. 180 and following: 'Sexual roles are constructed within the same general precariousness that marks the entire social fabric. Cross cultural comparisons of sexual conduct bring home to us powerfully the near flexibility that men [sic] are capable of in organizing their lives in this area. . . .'
3. John Berger, *Ways of Seeing* (London: Penguin/B.B.C., 1972), pp. 134–37.
4. Robert Giddings and Elizabeth Holland, *J. R. R. Tolkien: The Shores of Middle-earth* (London: Junction Books, 1981), pp. 58, 62, 63, 94–8, 138–39, 230–31.
5. See Christopher Caudwell, *Illusion and Reality* (New York: International Publishers, 1973), pp. 125–27; Raymond Williams, *The Country and the City* (London: Paladin, 1975), pp. 18 and following; and cf. Robert Giddings, 'A Myth Riding By', in *New Society*, 7 December 1978, and Richard Norton Taylor, *Whose Land is it Anyway?—Agriculture, Planning and Land Use in the British Countryside* (Northamptonshire: Turnstone Press, 1983), pp. 269 and following. The destruction of the unique character of the British countryside is the subject of Marion Shoard's provoking book, *The Theft of the Countryside* (London: Temple Smith, 1980). The contemporary fascination with the past is discussed on pp. 178 and following.
6. George H. Ford (ed.), *Victorian Fiction: A Second Guide to Research* (New York: Modern Language Association of America, 1978), p. 34.
7. See Robert Giddings and Elizabeth Holland, op. cit., pp. 7–9.
8. Bob Dixon, *Catching Them Young: Political Ideas in Children's Fiction* (London: Pluto Press, 1978), p. 149.
9. See Umberto Eco, 'The Narrative Structure in Fleming', in Tony Bennett and Graham Martin (eds.), *Popular Culture: Past and Present* (London: Croom Helm, 1982), pp. 242–62.
10. Roland Barthes, *Essais Critiques* (Paris, 1964), p. 156, in *Critical Essays* (Northwestern University Press, 1972); see also Diana Laurenson and

22

Introduction

Alan Swingewood, *The Sociology of Literature* (London: Paladin, 1972), pp. 11–12; and Pierre Macherey, *A Theory of Literary Production*, translated by Geoffrey Wall (London: Routledge and Kegan Paul, 1978), pp. 32–40.

11. Erskine Childers, *The Riddle of the Sands* (London: Penguin, 1978), pp. 320–21.

12. Childers, op. cit., pp. 304–5.

13. Terry Eagleton, 'Form, Ideology and "The Secret Agent" ', in Diana Laurenson (ed.), *The Sociology of Literature: Applied Studies* (University of Keele: Sociological Review Monograph, 1978), p. 55.

14. J. B. Priestley, *The Edwardians* (London: Heinemann, 1970), p. 88.

15. Claud Cockburn, *Cockburn Sums Up* (London: Quarto, 1981), pp. 1–2.

16. E. D. Morel, *Truth and the War* (London: National Labour Press, 1916), pp. 161 and following.

17. *Grierson on the Movies*, edited by Forsyth Hardy (London: Faber, 1981), p. 165.

18. John Russell Taylor, *Hitch: The Life and Work of Alfred Hitchcock* (London: Faber, 1978), p. 129; see also K. R. M. Short (ed.), *Feature Films as History* (London: Croom Helm, 1981), p. 103.

19. *Halliwell's Filmgoer's Companion*, 7th edition (London: Granada, 1980), p. 616.

20. Ibid.

21. Robert Blair Kaiser, 'The Case is Still Open', in Peter Dale Scott, Paul L. Hoch and Russell Stetler (eds.), *The Assassinations: Dallas and Beyond: A Guide to Cover-Ups and Investigations* (New York: Vintage, 1976), pp. 330–31.

22. *Ronald Reagan's Call to Action* (New York: Warner, 1976), p. 40.

23. 'America's Europe: A Hobbit Among Gandalfs', in *Nation*, 24 January 1981. I am indebted to Jessica Yates of the Tolkien Society for bringing this to my attention.

24. This was the claim made in a radio broadcast by Humphrey Carpenter. In conversation with Michael Oliver he said: 'You must remember that Tolkien's professional work was concerned really with, technically at least, with language rather than with literature and really all his literary academic work, his edition of *Sir Gawain and the Green Knight*, his lectures on *Beowulf* and on the *Ancrine Wisse*, and things like that, these are almost thrown off by a detailed study of the language so the academic work gets spun from the language, now so did the imaginative writings. He often said that he found it hard to convince people that *The Lord of the Rings* had really grown from a wish to express certain aesthetic linguistic preferences, by which he meant he wanted to create a world in which it was possible for certain sounds to exist. Now those sounds exist in fact, manifest themselves in his books as the various elvish language is spoken by elves in the stories and they are the centre of it, he began to make up these languages when he was in his teens and the language has developed so much and so fast they required a history and a habitation so again it was the imaginative writing that sprang from the language' (*Kaleidoscope*, B.B.C. Radio Four, 2 January 1981).

25. *Selections from the Prison Notebooks of Antonio Gramsci*, edited and translated by Quintin Hoare and Geoffrey Nowell Smith (London: Lawrence and Wishart, 1971), pp. 326 and following.
26. David Lodge, *Working With Structuralism* (London: Routledge and Kegan Paul, 1981), pp. 136 and following.
27. Evelyn Waugh, *A Handful of Dust* (London: Penguin, 1983), p. 203.
28. Cf. John Bunyan, *The Pilgrim's Progress* (London: Penguin, 1976), pp. 202 and following, and the *Bible Designed to be Read as Literature*, edited and arranged by Ernest Sutherland Bates (London: Heinemann, 1963), pp. 1224 and following.
29. J. R. R. Tolkien, *The Lord of the Rings, 3. The Return of the King* (London: Unwin Paperbacks, 1974), pp. 212 and following.

1

Gentility and Powerlessness: Tolkien and the New Class

by FRED INGLIS

1

The old, round way of dealing with bestsellers of Tolkien's magnitude was to *assume* that with the advent of mass produced literature came the debility of taste, and that if anyone sold enormous numbers of books then there must be something wrong with the books, because it was a datum of interpretation that mass taste was degraded. Q. D. Leavis, famously and polemically, made this position methodical in *Fiction and the Reading Public*, and given that she was of a view that her version of practical criticism afforded her a unique and transhistorical exemption from the little local difficulties of historicity, she was able to vindicate her judgements merely by quoting shrewdly from the bad books to hand, leaning on the solidarity of *Scrutiny*, and waiting for laughs. Well, in the case of her victims—H. M. Tomlinson, Edgar Rice Burroughs, Ethel M. Dell, Marie Corelli, and the company of those writers whose characters went in so much for country-house weekends and bouncing about on tiger-skin divans—laughter was the best criticism. When we turn to the grislier manifestations of today's bestsellers, to the headless horrors, monster vermin, and lavish suppurations of *The Dark*, *The Fog*, *The Shining*, and other extra-meteorological goings-on, then the laughter is likely, as novelists used to say, to die on your lips. Either way, however, the old method stands: quote the enemy, and say, how awful.

It is a notorious truth that Mrs. Leavis's method—which really *was* a method, with a full-blown conceptual framework and clear, usable criteria of relevance and conclusiveness—led amongst its successful practitioners to a deeply priggish and supercilious self-righteousness, tremendously helped out by the readiness with which literary commentators from the other ancient university lacking the privileges of Fenland election so reliably convicted themselves of the offences Mrs. Leavis most condemned as venal, or cardinal, or worse. But it is also true that what she identified as pretentious, snobbish, self-deluding, feebly consolatory, philistine, and grossly sentimental, was all these not very dreadful things, and sometimes worse. Today, faced with the tidal wave of cultural effluent from the grislier channels of video technology, one can only think ruefully, as the next generation always does, 'never such innocence again'.

Although her particular method in the human sciences had its inevitably ideological distortions inscribed in its premises, what concerns us is less these peculiarities of that English-woman, and more the fact that she saw clearly that in order to validate her judgements, both on the novelists and on the culture, she had to provide both a speculative psychology and a theory of cultural production—however little she would have recognized her own endeavour under these headings. That is, to give an explanation of why the *Tarzan* books sold as they did, she had, first, to identify in mass industrial society the market conditions which lent themselves to the Taylorized production of literature at high speed, low unit-costs, simple interchangeability of parts, and easy emulation by a range of socially differentiated producers and products. Secondly, she had to theorize a homology of feeling, purpose, and motive between the product designers (novelists and publishers) and their consumer audience. In a categorial framework and with a critical vocabulary surprisingly like that of the Frankfurt Institute then (1920s) at work on the same problems,[1] she and her consorts in the early volumes of *Scrutiny* (notably Denys

Thompson) sketched a model of the modern man and woman whose identity-formation, wounded and etiolated by being cut off from the language and the belief of their pre-agrarian parents, starved by lack of any creative work, and homeless and friendless in the waste land of industrial townscape, sought its emotional life 'at the novelist's expense' in a fantasy world (swear word) whose emotional gratifications (ditto) compensated for (school-teacher's report judgement) the emptiness of everyday life (guerrilla slogan).

Naturally enough such a view commits its holder to seeking election to one of two élites: in the first, the élitist in her dugout battles for a better world by warrening the enemy's position from end to end (the Left); in the second, the élitist takes to the hills from which he may look down upon the cities of the plain, the deturpation within, and the beast slouching roughly along which will make a good riddance of the awful human beings down there (the Right). It is a conclusion printed out from the premises of the second position that there is no remedial action that can be taken; people just are, as Beckett puts it in Estragon's mouth, 'bloody ignorant apes', and all anyone can do is discover like-minded subjectivities in the mass of the population, and rescue them for life in the ivory tower up in the hills.

It is the first form of action, deriving variously from one reading of *Fiction and the Reading Public*, but much more broadly and strongly from the well-known tradition of a post-Romantic and neo-socialist dissent from industrial-finance capitalism in which Morris and Ruskin are the earliest English names, which has been the ground for the most recent and tolerably impressive advances in the human and cultural sciences.[2] Its practitioners have acceded, certainly, to the judgement that industrial-finance capitalism has produced (*sic*) some horrible, much trivial, and a portion of distinctly evil cultural expressions. But it is all too clearly the merest cowardice masquerading as hauteur which dismisses so much of the culturally expressive and imaginative life of the times. Not only that. If these are human *sciences* that we profess, then such dismissal by definition refuses the understanding which is presumably cognate with science.

These preliminaries are a necessary part of an essay in what

27

Raymond Williams has happily called 'cultural materialism'.[3] But in nominating this as a field of inquiry whose very designation announces certain absolute presuppositions, it is worth repeating that the political echoes of such a name recall that politics as a subject has at its best combined a proper understanding with a picture of how the good life may yet be lived in the future. Practising a politics of literature is very far from refusing judgement, but judgement itself is only crassly the business of attaching a tick or a cross to the subject in hand, and very much more the reflexive determination of plausible meanings, meanings which can only be what they are in a field and for a class of subjects.[4]

This rather fearsome-sounding vocabulary is the speech of hermeneutics, a long-standing discipline which intends no more than the interpretation of texts according to their assurance or congruence with the human resource of meaning. It sorts well enough with the best literary criticism as produced since 1930 or so to say of J. R. R. Tolkien, our immediate subject, that his monumental work constitutes the residual statement of that well-known formation of Victorian Arthurians and ruralists whose great legacy was inscribed in the many forms of the Gothic, from architecture to poetry: *Idylls of the King*, 'the Forsaken Merman', all of W. B. Yeats (who knew what he was doing and should have known better), 'the Nature of Gothic', *The Dynasts*, Voysey's and Lutyens' home county houses, the best of Delius and Butterworth.

To write of Tolkien's version of this tradition that it is residual is not in the least to say that it has no life, or that it is a mere survival, or that in a now familiar but entirely empty putting-down, it is nostalgic. Nostalgia is an intense, powerful, and mobilizing emotion. It connotes, presumably, a yearning regard for a lost social and personal order which promised a human membership, a happiness and fulfilment, which life in the present signally fails to provide. The content of nostalgia is keen, vivid, and saturating. But it is commonly acknowledged that it implies not only some distortion of vision, but also a privileging of the past over the present such that the present can only be lived in terms of its failure to measure up to the past, or in such a way that it is successfully (but always temporarily) restored to the past. Nostalgia, we may say, aestheticizes experience by re-presenting the past (*sic*) as a series of separate moments. The supreme nostalgist is by now the television advertisement, but such supremacy, although no doubt aided by the structures of television programming as well as by the technology, is no more that symptomatic. The sweet nostalgias of glimmering girls and landscapes, porkpies and pubs, prefigure a deep wistfulness of the culture, and have no particular necessity of their own. What is important about them is their *aesthetic*, which is to say, non-narrative, dislocation.

The distinction was originally Kierkegaard's, in *Either-Or*.[5] He argues there that the aesthetic life is one in which experience is disjoined into a series of separate presents, each beautiful and entrancing, and that by contrast the ethical life is one in which commitments and responsibilities *to the future* are continuously made, broken and reaffirmed as the present becomes a past which holds the agent in a sequence whose unity he or she struggles to create as every action enters history.

Kierkegaard's sundering of moral history and aesthetics has its heedlessly puritanical cadence, no doubt, as well as being made at a date prior to the main achievements of European novelists in bringing solidly and inextricably together the life of personal experience and the great movements of a larger history. But he is usable for my purposes in identifying at its earliest point the urge of Romanticism to become narcissistic by picturing the self at the centre of the beautiful, and lapsing into self-congratulation accordingly. This is the deep drive of post-Romantic aesthetics, and it becomes institutionalized by the dynamics of modern compulsory education which knitted together the amiable doctrines of a rather rinsed-out liberalism and a domesticated Romantic poetic, and by and by placed them in the care of a new division of labour. Its staff were the curators of the meaning industry, assigned by the state to produce and reproduce the cultural expressions which keep individuals resolute in defence of an individuality circumscribed by the limitedly creative life of domestic privacy, and by ignorance of a larger destiny from transcending its collective interests and looking up to a civic good.

These honest worthies are those English teachers, television producers, journalists, interior designers, clergymen, town and country planners, restaurateurs and publicans, advertising agents, novelists, painters, craft centre entrepreneurs, and several dozen other representatives of the class, from Mrs. Laura Ashley all the way to Emmerdale Farm, who bind consumer individualism in the deadly-sweet susurrations of the English iconography. Theirs is, with a rueful irony, the English Tourist Board menu of the tranquil, green cathedral close, the iron-black and gleaming brass of a suitably distant steam train, the crunch of gravel on a wide, privetted drive, the twinkling reflection of a great bank of fire in an immense grate thrown back by the heavy engravures of a grand decanter, half full of the tawny spirit . . . the colour supplements do it all better.

Within this enchanted topography move handsome, upright, thirty-five year old and morally autonomous individuals. They live freehold but, comparatively speaking, landless; they are decent, faithful, independent, and sunburned in a homely way. They long for the chance to pledge their freely given allegiance, however, to transcendentally higher ideals carried by a superior order of officer-gentlemen-knights who are mostly lean and hawkeyed and sunburned in an exotic way, and whose rare, chaste, sister-in-arms is slender, hauntingly beautiful, boyish withal, and a wonderful horse-person. Their earlier incarnations were Buchan's Sandy Arbuthnot and Mary Hannay, R. F. Delderfield's crippled hero-subaltern[6] and Georgette Heyer's pert Rosalind-Viola heroines.

2

Once we have set the irony-stereotypewriter to work, it is easy for any bookish person who lives within the London-Bristol ellipse of thriving capital to go on remorselessly in this vein. By Hegelian example, all the stereotypes I have cited have their strong, familiar negations: the vast, empty, dark and shattered prairies of the waste land, the splendid storms, the hawkeyed, sunburned, black-cloaked *villains*, the black stallions counterposed to the white mares. Each gesture has its mirror-gesture, each mountain its corresponding underground abyss, all alike in their sweeping, disembodied and wholly insubstantial picturesquerie.

It will be clear that I am writing of the cultural realm—the word is apposite—of which Tolkien is King on this side of the water. But to name his cultural organisms and materials as 'residual' and 'nostalgic' is not to consign them to the rubbish bin of history; if we do, they insist on climbing out. They are residual in the sense that Tolkien speaks from within this well-kept protectorate of the English mind against the whole project of modernism, and on behalf of the tradition in the culture some of whose masterpieces I have listed. The new formation has taken him up so eagerly since the trilogy was completed at the end of the 1950s because his version of anti-modernism filled the space in their social identity left vacant by cultural convention for imaginative exercise by a self otherwise kept perfectly busy in the market's design for consumer living.

This is not simply to utter a malediction over this large, dispersed, and somnambulist class: we are, after all, members one of another. It *is* to claim, however, the truthfulness of a particular phenomenology of imagining, which in the process of reading Tolkien goes something like this.

A man sits on a Bertoia chair, at the working counter of a new, pine-panelled unit in a small complex of converted stone farm buildings, somewhere near (shall we say) Salcombe Regis. Formerly, he was head of art in a market town's shabby long-lived grammar school but left (with mixed motives) to set up this business, turning out neat and tiny pen, ink and water-colours of the Devon landscape, suitably purified of any but natural forms and colours, together with a little jewellery, quickly made but rather delicate. In the next cubicle, his wife serves Cona coffee and homemade scones to go with Tiptree jam and clotted cream at £1.30 a go.

Our man has read *The Lord of the Rings* half a dozen times; just now, he is reading, maybe, *The Eye of the Needle* or *Kramer's War* for himself—a meaty, tasty, sex-and-heroic-violence which mixes up Germans and English in expert equivocation. But he is reading aloud the trilogy, right through, to his two sons, aged nine and eleven, and they love it. He is a decent craftsman, fond of painting and paintings rather than passionate about them, enjoys the geniality of the local pub, the small respectabilities of the watering place, is quietly content and rarely fervent with his own hours to keep, his battered Cortina, and just occasionally hemmed in by the small compass of productive relations defined by formula water-colours at £15 each, wholemeal bread, veneer Welsh dressers, and the varying crowds of tourists. But when he reads Tolkien aloud to the boys in the sparklingly varnished attic bedroom with the dark beams and dormer windows, wanting them urgently to feel the surge of that round prose go thrilling along the nerves, then his voice fills to the brim with a rich, strong, nameless longing which makes it thicken and tremble a little, and creates in him a great rush of love and warmth for the little boys listening so raptly.

> There waiting, silent and still in the space before the Gate, sat Gandalf upon Shadowfax: Shadowfax who alone among the free horses of the earth endured the terror, unmoving, steadfast as a graven image in Rath Dinen.
>
> 'You cannot enter here,' said Gandalf, and the huge shadow halted. 'Go back to the abyss prepared for you! Go back! Fall into the nothingness that awaits you and your master. Go!'
>
> The Black Rider flung back his hood, and behold! he had a kingly crown; and yet upon no head visible was it set. The red fires shone between it and the mantled shoulders vast and dark. From a mouth unseen there came a deadly laughter.
>
> 'Old fool!' he said. 'Old fool! This is my hour. Do you not know Death when you see it? Die now and curse in vain!' And with that he lifted high his sword and flames ran down the blade.
>
> Gandalf did not move. And in that very moment, away behind in some courtyard of the City, a cock crowed. Shrill and clear he crowed, recking nothing of wizardry or war, welcoming only the morning that in the sky far above the shadows of death was coming with the dawn.
>
> And as if in answer there came from far away another note. Horns, horns, horns. In dark Mindolluin's sides they dimly echoed. Great horns of the North wildly blowing. Rohan had come at last.[7]

And the thrill of that moment courses down their skin, and crepitates at the nerve-ends.

What is it that stirs them to this high, rippling, idealized and curiously objectless flow of feeling? It is cool and easy for the devout critic to analyse the *Star Wars* imagery, the Darth

Vader figure, the vaudeville staginess ('Old fool'), the phoney biblicality ('. . . a cock crowed'), the sonorous anachronisms and alliterations ('recking nothing of wizardry or war', 'dark . . . dimly'), the Celtic nomenclature (Mindolluin), the sugared brass music, like Wagner played by Victor Sylvester—easy enough: all done in a few lines like that. But the practical criticism doesn't answer the question. Any answer must invoke instead some such metaphor as a vast reservoir or field of feeling perpetually in play in British culture, earthed for a moment in such prose and given its terminal or junction point.

Such a feeling does not transcend the culture, it is created by it. That is to say, the language learns to carry and express such a feeling, itself the product of centuries of iambic minstrelsy, but brought to a very particular undulation by the over-determining of Victorian poetry, the cultural moment at which the new divisions of industrial labour pushed poetry off Skiddaw into the Salon-Palace of (Ladies') Art, and the invention of new and necessary traditions[8] called old rough legends to the service of an innovative cadenced nationalism and its spreading military empire. This abrupt synopsis may stand for the history of a realm of feeling which found its official institutions in the public schools, themselves the product of the same cultural moment. They invented the traditions which created in a few decades after 1832 the myth of an atavistic, trans-historical Englishness embodied in the form of its youngish bourgeois men, and given content by a high, objectless and yearning idealism obliged always to keep its gaze on the high windows of an endless blue horizon[9] for fear of seeing too closely the material immediacy of (as they say) its historical genesis. The insubstantial pageants of knight-errantry and its timeless courtesies served these necessities well, especially when dosed with that odourless saevicide which removed the coarsenesses of Sancho Panza, Falstaff, Villon and Pantagruel from the stories.

Tolkien and C. S. Lewis were lesser figures in a formation which was made by this moment and included Vaughan Williams and Britten, John and Paul Nash, Winston Churchill and Lord Reith. The language in which that formation expressed its strongest feelings of idealism, heroism, manliness and womanliness may be said to have reserved a space in the

33

many forms of social identity which our culture makes possible. When that fraction of our class structure which I have designated 'the meaning-minders' needs a language which is capable of connecting these ideals to the relevant feelings, thereby releasing a current to keep their characters straight and upright, they turn to Tolkien. He provides a way of imaginatively living through a range of emotions whose cognitive content and objects are so contradictory or so implausible that they can find no domestic expression. Once acknowledged, they would have to be dropped. To understand why this is so requires a brief history of the autonomous individual since the modernist project really began to falter.

3

The autonomous individual first surfaces in a recognizably modernist style with Romanticism and the Enlightenment. Kant is his ideologue, Wordsworth his diarist, and Beethoven his formalist. Adam Smith, however, is his canny economist, and as the debate over the human meanings of political economy devolved itself into the many camps of Left and Right during the nineteenth century, one substantial guerrilla began to organize in subversion against the baleful works of industrial capital while trying to hold onto the great freedoms won by the new contractarian liberals for the idea of a creative, self-propelling, self-aware and fulfillable individual identity.[10] Give or take a bit, the best versions of the modern project were held to be those which resisted the awful depredations of that juggernaut named capitalism on the Left and mere industrialism elsewhere. Both versions of the critique hung onto the notion of the autonomous individual, while finding it harder and harder to position him anywhere other than in the margins outside both domestic and political life as, variously, dandy, artist, revolutionary, intellectual, or exile.

For the idea of autonomy came under breaking strain from two quarters of the present century's heavens. On the one hand, the histories of the Soviet Gulag and the Third Reich's charnel houses, to say nothing of the liberal democracies policing the globe in Vietnam, Africa, Latin America, and elsewhere, made it horribly clear that autonomous individuals may be creatively loathsome. On the other hand, the growing awareness in both popular and intellectual life of the power of structures in social life to 'de-centre', dissolve, and re-make to fit their own mechanism the purportedly free individuals, went a long way to tarnish liberal individualism as a master-doctrine of the rich countries. After barely a couple of centuries, the establishment of the individual's rights to unencumbered self-fulfilment and the defeat of tradition, status, and superstition are rejected at least by a cultural élite before it is even within sight for the new nations of the world's poor.[11]

The meaning-minders are, unevenly and contradictorily, living that rejection. Horrified by what individuals may do out of their free subjectivity, and repelled by the destructiveness of the reified structures of political economy, they have proposed a partial withdrawal into an enclave culture, where they battle to keep the relations of production on a personal scale and in a domestic setting. The implicit comparison of a good primary classroom is with the family home; the node of reference for our craft centre producer is the guild journeyman. (The distance between him and William Morris or Gustave Courbet,[12] whose claims on journeyman status really had substance, is one measure of how much the Utopias of the counter-culture are thinned out.) *The Lord of the Rings* is the political fantasy of a consolatory kind for this non-political class; it is the negative relief of a now legendary liberalism.

On this analysis, the enclave master-symbolism of Mexican gastronomy, Celtic furniture, late medieval systems of production, and Romantic metaphysics, has the courage to see that there is no redemptive dialectic inscribed in any historical process. The best you can do is to keep your moral horizon within the scale of your family—hence the commitment of the enclavist to the peace movements. But if modernism cannot fulfil its larger promises, the best you can then *imagine* as an image of the action that failure denies you is the world of Middle-earth.

Like all popular cultures, Middle-earth's Utopia is pre-historic and classless.[13] It constates a rejection of 'the brief intermezzo of liberalism', in Horkheimer's phrase, by returning its leading individuals to membership of a city state (the Shire) without a city, exonerated from production, and guaranteed

35

abundance of food. It solves the problem of individuality itself by simply dissolving the category into the freely given allegiance of an honourable and unquestioning militia, which is also a free association of friends. It is a picture which draws a little from the tale of Robin Hood (to vanquish is to command fealty) and a little from Jefferson's post-independence farmer-army. Its principle of legitimacy is sacred, traditional and reassuringly charismatic: Aragorn is the one true king, sage and just. But more importantly he restores with Gandalf the Freudian authority to the figure of the father, latterly ether-ealized by bureaucratic distance and stripped of his rank by the discrediting of the concept of wisdom. Above all, however, Tolkien's prose abjures any corporeal solidity: the action is bodiless, the blood colourless, the corpses as unreally pic-turesque as the rocks and thorn trees, the dark clouds of Mordor, the sweet comforts of Rivendell.

The contrast comes out if we accept C. S. Lewis's com-parison of Tolkien with Ariosto and Malory. Malory's fighters in the *Morte D'Arthur* are often comically repetitive—all that traversing and foining puts one more in mind of Wodehouse's heroes than those of Camelot. But while Malory can only be pretty boring to most people, and—by all accounts—bookish and unrealistic to his own, he spoke from a culture in which, as Isaiah Berlin puts it for all pre-industrial narratives,

> men naturally talk of the lips of a vase, the teeth of a plough, the mouth of a river, a neck of land, handfuls of one thing, the heart of another, veins of minerals, bowels of the earth, murmuring waves, whistling winds, and smiling skies, groaning tables and weeping willows—such a world must be deeply and systemati-cally different from any in which such phrases are felt, even remotely, to be metaphorical, as contrasted with so-called literal speech.[14]

Tolkien, writing in a much later culture, technologized and instrumental as it is, as well as being in himself (I would guess) fairly timorous of and repelled by bodily immediacy and physical contact, writes of heroes and heroic action whose bodily actuality, vividness, and concrete weight of presence and experience are entirely spiritualized and naïve. Naïve, that is, in the sense Schiller famously defined in his essay of

1777 on 'naïve and sentimental poetry', in which 'sentimental' connotes to be self-reflexive and thickened by historicality, and 'naïve' means straightforwardly narrative, undialectical and unself-consciously spontaneous.

It is rightly hard, in a complicated world, not to attach pejorative weight to 'naïve' although perhaps as great a novel as *Little Dorrit* is on this score naïve. But Tolkien is categorically naïve in that none of his characters reflect on their actions for a moment; they see what they have to do as being a consequence enforced by the structure of the action and as inescapable as the calendar. By the same token, the trilogy is almost empty of the description of emotions. That is not to say it is unemotional: the whole book is suffused with an intense emotionality which, in much the way that musical narrative works in opera, spiritualizes the action and transposes what is physical into the soaring splendours of musical experience which, having no referent, cannot *signify* but only move. A parallel might be found in some of Verdi's operas as well as Wagner's, as I have already suggested. But Tolkien is entirely without the weight and density of Verdi's mature cadences: the lived sexuality of Falstaff or Otello, the pain of Violetta, are precisely what he has excluded from the treble sexlessness of the Shire. And similarly, the harshness, cruelty, and consciousness of power which pervade Wagner's *Ring* have no place in the simple, motiveless and dispositional evil of the Nazgul or Saruman. Perhaps we can say that Tolkien's is an opera nearest in spirit to Britten's church parables— *The Burning Fiery Furnace* and even *The War Requiem*— which I have claimed as a product of the same social formation. Nothing too much turns on my comparison: what I am trying to identify is Tolkien's fervently emotional and boyish innocence which his musical prose so constantly reaffirms. The innocence of his characters keeps them purified of the effects of experience, and this is not only true of the Hobbits. Aragorn's splendid gravity and courage, Gandalf's resourcefulness and dauntlessness are alike innocent in their unreflective fixity, their serene calm in the face not just of mortal danger (only to be expected of heroes) but of the end of their world. Theirs is not resolution because the presence of dissolution is unknown in this world. They have, so to speak, pre-Nietzschean selves petrified in a given role.

Such selves, if they have ever had historical existence, belong to a pre-historic world. Tolkien, who isn't writing history, can amalgamate the best traits of an imaginary self (whether Meriadoc's, Sam Gamgee's, the Prince Imrahil's, or the dwarf Gimli's) compounded of Homeric Athenian, Renaissance Burgundian, and Victorian Harrovian.[15] That combination of role-defined honourable soldierliness (Hector), graceful court-liness of speech and bearing (Chrétien de Troyes), and eager, boyish allegiance and unquestioning servitude (Julian Grenfell) is the ideal self of a bookish, reclusive, pre-sexual Oxonian born before the First World War. That incorrigible blend of quest and lark which is the adventure requires for fulfilment a peculiar immunity to consciousness especially in its self-doubting forms, and at the same time a spontaneity of generous feeling issuing in quick, decisive action. Without reflection but within a given set of roles and a fixed, classless social structure such action can only be physical. We end with a truism—the only valid version of the public school hero is the soldier.

4

Is this the banal source of Tolkien's pulling power? That he returns us to the longed-for simplicities of military action? Well, yes; but it is more precise and illuminating to say that he does so within the structure of feeling of 1914 and, more briefly and less broadcast, of 1940. His subalterns and commanding officers are all in the field; there is no General Staff. Tolkien's are the battle manoeuvres of the first year of the war in Belgium or of the Italian campaign: rapid movement by masses of men across a wide plain, the fall of key cities, infiltration behind the lines by a daring commando, a single mighty engine (the tank Grond), hand-to-hand fighting, a small Flying Corps (the Eagles), a vast final explosion in Command headquarters. Tolkien archaicizes these images, settled so deeply in the modern memory,[16] which *are* indeed what people mean by war. The archaism moves the warfare from the domain of political history to that of aesthetics. Warfare becomes a series of separate, magnificent moments fixed in the gesture of a tableau or a diorama. That is what the word 'picturesque' means.

Yeats lived off his understanding of this process—made it, glancingly, his own subject, in *Easter 1916*.

> This other man I had dreamed
> A drunken, vainglorious lout.
> He had done most bitter wrong
> To some who are near my heart,
> Yet I number him in the song;
> He, too, has resigned his part
> In the casual comedy;
> He, too, has been changed in his turn,
> Transformed utterly:
> A terrible beauty is born.

He knew that his cadence, momentum and flourish made a picturesque image out of the squalid facts of living history—a mother crawling in her own blood, a drunken, vainglorious lout, both set in the golden lozenge of the icon. Tolkien, much less wide-awake, softens 1914 and 1940 into the entirely unphysical, bloodless, corpseless ceremonies of stirring names, ritual swordplay, stately parades, and grave orisons: the arias and ensembles of spiritualized combat. And at the long close, he brings his boyish young men home to a perfect Oxford and Oxfordshire, tawny stone courts and deep green lanes, cloister and cottage.

Thus and thus does Tolkien's irresistible appeal work for his wide constituency. Understood so, he is ineffably English, with England's old and grim snobbery and stupidity, and England's excellent idealism and high-mindedness. This comes out in the hastiest of comparisons with his American imitator, Stephen Donaldson and his bestselling *Chronicles of Thomas Covenant*.[17] Tolkien, of course, has long been hugely popular on American campuses, but it is a premise of this paper that his popularity must be culturally situated. Donaldson's hero is a lonely frontiersman, the action takes place in a dream, and the hilariously dismal plot is much nearer *The Deer Hunter* than to Tolkien.

What Tolkien does for such a mixture of admirers is hold open a space in which his readers may feel with particular force a generalized but intense idealism, a longing for in-expressible bravery, a keen fearfulness with no physical object to define it, a chokey, brimming, wanting-to-give-of-oneself which is most like the beginning of a love affair, when the whole point and excitement is that the other person is a perfect (*sic*) stranger. To bring this off, it is necessary that the novelist be as unspecific and generalized as possible.

The other side of contemporary individualism is the longing for a lost Eden of membership, community, ceremony, and a commitment of the self to and loss of its strangeness in the larger movements of a whole people, even at the expense of rationality. All political leaders need myths which rouse this longing, but Fascism is founded on it. Tolkien is no Fascist,[18] but his great myth may be said, as Wagner's was, to prefigure the genuine ideals and nobilities of which Fascism is the dark negation. Instead of the raucous bawling of *Il Duce*, the pentameter; instead of tanks and the goose step, horses and cloaks and lances; instead of Nuremberg, Frodo's farewell. But I noted Tolkien's Englishness, and if Fascism were to come to England it would, in E. P. Thompson's phrase, come by 'steady vegetable pressure' rather than by murder and burning down the House of Commons. The realm of deep feeling which Tolkien so tellingly gives form to found its most recent English moment at several thousand miles distance in the south Atlantic in 1982.

NOTES

1. I am thinking particularly of Leo Lowenthal in *Literature, Popular Culture and Society*, Doubleday translation, 1961.
2. The first, best catalogue of this tradition is, of course, Raymond Williams's, in his classic *Culture and Society 1780–1950* (Chatto and Windus, 1957). I have attempted some revision and restatement of this in my *Radical Earnestness: English Social Theory 1880–1980* (Martin Robertson, 1982).
3. *Problems in Cultural Materialism* (Verso, 1981).
4. A definition of meaning in social action which is taken from Charles Taylor 'Interpretation and the Sciences of Man' in *Review of Metaphysics*, January 1971.
5. But I take the point, and the preliminary argument from Alisdair MacIntyre, in *After Virtue: A Study in Moral Theory* (Duckworth, 1981), especially Ch. 16 and p. 225.
6. Still going strong in John le Carré, *Tinker, Tailor, Soldier, Spy* (1977).
7. *The Return of the King*, p. 103.

40

8. See Eric Hobsbawm (ed.), *The Invention of Tradition* (Cambridge, 1983), for evidence of the (surely correct) case that our culture was largely made up in the second half of the last century.
9. Philip Larkin's celebrated collection *High Windows* (1974) is an interesting example of a poet trying to sing in the olde English voice, and constantly choking on it, when he realizes what he's doing.
10. A cutting obloquy is read over this history by John Dunn in *Western Political Theory in the Face of the Future* (Cambridge, 1979). Dunn, however, appears to believe that individuals are really there even though he treats them with unyielding sarcasm.
11. I take theoretic points here from Joel Whitebrook, 'Saving the Subject: Modernity and the Problem of the Autonomous Individual', *Telos* 50, 1981, 79–102. The novelists tell two versions of the same story in Africa, the first as tragedy, the second as thriller. Nadine Gordimer, *A Guest of Honour* (Penguin, 1970); V. S. Naipaul, *A Bend in the River* (Penguin, 1979).
12. On whom, see T. F. Clark, *Image of the People* (Thames and Hudson, 1977).
13. A point I take from Walter Benjamin's programmatic note in his study of Baudelaire, *A Lyric Poet in the Era of High Capitalism* (New Left Books, 1974). See especially p. 159.
14. In Vico and Herder, *Two Studies in the History of Ideas* (Hogarth Press, 1976), pp. 46–7.
15. I am thinking of the heroes of H. A. Vachell's *The Hill*.
16. As finely documented by Paul Fussell, in *The Great War and Modern Memory* (Oxford, 1975).
17. E.g. Volume I, *Lord Foul's Bane* (Fontana, 1974; 14th impression, 1982).
18. I am trying to correct a speculation about Fascism which I made in my *The Promise of Happiness: Value and Meaning in Children's Fiction* (Cambridge, 1981), and for which I was accurately criticized by Claude Rawson, to whom I am grateful, in the *Times Literary Supplement*, 26 July 1982.

2

Recovery, Escape, Consolation: Middle-earth and the English Fairy Tale

by ROGER KING

Cultural fashion can begin in the strangest places; and one of the most extraordinary examples of this is the cultish popularity achieved by Tolkien's two novels *The Hobbit* and *The Lord of the Rings* during the late 1960s and early 1970s in both Britain and America. *The Hobbit* was, after all, published as early as 1937, waiting thirty years for its popularity to be established as an important literary achievement, and the three volumes of *The Lord of the Rings* were published originally between 1954–55. They were hardly overnight successes, and neither was their popularity the result of explicit commercial manipulation. They arrived, as it were, out of nothing—what the record trade describes as 'sleepers'—and both of them had slept for a very long time, particularly *The Hobbit*.

Yet for Tolkien himself they represent the culmination of a deliberate and consistent attempt to resurrect English mythological literature. His own literary works are entirely consistent with the defence of the fairy story which he elaborated as early as 1938 in the Andrew Lang lecture at the University of St. Andrews, later reprinted in a revised version in *Tree and Leaf* (1964). 'The world of *Faërie*, the realm or state in which fairies have their being . . .' is recognizably the world Tolkien deliberately recreates in both *The Hobbit* and *The Lord of the Rings*:

> Faërie contains many things besides elves and fays, and besides
> dwarfs, witches, trolls, giants, or dragons: it holds the seas, the
> sun, the moon, the sky; and the earth, and all things that are in it:
> tree and bird, water and stone, wine and bread, and ourselves,
> mortal men, when we are enchanted.[1]

The lecture also reveals Tolkien's views not only on the
imagined worlds of the fairy story, but also on the functions
the fairy story has in the modern world. These he terms
'Recovery, Escape, and Consolation'. 'Recovery' consists of a
're-gaining of a clear view'.[2] 'Escape', escape from the 'Robot
Age',[3] and 'Consolation' the bringing of a 'sudden and
miraculous grace' in the fairy story's Happy Ending.[4]

It might be possible to object to the functions that Tolkien
claims for the fairy story, but for our purposes I want initially
to accept them—at least in a modified form—using tales from
the collection *English Fairy Tales* compiled by Joseph Jacobs in
1890.[5] I have not chosen this particular collection accidentally:
Jacobs' intention, to collect and rewrite specifically *English*
fairy tales, closely parallels Tolkien's own. (Tolkien explicitly
claimed that one of the reasons for his writing was the poverty
of English folk tales, and his desire to write some of his own.)[6]

Firstly, then, 'Recovery'—the 're-gaining of a clear view',
'so that the things seen clearly may be freed from the drab blur
of triteness or familiarity'.[7] There are two separate notions
here, and they need disentangling. Firstly, freedom from
familiarity. The fairy story, Tolkien is claiming, allows us to
recover our sense of the unfamiliar. This seems to be true: the
fairy story presents us with a world of supernatural beings and
events, enchantment, riddles, transformations. We live vicari-
ously while we read a fairy story in the unfamiliar world of the
irrational. But if unfamiliar at one level, it is at a deeper level
highly familiar: once inside Dick Whittington's London, for
example, we know exactly where we are, because we have
been there so often before. We know—and can anticipate—
the point at which, leaving London in utter dejection, Dick will
sit down on a stone, and the bells of Bow Church will ring out:

> Turn again, Whittington,
> Thrice Lord Mayor of London.

43

Similarly in *Jack and the Beanstalk* we await with relish for the giant to smell Jack and roar out:

> Fee-fi-fo-fum,
> I smell the blood of an Englishman,
> Be he alive, or be he dead
> I'll have his bones to grind my bread.

We know where we are because both fairy stories—their characters, narrative trajectories and specific incidents—are part of our general cultural apparatus, part of our common cultural consciousness. We only need, as it were, to be reminded.

But how far is this true of either *The Hobbit* or *The Lord of the Rings*? Not, I would have thought, at all. What common consciousness is reawakened by Anborn, Faramir, Aragorn, Gimli, Ringwraith, etc., etc.? Far from operating on commonly held responses, we enter a world of bizarrely unfamiliar mythology, and our problem—which never exists in fairy tales—becomes one of intellectual decoding as we struggle to give meaning to characters, narrative trajectories and specific incidents which have no apparent meaning whatsoever. Paradoxically, while attempting to ressurrect the mythological, Tolkien's writing in fact results in its replacement by the purely intellectual: myth has been reduced to a literary Rubik's cube.

The second notion contained in Tolkien's concept of 'Recovery' is that of increased clarity of vision. Again, there is a sense in which, on a moral level at least, this seems to be an accurate observation of the fairy story as a literary form. Ambiguities and complexities are replaced by a moral universe where Good and Evil are never in doubt, and where cruelty, foolishness, idleness are punished, virtue rewarded with wealth and public honour. Yet once again, this world of moral absolutes is not one that we have great difficulty in regaining; the moral principles of the fairy story that Good and Evil are absolutes, and that the Good shall inherit the earth, that the Evil be destroyed, are fundamental moral principles implicit in our culture. We understand the moral universe of the fairy story as easily as we enter its imagined world. We rejoice that Jack's courage in chopping down the beanstalk is rewarded with financial and social success, and that Dick's persistence eventually gains him the position of Lord Mayor of London.

Yet Tolkien's moral universe simply doesn't work like this. His world is populated with such a baroque proliferation of different types of mythological being—elves, dwarfs, orcs, trolls—that we simply never know where we are in any detailed moral sense. We can isolate evil in the form of Sauron, and heroic goodness in the characters of Frodo and Bilbo: Sauron is duly condemned to the chambers of Fire, and Frodo and Bilbo duly rewarded. But what of the rest? Far from achieving the clarity of moral vision represented by the fairy story, Tolkien's work—and particularly *The Lord of the Rings*— largely baffles the reader's moral responses. We become as confused morally as we do in interpreting character and incident.

But if Tolkien's own work fails to achieve 'Recovery', perhaps we ought to examine his second function of the fairy story, that of 'Escape'. It goes without saying that all fiction represents a kind of escape, and that mythological literature represents a particular type of escape; when we escape into *Dick Whittington* or *Jack and the Beanstalk*, we escape into a more irrational substitute world than when we escape into *Middlemarch* or *The Rainbow*. But it is never simply the extremely limited escape defined by Tolkien as 'an escape from the Robot Age', an alternative to our modern experience of 'play under a glass roof by the side of a municipal swimming-bath'.[8] The distaste for modern technology—'a glass roof'—and for the urban—'municipal'—is evident here, as it occasionally is in as explicit a way in his novels, as in this description of Hobbiton after industrialization:

> The great chimney rose up before them; and as they drew near the old village across the water, through rows of new mean houses . . . they saw the new mill in all its frowning and dirty ugliness: a great brick building straddling the stream, which it fouled with a steaming and stinking outflow.[9]

In *The Hobbit* Tolkien's distaste for the urban is presented more obliquely—but it is nonetheless there. It is no accident that the man-eating trolls talk in Cockney accents:

45

'Mutton yesterday, mutton today, and blimey if it don't look like mutton again tomorrer', said one of the trolls.

'Never a blinking bit of manflesh have we had for long enough', said a second. 'What the 'ell William was a-thinkin of to bring us into these parts at all, beats me—'[10]

A more complex example from *The Hobbit* is the description of the human lake-town near the mouth of the Forest River in which Thorin and Bilbo rest on their journey. They are welcomed with civilized hospitality, but Tolkien's initial description of the town is ambiguous, to say the least. The human inhabitants still thrive on 'the trade that came up the great river from the South', but it is not as in 'the great days of old' when

> . . . they had been wealthy and powerful, and there had been fleets of boats on the waters, and some were filled with gold and some with warriors in armour, and there had been wars and deeds which were now only a legend. The rotting piles of a greater town could still be seen along the shores when the waters sank in a drought.[11]

Why this deliberate emphasis on the decay of a prosperous commercial urban society? It is unnecessary for the narrative; one feels that Tolkien rather relishes the collapse of a technically superior human society and the recovery of a simpler world.

This anti-urban emphasis reflects the escape from the modern which he claims is one of the central functions of the fairy story. Yet there seems little justification for the claim. There is nothing necessarily anti-modern about the English folk tale; *Dick Whittington*, for example, is heavily committed to the city as an arena for social success. It is true that Dick's original view of urban utopia,

> that folks in London were all fine gentlemen and ladies; and that there was singing and music there all day long, and that the streets were all paved with gold . . .[12]

is undermined by his experience of urban poverty, but the resolution of the tale is a celebration of urban financial social and political power.

Of course *Dick Whittington* is rather a special case in this stress on the urban, but other English folk tales demonstrate similar commitment to the modern. In the *Three Little Pigs* it is the most sophisticated building technology—a brick-built house—which provides the best refuge against the Wolf; there is no sentimental appeal to earlier technologies. And even in a tale such as *Jack and the Beanstalk* it is rural poverty that forces the widow to sell the cow at market in the neighbouring town. It is an urban commercial transaction which provides Jack with the magic beans. Similarly, it is another trip to the same market selling the golden eggs, presumably for cash, that enables Jack and his mother to achieve the prosperity which gains him the hand of a great princess. In their different ways these three folk tales demonstrate, not a withdrawal from the modern, but a commitment to it, to the possibilities inherent in an urban technically sophisticated and commercial world. In this sense, they are diametrically opposed to the works of Tolkien.

The third function Tolkien ascribes to the folk tale is that of 'Consolation': 'the bringing of a sudden and miraculous grace' in the Happy Ending of all fairy tales.[13] We must agree with Tolkien here: the Happy Ending of a fairy tale does have a consoling function. Let us examine two such endings in more detail:

> Then Jack showed his mother his golden harp, and what with showing her that and selling the golden eggs, Jack and his mother became very rich, and he married a great princess, and they lived happily ever after.[14]

> . . . Mr. Whittington and his lady lived in great splendour and were very happy. They had several children. He was sheriff of London, thrice Lord Mayor and received the honour of knighthood by Henry V.[15]

In both cases, our heroes' persistence and courage are rewarded with financial success and social prestige. They achieve a public recognition for their efforts—and in the case of Dick, if not of Jack, gain explicit political power. But the crucial element of the consolation is the public nature of the resolution; individual achievement has been recognized, acknowledged and rewarded by society as a whole.

How far does this correspond to the consolation offered by the Happy Endings of *The Hobbit* and *The Lord of the Rings?*

Certainly, there *are* parallels. At the end of *The Hobbit*, Bard sends 'much gold to the Master of Laketown', and he rewards 'his followers and friends freely'. He wishes to reward Bilbo more: 'I would reward you most richly of all', but 'in the end he would only take two small chests, one filled with silver, and the other with gold.'[16] Bilbo comes into a financial reward just as Jack and Dick, although Bilbo's reluctant acceptance of only a portion of it makes it far more problematic than either Jack's or Dick's financial success.

But what does Bilbo do with his justly acquired wealth? Very simply, he retires: not for him the social or political success of marrying a princess, or becoming Lord Mayor. He retreats to his hobbit-hole, hanging his sword over the mantelpiece, and receiving the occasional visitor. When in the final lines of the story, Gandalf visits him, he reminds Bilbo

> 'You are a very fine person, Mr. Baggins and I am very fond of you; but you are only quite a little fellow in a wide world after all!'
>
> 'Thank goodness!' said Bilbo laughing, and handed him the tobacco-jar.[17]

This retreat from the public world into private retirement is in direct contrast to the public endings of *Jack and the Beanstalk* and *Whittington and his Cat*, and is paralleled by the ending of *The Lord of the Rings*, in which the renunciation of public power is exemplified explicitly by Frodo's getting rid of the ring. Bilbo momentarily forgets this:

> 'Now where were we? Yes, of course, giving presents which reminds me: what's become of my ring, Frodo, that you took away?'
>
> 'I have lost it, Bilbo dear,' said Frodo. 'I got rid of it, you know.'[18]

Frodo and Bilbo subsequently retire: Bilbo to Rivendell, and Frodo to the West where he beholds 'white shores and beyond them a far green country under a swift sunrise'.

If there is a consoling function in Tolkien's Happy Endings, it is not the consolation of public social success, but of privacy and retirement. Not, of course, that wealth has been rejected entirely; neither Bilbo in *The Hobbit* or Frodo in *The Lord of the*

Rings elect poverty. Bilbo has his small chests of gold and silver (some of which he redistributes as presents) and Frodo his white gem on a silver chain given to him by Queen Arwen. In both cases, their retirement is relatively well-heeled.

'Recovery', 'Escape', and 'Consolation': Tolkien's two fairy tales represent an attempt to embody these three functions, but do so in an extremely limited way. Far from recovering the unfamiliar—but deeply familiar—narrative and moral universe of the fairy tale, the reader is involved in the intellectual deciphering of a bewildering and individualistic *pot pourri* of mythological beings. We escape—but only into Tolkien's general distaste for the modern. We are consoled not by the public success of rewarded virtue, but by the solace of quietly affluent retirement. To sum up, reading Tolkien's works is to enter a private world, where we are invited to value privacy above all things public and modern. The English fairy tale, as we have tried to demonstrate, is not like this at all.

But the popularity of *The Hobbit* and *The Lord of the Rings* was not unaccompanied; parallel developments were occurring in other contemporary cultural forms. The most striking example, of course, is rock music. Rock, as Charlie Gillett's definitive account *Sounds of the City* establishes, was essentially an urban musical form. True, it was partly dependent upon and assimilated the musical structures and vocabulary of American White country music, but the resulting amalgamation of these with the structures and vocabulary of Black American music produced an essentially urban American musical form. This is paralleled by the growth of a specifically English rock music in the early 1960s, which was similarly urban; London, Manchester and, above all, Liverpool provided the social context for its development.

Yet a funny thing happened: a music born in the city and based on public performance retreated in several ways at the same time. Firstly—and the Beatles L.P. *Sgt. Pepper's Lonely Hearts Club Band* was perhaps the most dramatic example of this—rock music retreated into the recording studio, developing techniques which were irreproducible live, as the L.P. record became the central medium of cultural exchange between artist and audience. This also implies a retreat on the audience's part; the consumption of rock music becomes an increasingly privatized experience, as you listen to sounds on your headphones in the privacy of your home.

This privatization of both rock music production and consumption is paralleled by increasingly individualistic content. The lyrics of bands like the Beatles, Matthews' Southern Comfort, the Incredible String Band, become increasingly self-consciously 'poetic', increasingly a *pot pourri* of personal fantasy. The record listener is involved in the same process of intellectual deciphering of meaning as in *The Hobbit* and *The Lord of the Rings*. What does *Lucy in the Sky with Diamonds* mean? 'Tangerine trees', 'marmalade skies', 'rocking horse people'— this is an exact parallel to the readers' problem in interpreting Gimli, Ringwraith and Faramir. It is not surprising to discover that an audience deriving aesthetic pleasure from the rock music of the late 1960s finds a suitable literary equivalent in the writing of Tolkien.

Even more than this, much of the rock music of the late 1960s evokes a similar disenchantment with the urban, a similar evocation of the rural that we have already identified with Tolkien's work: listen to the lyrics of the Incredible String Band's *'Mercy' I cry 'City'* on *The Hangman's Beautiful Daughter* (1968) or Steve Barlby's and Ian Matthews' lyrics in songs like 'The Castle Far' and 'What We say' on *Matthews' Southern Comfort* (1970).

Neither is it simply a matter of lyrics—the instrumentation of rock at this period increasingly incorporates explicitly 'folk' instruments. There is a self-conscious return to the acoustic guitar, and the introduction of flutes, citars, concertinas, tambourines, etc. and, in many cases, folk musicians join the recording sessions in order to play these particular instruments. At the same time, recording groups retire into the English countryside, either emulating the lifestyle of the English landed gentry or getting their sounds together in their elaborately equipped mobile recording studios.

Yet there is a paradox here: the retreat from the modern is only possible because of increasingly sophisticated recording equipment and an increasing amount of capital outlay for the production of records, as well as a sufficiently affluent audience to buy L.P.s to play on their sufficiently sophisticated domestic equipment.

The popularity of Tolkien and the development of rock music demonstrate parallel characteristics, but both take place in a wider socio-economic context. Establishing the precise nature of the relationship between cultural phenomena and their socio-economic context is of necessity a difficult and inevitably tentative one—like 'gathering samphires—dreadful trade'; but the retreat into the private demonstrated by both does correspond to developments in English patterns of cultural consumption that have taken place generally since the Second World War. Cinema audiences have declined as television has become the more popular medium of visual entertainment, and the national duopoly of television distribution is now under increasing threat from cable T.V., video entertainment and domestic computers. This privatization of cultural consumption shows no sign of waning. The popularity of Tolkien, paralleled by developments in contemporary rock music, represents one moment in this process.

But only a moment: the rock music of the later 1970s represented a self-conscious reaction to the developments outlined above—stressing the record as a deliberate reproduction of live performance, using deliberately crude and unsophisticated recording techniques and, above all, reaffirming rock's role as an urban and politically explicit cultural form. The distaste for the urban, the emphasis on the rural, the suspicion of advanced technology has hardened into organized political action, into the Ecology Party, into conservation movements, into Friends of the Earth.

But there are still echoes of that cultural moment in post-War British literary culture: Kit Williams's *Masquerade* bears a strong resemblance to Tolkien's work. Here an extremely lavishly produced jumble of mythology provides the basis for the individual reader's quest for the ultimate reward, a Golden Hare hidden somewhere in England; this represents the reduction of myth to a game of intellectual deciphering even more explicitly than in Tolkien's work. When finally found, it was presumably hung up on the mantelpiece like Bilbo's sword.

Although the success of *Masquerade* in contemporary fiction is a lone echo, works like Richard Adams's *Watership Down* and its imitators establish more 'realistic' rural worlds. Rabbits have replaced hobbits, and warrens replaced hobbit-holes.

51

They are 'real' rabbits with their niche in a Downland eco-system; they are part of a food-chain and subject to the laws of population dynamics. This increasingly realistic emphasis in fiction of the natural world is paralleled by the success of the reprint of Edith Holden's nature notes as *The Country Diary of an Edwardian Lady* and of the Collins' *Field Guides of Birds, Flowers and Butterflies*. These works demonstrate a withdrawal from the urban as clearly as do Tolkien's novels, but Tolkien's mythological world has been replaced by an emphasis on observation and identification, reinforced by the popularization of environmental biology by Radio 4, the B.B.C. Bristol Natural History Unit, and Oxford Scientific Films. In short, the interest in the natural world has become scientific, rather than mythological, or in the classification of the public library, non-fiction rather than fiction. Gardening books, D.I.Y. Manuals and Cookery books, as well as Nature Guides, represent the four most popular genres of contemporary best-selling hardbacks. Contemporary reading habits confirm an increasing privatization but with an increasingly practical emphasis.

But there are other echoes. St. Valentine's Day is cele-brated, at least in the 'serious' newspapers and particularly the *Guardian*, by coded messages of love—hobbits, elves and goblins mingle with floppy bunnies, white seagulls, Camber-well Beauties and buttercups. The mythological world evoked is occasionally directly dependent on Tolkien, but more generally it represents a similar mix of English pastoral and medieval epic. The reader (unless sending or receiving such a message) derives pleasure from deciphering the relationship concealed by the code. If the Spring Love Festival is cele-brated in this way, then so is the Summer Festival, at least as far as Open University students are concerned, who celebrate their Summer School loves in similarly coded messages, par-ticularly in the mythology of *Midsummer Night's Dream*—with Puck, Titania, Peaseblossom and Mustardseed. In this area at least, Tolkien need not have feared the demise of a particularly English folk mythology.

It is among the educated that the echoes of Tolkien still resonate. As we have tried to demonstrate earlier, it is primarily an intellectual pleasure that is satisfied by Tolkien's works and by the rock music of the late 1960s and early 1970s. The retreat into personally idiosyncratic lyrics and into the technically sophisticated recording studios were two of the means by which rock attempted to establish itself as a 'respectable' art form, making its claim to appeal to the intelligentsia, to an educated audience. Although, of course, this audience was already there, the generation whose adolescence had been spent listening to rock music were now the beneficiaries of mass higher education, as the recommendations of the Robbins' Committee had been implemented. Producers of rock music—and their audience—had done their 'A' Level English, were going to University, and provided the audience for rock and the readership of Tolkien. The moment of Tolkien is partly explained by the sudden expansion of a young, literate and educated readership. Since then, public support for and confidence in higher education has soured; perhaps it is not surprising to find these dying echoes of Tolkien in the columns of the *Guardian* and *Sesame*, committed as they are to the ideals of an open liberal education in an increasingly—in their view—technocratic society. Their readers are perhaps escaping from Tolkien's 'Robot Age'. Yet an ambiguity remains: the O.U.'s commitment to open access to a higher education is only possible because of its technological sophistication, the packaging of its learning materials and, above all, its computer.

There are, it is true, minor echoes in the visual arts: Peter Blake—designer of the *Sgt. Pepper* L.P.—retreated into self-styled 'ruralism', producing book illustrations of *Alice in Wonderland* and a sequence of paintings of Titania. Richard Long's artistic walks through the British landscape, up rivers, over moors, rearranging stones, noting placenames, combine an emphasis on the English rural with an intense sense of privacy, since he never reveals the rearrangements for which he has been responsible.

But all is not lost; the strongest resonances of Tolkien lie elsewhere in our contemporary culture. If you own a 48K Sinclair Spectrum, for example, you can buy a *Hobbit* programme for only £14.95. A free copy of the book is provided with it, giving the clues to help solve the adventures. Similarly, if you own a ZX 81 (16K) you can play *Frogger*; the object of this game is to guide your frog across the road, then to cross the river by jumping onto turtles and logs to reach a safe haven in a frog-home. If you fill all five frog-homes, you earn a new 'screen' with more hazards, including moving cars and diving turtles. Saving a baby-frog earns you a bonus. In a more elaborate programme *Kingdom*, you are given a rural realm to control (your name, sex and age determine whether you will be King, Queen, Prince or Princess). Your object is to protect your people against flood, famine and the ruthless local banditry. The similarity between these computer games and the world of Tolkien is striking; we enter a world of bewildering mythology to perform our decoding quest in the increasingly privatized world of cultural consumption which is determined by the sophistication of our domestic equipment.

Even more than this: we are no longer dependent on the mythologies of others, whether Tolkien's or anybody else's. For the domestic computer allows us to construct our own quests, our own mythological worlds, our own rewards, to build our own moral universe. The privatization of cultural consumption has completed itself: everyone can not only make their own L.P., everyone can construct their own Middle-earth. But this freedom is still based on comparative affluence and increasingly on the education necessary to programme your machine, in your increasingly sophisticated hobbit-hole. Tolkien's popularity represents one moment in this post-war process of cultural privatization and, perhaps more tentatively, in the growing scientific interest of the English intelligentsia. Yet a certain ambiguity remains: in order to rule your kingdom of peasants on the 16K ZX-81, you need 2Ø1Ø lines.

On the other hand, the English fairy tale is still alive and well—in the *Ladybird* books at your newsagents, in the pantomime at the Wimbledon Theatre. Jack and Dick still come into their deserved public reward, Jack still marries the Princess, and Dick becomes Lord Mayor of London. But this has nothing to do with Tolkien.

NOTES

1. J. R. R. Tolkien, *Tree and Leaf* (London: Allen & Unwin, 1964), pp. 15–16.
2. *Tree and Leaf*, op. cit., p. 52.
3. *Tree and Leaf*, op. cit., p. 56.
4. *Tree and Leaf*, op. cit., p. 60.
5. Joseph Jacobs, *English Fairy Tales* (London: David Nutt, 1890). The edition cited here is that published by the Bodley Head (London, 1968).
6. *Los Angeles Times*, 9 April 1972.
7. *Tree and Leaf*, op cit., p. 52.
8. *Tree and Leaf*, op. cit., p. 56.
9. J. R. R. Tolkien, *The Lord of the Rings*, revised 2nd edition (London: Allen & Unwin, 1966), Vol. III, p. 296.
10. J. R. R. Tolkien, *The Hobbit*, 3rd edition (London: Allen & Unwin, 1966), p. 33.
11. *The Hobbit*, op. cit., p. 177.
12. *English Fairy Tales*, op. cit., p. 144.
13. *Tree and Leaf*, op. cit., p. 60.
14. *English Fairy Tales*, op. cit., p. 45.
15. *English Fairy Tales*, op. cit., p. 110.
16. *The Hobbit*, op. cit., p. 268.
17. *The Hobbit*, op. cit., p. 279.
18. *The Lord of the Rings*, op. cit., Vol. III, p. 234.

3

Middle-earth and the Adolescent

by JANET MENZIES

When I was small we had a house with a breakfast room fire. The fire sometimes used to smoke, and the room smelt of coal-dust. With bits of bacon rind on it the fire used to crackle up with a blue flame, though staying a little greasy. In one corner of the breakfast room was a bookcase.

I looked at it, but the books were very dull. Shabby volumes in dusty red, green or blue clothboard, they were histories or biographies or collected poems. One old day when I was bored and there was nothing to read or be read aloud, my mother told me to pick a book from the bookcase.

Without much hope I had another look and came across an ordinary little black book with 'Alice's Adventures in Wonderland, and Through the Looking Glass and what she found there' stamped in gold lettering on the front. That is how I remember the moment when I made my first real discovery in the world of books. Ever afterwards I used to scour that bookcase for another glorious find, a nugget of gold in the faded clothboard ore, but I never have. The bookcase, transplanted several times, still exists and I always have a quick search through when visiting my parents.

' "What is the use of a book", thought Alice, "without pictures or conversations" ', and *Alice in Wonderland* was well-supplied with atmospheric Tenniel pictures and memorable conversations. The best picture of all, though, was that conjured up by the book itself. The words were marvellous living pictures, a real world which you stepped into entirely when you began reading. It is this thrill of genuine experience and sensation, produced just by words on paper, which I look forward to every time I begin a book.

C. S. Lewis remembered with affection that his childhood home was crammed with books stacked two deep in the bookcases and how eager he was to read them. Once I knew about the reality of words and how you could go on true adventures in actual, personal experience, I hardly stopped reading. That is how I came across *The Hobbit*. As usual I was plaguing my mother for more reading matter and she suggested I look out for *The Hobbit*. I was about 9 then, and quickly found it in the quiet little book room of my junior school.

On opening *The Hobbit* and entering Tolkien's Middle-earth I once again experienced that extreme joy of revelation which started me on the reading path two or three years before. Here I was opening an ordinary, unexciting hardback book with a blue and green drawing of a mountain on the cover, but at the same time I was actually walking, running, fighting and breathing in Middle-earth. I stress the concrete details of my getting hold of these books because to me the experience of reading them was just as real as was the physical handling of their covers.

By the time I was 11 I was already setting out from Rivendell on my way to the Misty Mountains—although finding all three separate books in the library was a problem. The one volume paperback came out when I was about 10, but I did not get hold of it immediately. At that age the world of sensation and of landscape is very important. It is on these levels that I still think *The Lord of the Rings* makes its primary impact. So I was very lucky to read it when young, and to be able to grow up with the book, unlike many of its contemporary critics.

Mine was an instant reactive response, unalloyed by any notion of critical analysis. The memory of that response, and the conviction that reading is real, find a fuller exposition in Tolkien's own theories of 'sub-creation'.

There are two important things about grass, discovered

Tolkien—its grassness of course, but also, and especially, its greenness. Then he realized that the mind which can separate the greenness of grass from its general grassyness has the perception to make anything of that grass:

> The human mind, endowed with the powers of generalization and abstraction, sees not only green-grass, discriminating it from other things (and finding it fair to look upon), but sees that it is green as well as being grass. But how powerful, how stimulating to the very faculty that produced it, was the invention of the adjective; no spell or incantation in Faerie is more potent.[1]

Sub-creation is an ability to make real the external sensations of a story. Ordinary description, by comparison with sub-creation, is a photographic process of transporting an image from one place to another by recording it. Sub-creation reveals to the senses a place, a landscape, which has previously been no-place. Tolkien called it, 'the power of making immediately effective by the will the visions of "fantasy"',[2] but my own experience with *The Lord of the Rings* warns me against implications of the visionary or purely imaginative.

When the hobbits walk across the Barrow-downs on the early part of their journey, they find themselves in 'a country of grass and short springy turf, silent except for the whisper of the air over the edges of the land, and high lonely cries of strange birds'.[3]

As evening overtakes them, the weather closes in:

> The sun, a pale and watery yellow, was gleaming through the mist just above the west wall of the hollow in which they lay; north, south, and east, beyond the wall the fog was thick, cold and white. The air was silent, heavy and chill.[4]

These downs are similar to some unpopulated parts of England, the Pennines especially; or they may be like some of the countryside Tolkien would tramp through with his fellow Inklings.[5] No matter how far you search, though, you will not find the Barrow-downs in England, Wales, Scotland, Ireland, Europe, America or wherever. Tolkien tells us quite specifically where they are—just to the east of the Old Forest, on the borders of the Shire in Middle-earth. That is where you find them, just as you find the curious low brown hills of Kerry on the south-west coast of Eire.

To me the effect of reading the quoted passages is the same as going for a walk on the Lancashire moors. I experience the turf of Barrow-down just as I experience that of Deerplay moor. The isolation is the same, the air is as quiet in both places because both places do have air. Analysing Tolkien's 'sub-creation' here we find that adjectives make the description concrete, as Tolkien has pointed out. Without them, we would see a country of grass and turf with air at the edges of the land and cries of birds—emotive, yes, but it would take the reader's previous experience of some like place to supply an imaginative reality. Tolkien's description is complete as it stands. Its quality of reality is its own: independent of what a reader may bring to it. Before Tolkien wrote it down that landscape was not; now it is.

The ability, highly developed in Tolkien, to create entity, may be closely related to the anti-analytic stance towards literature among his academic friends which is highlighted in Humphrey Carpenter's *The Inklings*. Carpenter, simulating a discussion among the Inklings, has C. S. Lewis decrying the critical habit of constant analysis of meaning; and saying of *The Lord of the Rings*:

> Story—or at least a great story of the mythical type—gives us an experience of something not as an abstraction but as a concrete reality. We don't understand the meaning when we read a myth, we actually encounter the thing itself. (p. 143)

Carpenter also quotes Charles Williams on the same theme 'it isn't what poetry says, it is what poetry is', describing the belief in poetry as a 'storehouse of emotional or even supernatural power' (p. 102). Under these conditions criticism should concentrate on the discharge of that storehouse, embodied in its effect upon the reader. How the battery was charged up would become a secondary matter.

Meaning and being are fused:

> As he fell slowly into sleep, Pippin had a strange feeling: he and Gandalf were still as a stone, seated upon the statue of a running horse, while the world rolled away beneath his feet with a great noise of wind. (p. 624)

This image made a great impact on me as a child. It altered and expanded my perception of the external world. My appreciation deepened of the huge potential of what could be concretely sensed. The value of Tolkien's sub-creation is to develop the reader's response to his environment, that extra sense which sees the dragon round the corner.

I think Tolkien underestimated the power of his sub-creation:

> I desired dragons with a profound desire. Of course, I in my timid body did not wish to have them in the neighbourhood, intruding into my relatively safe world, in which it was, for instance possible to read stories in peace of mind, free from fear.[6]

The achievement of *The Lord of the Rings* is that it is not possible to be free from fear or in a peaceful state of mind. In a footnote Tolkien decides that 'The answer, "There is certainly no dragon in England today", is all they [children] want to hear.' The success of *The Lord of the Rings* is the reverse, it makes you aware that there are certainly dragons in Middle-earth, which is as real as England—so you begin checking around the garden for tracks!

In an Inklings' 'conversation' Carpenter has Lewis make the point that a child's reading about enchanted woods 'makes all real woods a little enchanted', but through reading the very books written by Lewis (and Tolkien), I discovered that the 'real' woods had been enchanted all the time, which the books enabled me to see. Equally the 'enchanted' woods were perfectly real. The reality of a wood, any wood, is its enchanting sensation—the writer responds to this, and the pure image comes across in the book.

The reader's sensory path is the same whether he is reading a book or admiring a tree. The image is fielded by the eyes, translated into impulses and then digested by the brain. Whether words printed on a page or leaves growing on a tree the process is the same. Who is to say that the images in our brain on reading words may not be more real than the images on seeing leaves? Perhaps indeed the brain fails to translate leaves fully, so that we never experience the whole tree as we do the whole story. I often find leaves more difficult to 'read' than words. Yet stories (Tolkien's especially) help us to learn the language of leaves—so that we can translate trees fully when we see them. The natural reaction of the reading child is to get into the habit of reading everything—words in a book; leaves on a tree; bricks in a wall; clouds on a sky; pebbles on a beach—and, of course, people on a street. Oh yes, dragon spotting is very important when it comes to people reading!

Yet Tolkien's conjecture that *The Lord of the Rings* could be read without disturbance of spiritual equilibrium (p. 144, *The Inklings*) may point towards an area which the Inklings were conscious the book did not enter. Not very long after reading Tolkien's story I began to make up my own tales about a great hero who rode out on quests in wild lands. He was rather untrustworthy, occasionally unmerciful, inclined to depressive moods and definitely irresponsible. In spite of that he was indisputably noble, courageous and kind, with a supreme joy in life: in fact a complete, and I still think, convincing hero. A hero was what *The Lord of the Rings* did not supply.

Aragorn is initially attractive; when we meet Strider at Bree he has an alluring doubleness which hints at a romantic hero. The first description of Strider, 'His legs were stretched out before him, showing high boots of supple leather that fitted him well, but had seen much wear and were now caked with mud' (p. 172), has a highwayman sexyness in its appeal. There is also a mystery about him: 'For a while he sat with unseeing eyes as if walking in distant memory or listening to sounds in the Night far away' (p. 181). Then comes the revelation of his hidden power: ' "If I was after the Ring, I could have it—now!" He stood up, and seemed suddenly to grow taller, in his eyes gleamed a light, keen and commanding' (p. 187); but his mightiness is also accessible, because he is dispossessed, and his sword is broken.

During the journey towards the Misty Mountains Aragorn's internal character develops as we see him in conflict with Gandalf about the choice of road. While the company are staying in Lothlorien Aragorn is reavealed again as 'a young lord tall and fair' (p. 371). The revelation technique is also applied to Galadriel in this section, when she defies the eye of Sauron and reveals her ring: 'seeming now tall beyond measurement—. . . terrible and worshipful. Then she let her hand fall . . . and lo! she was shrunken' (p. 385). Once more in Lothlorien Tolkien repeats the technique with Aragorn: 'those who saw him wondered; for they had not marked before how tall and Kingly he stood' (p. 395); and yet again, this time with Galadriel: 'he saw her again standing like a queen, great and beautiful, but no longer terrible' (p. 397).

The next revealing of Aragorn follows quickly; on the river journey, as the company pass through Argonath: 'the weather-worn Ranger was no longer there. In the stern sat Aragorn son of Arathorn, proud and erect . . . his hood was cast back and his dark hair was blowing in the wind . . .' (p. 413).

With the chase of the Three Kindreds we come into much closer relationships with the three chasers. The stirring and rhythmically exciting account of the chase is moving because it is told on an intimate, personal level. Aragorn comes to combat the moral problem of choice-making. As the chase comes to an end, though, Tolkien repeats his favourite trick of revelation:

> Gimli and Legolas looked at their companion in amazement, for they had not seen him in this mood before. He seemed to have grown in stature while Eomer had shrunk; and in his living face they caught a brief vision of the power and majesty of the kings of stone. (p. 454)

This device of giving brief glimpses of the true nature of a veiled character can be very eye-catching. Used sparingly it is both dramatic and convincing, but Tolkien repeats it so often that it becomes at first irritating and eventually ridiculous. It is used at the return of Gandalf: 'there he stood, grown suddenly tall, towering above them' (p. 515). After the return of Gandalf the character of Aragorn diminishes. He becomes a remote paragon of kingliness, and any inner self is gradually lost as he inherits the selflessness of regal responsibility.

Gandalf's descent and resurrection during the Balrog episode make him too unapproachable to be a central hero. He is even described in terms which make him a Christ figure. We hear that 'he has passed through fire and the abyss' (p. 522). Gandalf describes how 'naked I was sent back . . . and naked I lay upon the mountain-top' (p. 524). It is as though Gandalf's fall with the Balrog was a descent into hell, and now he has risen again. Like the risen Christ, too, his disciples doubt him when he first comes among them. Tolkien loses his sure concrete touch for description in the battle on the stair. The visual detail is vague, a weird impression of a fiery nostrilled creature with a whip, which seems to play very heavily on human nightmare phobias of high staircases suspended over nothingness; fear of falling; whip-bearing monsters; and fiery darkness.

Frodo shares with Gandalf many Christlike, but not heroic, features. As ringbearer it is just convincing that Frodo should succeed in his quest, mainly through the Christian fallacy that meekness, innocence and humility are the conquering strengths of humanity. Yet as the bearer of the onus of interior development in *The Lord of the Rings* Frodo is too weak a vessel. Frodo is an urbane and sophisticated, if introverted, member of the very natural hobbit world. His role requires him to operate convincingly on a supernatural plane—so Frodo's character changes very rapidly.

His first wound, received on the way to Rivendell, marks him out and sets him apart as if it had been the kiss of Judas at Gethsemane. Recovered from the wound Frodo says, 'I feel much better, but I don't think I could sing, perhaps Sam . . .' (p. 222). His rejection of the material here smacks more of the pietistic than of a gradual withdrawal to be expected in the ring-bearer. More convincing would be to hear these words after entering Frodo's internal struggle, his equivalent of Christ's 'let this cup pass.'

As Frodo's quest proceeds Tolkien's vocabulary is increasingly inadequate. When the hobbits enter Ithilien we are told they 'breathed deep, and suddenly Sam laughed, for heart's ease not for jest' (p. 677), language which is not in keeping with hobbit experience—no matter where. Suspect diction is most apparent in the sentimental, and frequently patronizing, portrayal of Sam and Frodo's relationship. Frodo, watched by Sam, sleeping in Ithilien looks:

> Old and beautiful as if the chiselling of the shaping years was now revealed . . . Not that Sam Gamgee put it that way to himself. He . . . murmured: 'I love him. He's like that and sometimes it shines through, somehow. But I love him, whether or no.' (p. 678)

The effect is half-way between a disciple honouring Christ and a First World War N.C.O. talking about his captain. Frodo is a sleeping hobbit—a leathery footed creature just over three feet high—and Sam, though unlearned and an employee, is not a gormless retainer.

The Victorian mawkishness of

> In his lap lay Frodo's head, drowned deep in sleep; upon his white forehead lay one of Sam's brown hands, and the other lay softly upon his master's breast. Peace was in both their faces. (p. 741)

is misplaced because there is no emotional necessity for it. Such false diction is often a clue of the writer's failure to engage fully with his subject. Tolkien makes Frodo the ring-bearer when he could have given the ring to Aragorn, Gandalf (even Sauron), or to a latter-day Beren. Hobbits were favourites with Tolkien, and they were what the public wanted. The most recent possessor of the ring was a hobbit. These positive reasons are, I think, outweighed by the negative impulse that Tolkien needed his ring-bearer to be a cipher.

If the ring had been given to a strong, fully developed character the whole emphasis of the story would be changed. The human character who carried the ring would have to be very convincing, with a large degree of internal development. The man's struggle would be all the greater because he was capable of bearing the ring. The reader would enter that struggle intellectually and be offered understanding of every element of the hero's journey to enlightenment. This moral dimension would raise the book's scope to the achievement of great novels (like *Moby Dick*, or *Nostromo*) where the epic narrative of stirring events is intensified through the focus of a moral burning glass.

That would certainly be a novel to carry through life! Tolkien, though, avoided this challenge by making Frodo carry the burden (of the book and the ring). He wrote a story, not a novel. Using Frodo he could still have internalized the presentation of the character's experience, which is expressed externally through physical hardship and atmospheric landscape.

Tolkien tends to deprive Frodo of free will as the book develops. Frodo feels the pull of the ring at Cirith Ungol:

64

> There was no longer any answer to that command in his own
> will, dismayed by terror though it was, and he felt only the
> beating upon him of a great power from outside. (p. 734)

This description gives the impression of the ring's power being
something external and physical, like magnetism, but we
know that the ring's magic works internally, bending men's
minds in a telepathic way, not moving their bodies tele-
kinetically.

Then Frodo steps out of his own mind, watching himself
from outside as we watch him:

> It took his hand, and as Frodo watched with his mind, not
> willing it but in suspense (as if he looked on some old story far
> away), it moved the hand inch by inch towards the chain upon
> his neck.

Frodo is non-participant, and the non-human objective pro-
noun operates the action. Nor does it relate directly to Frodo's
self; it moves 'the' hand, not Frodo's hand, and everything is
'far away' from Frodo:

> Then his own will stirred; slowly it forced the hand back and
> set it to find another thing, a thing lying hidden near his breast.

How, though, does Frodo's will work? What makes it stir?
How does Frodo feel as he begins to conquer the ring's power?
The acting of Frodo's will is expressed in the same terms as the
impulsion of the ring; it simply takes 'the' hand in a different
direction. Then the phial of Galadriel rescues him—again an
external agent.

Frodo is not the only character deprived of free will by the
ring and Sauron's demands through the ring. The under-
mining of human judgement is a general effect of the ring
throughout the story. The revelation technique which shows
Boromir hideously changed by the ring is reflected and con-
trasted in his brother, Faramir, who is one of the few characters able to master his response through conscious decision.
Yet despite its importance in driving the mechanics of the plot,
the ring does not provide the story's centre, nor does it act as a
hero substitute.

If we look at the ring as an image of the story's development we see it as a hollow circle—as Tom Bombadil shows it to be by putting his eye to it: 'the hobbits had a vision, both comical and alarming, of his bright blue eye gleaming in a circle of gold' (p. 148). With its repetition of patterns, themes and effects Tolkien's plot is circular rather than linear. It seems to spiral round and round, propelling its protagonists on inter-locking and reflecting courses. There are fairy-tale formulae: the giving of gifts; the enacting of prophesies; the meeting of helpers; the episodic bouts of action and respite; the repeating of ritual acts (like Merry and Pippin both becoming liege-men).

The interchanging patterns take up a circular motif, as though Tolkien himself were searching round as he wrote. In such a complex plot we would certainly expect a certain amount of authorial scouting around to keep loose threads of plot and straying persona in order, but is the circularity in Tolkien's plot more like an emotional search? The ring is simply a circle—it encloses nothingness, and can have no centre. Is Tolkien on a personal, moral quest for the centre of his own book?

The successes of Tolkien's 'sub-creation' in *The Lord of the Rings* are on an external level. He makes real a whole land-scape; it is the forces of the concrete environment of Middle-earth which drive his protagonists to endure danger and hardship. Each new episode comes as a battering blow of sensation on the reader, a breaker in which he struggles with the characters to keep his head above water.

There are many versions of external special sight in *The Lord of the Rings*, particularly in visions from high places. From the pinnacle of Orthanc Gandalf sees all the activity of Saruman's army. On the mountain-top of Celebdil Gandalf gathers 'the rumour of all lands'. In Rohan Legolas watches the riders at a great distance, yet sees them in tiny detail. Galadriel's mirror is not a high place, but in it Frodo sees the scenes of a vast history enacted. From Minas Tirith, Pippin sees all the movements across the field of Pelennor. All these sights give a sense of the large scale enactment of events and the movement of bodies of people across the vast stage of the physical world. This stage is itself the 'hero' of Tolkien's book: not the players, but the play's own changing landscape.

The Lord of the Rings has no fundamental moral or human centre because Tolkien's primary concern is not with the inner man, the social man, at all. 'All this stuff is mainly concerned with Fall, Mortality and the Machine. . . . by the last I intend all use of external plans or devices (apparatus). . . .'[7] Tolkien's preoccupation is with the external world, and moreover with an external world undergoing profound changes. Change, rather than human conflict, stands at the heart of *The Lord of the Rings*. Entropy is constantly at work in Middle-earth. Every landscape we enter is one that has been altered: the Barrow-downs have been depopulated; Moria is a dwelling place which has changed hands; Lothlorien is gradually fading; Fangorn has lost its womenfolk; Hollin and Ithilien are no longer elvish; Minas Tirith has a throne without a king; and the lands round Moria have been corrupted and made barren.

Middle-earth is a place of fading and passing-away, every victory there is pyrrhic. This sense of loss stems from Tolkien's belief in the Fall and his expression of the external state of being fallen. It is the fall which makes change inevitable, and which predetermines mortality—the second of Tolkien's themes.

Reluctant to let go of Middle-earth, Tolkien draws out the ending of his book while he tidies up various external details. The end of the ring quest is reached when Gollum falls with the ring into Mount Doom: 'even as his eyes were lifted up to gloat on his prize, he stepped too far, toppled, wavered for a moment, and then with a shriek he fell' (p. 982). This is the organic conclusion of the story and that vivid, almost Dickensian tableau, its artistic climax. Many a painter would put down his brush there and many a writer put the cover on his typewriter. It is significant that Tolkien continues for another six chapters.

In these chapters Tolkien stresses the third theme, his dislike of the machine age. The Shire is industrialized with the machines and bricks which Tolkien despises. Although it is re-created after its despoliation, we know that mechanizing forces cannot wholly be reversed. Frodo tells Gandalf (p. 1026) 'there is no real going back.' The trip back to the Shire is filled with a sense of nostalgia. As the companions retrace their footsteps they wistfully relive old memories which to some (not

67

Frodo) seem almost preferable to the present journey. They seem so because they belonged to a time of beginning, of setting-out, not the present period of ending. The emphasis is on the passing of the Third Age and the fading away of the elves.

The experience of nostalgia and the sense of loss are, I think, quite common features of adolescence. There is nothing wrong with nostalgia. At the end of an enjoyable walking holiday Tolkien and his friends would look back with some regret to think the good times they had shared on it were over. They would also appreciate, though, that there was nothing bad about its being over. Their positive response would be to enjoy their memory of the holiday, but not to allow excessive reflection to spoil the present moment. Just emerging from the physical, sensational world of youth, an adolescent lacks the emotional development for this reaction. Often nostalgia makes us try to cling on and fight the change. For where the moral centre which puts meaning into life is lacking, then external change is unacceptable.

In *The Lord of the Rings* the same conditions operate. There is the 'felt' world, experienced, by the brilliance of Tolkien's sub-creation, with all the vitality and glory of youth's waking days. Without a hero, though, without the exploration of man's inner being, the book lacks a moral centre. By this I do not mean that the story is immoral in the sense of being godless, or without standards of good and bad. It is rather that it is 'manless'. The dictionary tells us that what is moral is 'concerned with or relating to human behaviour'. I would describe morality as the central point of reference in a book. It is the inner matter which a reader will almost unconsciously strive to find. His attempts to find it are, I think, an essential part of reading. The reader should always be reaching out for the point of linkage, at which he and the writer are mutually engaged.

I have stressed before that we do grow from reading *The Lord of the Rings*. We grow in our response to our environment, which we perceive more acutely, but our inner judgement is not tested. It is important to be able to see dragons so that we can develop into the sort of person who can understand and cope with dragons, but the development of moral equipment is also necessary. This does not mean that you should read a book just because it is good for you. Of course we don't read *The Lord of the Rings* because we think it is doing us good, and leave off reading it when it has stopped having the effect—any more than we drink Guinness because it is good for us (despite the advertisements!). We read (or drink) because it pleases us.

Where Tolkien's book fails to please, and it does, can usually be tracked down to the lack of a moral centre. When the characters are unsatisfying it is because they lack internal development; when the plot is irritating it is because it lacks interior necessity. It is for the writer's own sake that his story should be moral, not for his reader's. If the story is not moral, where is the writer? His choices in description will not be guided. He writes the story for himself as well as for a reader. If the story is not moral, then the writer does not have to engage with it, and when he is not engaged he ceases to convince; his descriptive choices go wrong. Then the creative contact between the writer and the reader can be fragmented or lost completely.

I think it unlikely that Tolkien and his Inkling friends would have placed so much importance on internalization. Tolkien was a traditional Roman Catholic and Lewis eventually arrived at a basically Anglo-catholic faith. Lewis's major achievements in criticism were in medieval literature, Tolkien's in Early English—both pre-Renaissance periods.

These pointers, while perhaps not particularly significant within the Inklings, provide clues as to why we feel a lack of internalization in Tolkien's *The Lord of the Rings*. At the heart of Judao-Christian religion is the fall, stated by Tolkien to be one of the main themes of *The Lord of the Rings*. Thanks to Christ each Catholic individual can be absolved and achieve, if only for a while, a state of grace. Belief in the fall implies that fallen man has lost his perfect moral being. It could be argued that the fallen state of man is the most morally aware, and the internal dialogue which arises is the most creative. A traditional Catholic, though, will desire the state of grace as the most real and perfect human aspiration; to him the mind of fallen man is less important. Personality has little place in the Catholic faith.

In pre-Renaissance literature, whether pagan or Catholic, I

find a common external mode of expression. The private world of soliloquy and sonnet characteristic of the Renaissance had little place in either myth, saga or allegory. In sagas a man is defined more by his acts (*gestes*) than his thoughts. The practice of allegory is to externalize inner action by presenting it as a physical world.

Tolkien's principal males add up to a corporate identity where each represents elements or limbs of the complete organism. Boromir has pride, Faramir discernment; Aragorn has experience, Eomer instinct. Like ants in an ant heap, all these components join to form a successful unit, and again early society had little notion of the individual as a unity. Such circumstances, I think, may have contributed to a lack of inner causation in Tolkien's book.

The Lord of the Rings has now itself become a circumstance of daily life. The craze of the '60s and '70s is a seminal influence in the '80s. The blockbusting film *Star Wars* shows many signs of its influence. It concerns the epic theme of good fighting evil, and the movements and *gestes* of mankind caught up in the age-long struggle. There are wizards, too, in the shape of Jedi knights. Darth Vader is Saruman, a wizard turned to evil, and his adversary is Obi Kenobi, a Gandalf figure whose own death is eventually a triumph over evil. Gandalf fights the Balrog on the bridge of Khazad-dum:

> It stepped forward slowly onto the bridge, and suddenly it drew itself up to a great height . . . but still Gandalf could be seen. . . . From out of the shadow a red sword leaped flaming. Glamdring glittered white in answer. There was a ringing clash and a stab of white fire. (p. 349)

To see this battle reproduced on film you have only to watch the last fight between Darth Vader and Obi Kenobi in *Star Wars* (notice, too, how the red light-sabre of Vader leaps out of darkness).

The 'new romantic' pop wave also shows a Tolkienish desire for heroic figures. Adam Ant went back to fairy-tale roots for his Prince Charming; and Toyah's preoccupations are with white horses galloping across a Morder-like plain. Costumes are those of Norse war-lords, noble savages, Arthurian knights, princes and princesses: the heroes of earlier times. So many of today's pop videos could be the very landscape of Middle-earth; they show an impersonal, changed world of fantasy.

They possess the same concrete appreciation of a potent physical world which Tolkien inspired in me. This is not simply a response to having been brought up in a Tolkien generation. Nor does it wholly reflect the adolescent love of sensations. Today's experience is impersonal; Tolkien provides the trappings of heroism. His externalized outlook leads us into the abstract world of the *geste*. 'This means nothing to me' is a repeated phrase (listen to Ultra Vox's song 'Vienna') which voices a recognition of the baselessness of our situation. Actions are felt intensely, but they remain cold and remote; events are enthralling, but formalistic.

Then the attraction of alienation takes over: life is full of moving and doing, performing elegant and intricate rituals. The actors and the audience are all caught up in some larger dramatization. The more money, the more vivid and satisfying the drama. All this is pleasing like ritual, even the movement of the mind across emptiness becomes a wonderful pattern. The individual, having no inner core, watches his unpossessed self drift across the poignantly beautiful wastes of external artifice.

This is not the positive, but youthful, enthusiasm for felt experience; nor even the adolescent struggle for understanding. It is the winter lingering of one who stays beyond his time in the life of sensation, rejecting the creative search for meaning's centre.

As a child *The Lord of the Rings* meant everything to me; coming back to it as an adult I find it superficially attractive but ultimately unsatisfying. It is a book of and for adolescence. Of its author I can only say that Tolkien showed me how to perceive the world, but he did not convey to me an understanding of it.

NOTES

1. J. R. R. Tolkien, 'On Fairy-Stories', in *Tree and Leaf* (London: Allen & Unwin, 1964), p. 25.
2. Ibid.
3. J. R. R. Tolkien, *The Lord of the Rings* (London: Allen & Unwin, 1968), p. 151.
4. *The Lord of the Rings*, op. cit., p. 153.
5. I am indebted for this information about the Inklings to Humphrey Carpenter's *The Inklings* (London: Allen & Unwin, 1981).
6. *Tree and Leaf*, op cit., p. 40.
7. *The Letters of J. R. R. Tolkien*, edited by Humphrey Carpenter (London: Allen & Unwin, 1981), p. 145.

4

Tolkien and the '60s

by NIGEL WALMSLEY

The popularity of *The Lord of the Rings* has to be understood in the context of that group which most surely guaranteed its reputation, the young, disaffected section of the Western industrial middle class of the mid-1960s. The book was a seminal influence on the popular sub-culture of that period, an artifact as commercially enticing as a Bob Dylan record. As an apparent literary success it has perplexed some academics, and in 1967 a protracted correspondence on the merits of the book took place in the letters column of *The Times* between British University teachers anxious at what they saw as a sign of the collapse of their students' critical judgement in embracing Middle-earth. The key years in establishing Tolkien's popularity as a writer were from 1965 to 1968, during which period *The Lord of the Rings* sold 3,000,000 copies in paperback. Nothing succeeds like success and the sales momentum created then has ensured steady international sales since: 8,000,000 copies had been sold worldwide by 1980.[1] But the wide temporal and spatial span of the book's popularity has obscured the context of Tolkien's original sub-cultural impact in the mid-'60s from which this success stems.

To attempt to place some unifying significance on the '60s, on any decade, is a facile exercise in simplifying and making sense of time, compartmentalizing history, cataloguing the culture. To see the '30s as depression, the '40s as war and austerity, the '50s as affluence, the '60s as revolution, the '70s as consolidation, the '80s as decline and . . . depression, is neatly to complete a superficial cyclical view of the recent past but ultimately only to weigh down the donkey time with a pannier of clichés. The error of such facility lies in using isolated moments and events as indicators of cultural and social mood.

Thus, we can give the '60s no monolithic meaning, no arbitrary attribution of significance that will hold fast to analytical, ground: to understand Tolkien's apotheosis in the middle of that decade, eleven years after the first publication of *The Lord of the Rings*, it is necessary to look back to the late '30s to two separate, isolated yet coincidental developments.

In 1938, Tolkien in England and Albert Hoffmann in Switzerland began tentative, innovative experiments in unlinked, independently conceived, original creative works, Tolkien's literary, Hoffmann's chemical. Tolkien's work, of course, emerged in 1954 as *The Lord of the Rings*, Hoffmann's as lysergic acid diethylamide (LSD), the most potent of all psychotomimetic drugs.

In 1943, having unwittingly ingested a small quantity of the chemical, whose precise effects on the human nervous system were then unknown, Hoffmann took a cycle ride and rapidly became aware of an increasingly intense psychotic reaction as the faces of passers-by loomed like masks, colours intensified and his sense experience became exaggerated and distorted, the now familiar effects of LSD ingestion. Hoffmann had accidentally pioneered the use of a drug that was to be used first in psychotherapeutic research into schizophrenic conditions in the late '40s and early '50s, and then, as news of experimental use in the psychology departments of American universities spread to other, disinterested students, academics and campus frequenters, it began to acquire a social use, initially as an intensifier of awareness and then as an indispensable adjunct to hedonism.

With almost Koestlerian coincidence the works of Tolkien and Hoffmann formed a potent cultural conjunction in the mid-'60s, a quarter of a century after the early seminal experiments in each. For the sudden increase in popularity of *The Lord of the Rings* at this time, its fashionable status as a subcultural text a decade after it had first been published, can be directly attributed to the parallel increase in popularity of LSD with the same social group, the dissident, young, educated middle class.

Though the effects of LSD can vary widely between individuals and its street marketing led to a loss of purity and to adulteration with such additives as strychnine, subjective discussions at the time centred on whether it constituted a journey into or away from reality. Certainly it could pierce the skin of reality and reveal the underlying artifice and pretence of contemporary sophistication as grotesque. Significantly for Tolkien's popularity this led to an atavistic evaluation of the primitive and the ethnic over the modern. However, a mythology grew around LSD which was ultimately a more potent sub-cultural force than the drug itself. Few took it regularly, many once, others never; but the received perception of the chemical's effects began to texture and condition the style, manners and artifacts of the *soi-disant* alternative society or counter-culture.

From 1965 onwards the familiar alternative product of posters, comics and record album sleeves was increasingly marked by the imitation of the agreed spectrum of psychedelic experience, from alleged nightmare to avowed epiphany. For marketing purposes a set of signs evolved which emphasized intense visual pleasure by manipulating the shape and colour of content mythic, erotic or mundane, in order to create an aura of sensuousness and accessibility.

Unfortunately for the market, few books of any substance were being written in this genre. Publishers cast around for a writer to fill this gap, to do for LSD what Thomas de Quincey had done for opium or Aldous Huxley for mescalin, but apart from the outpourings of Dr. Timothy Leary and Carlos Castaneda's investigations of esoteric organic Yaqui psychedelics (complete with a parodied pseudo-philosophical structure for analysing the new reality) little emerged that was not unmarketable or ephemeral.

Naturally enough the decade-old work of an Oxford don had not been considered in this light, but the mass sales success of *The Lord of the Rings* following paperback publication in 1965 is not in retrospect surprising: like the popular artifacts of psychedelia it was the product of strong visual imagination and encompassed the mundane and the mythic. It was readily assimilable through a clearly etched plot and, most importantly, dealt with an ethnic, primitive other-world: it was read by millions in eschewal of the artificiality of modern industrial society and in pursuit of atavism.

One of the ironies of the growing wealth and affluence of the western industrial middle class in the '60s was that many of its sons and daughters, assured of a material and psychological safety net from their parents, temporarily rejected comfort and indulged in the atavistic pursuit of a false ethnicism. This atavistic tendency was the natural outcome of the growing rejection of materialism amongst the post-war bulge generation, raised from austerity in the doctrine of the pursuit of prosperity, and formally educated to a level beyond that of their parents, only to deny the belief that happiness was a warm television set. A consumer society can be enjoyed uncritically and without irony only by those lacking the awareness to perceive its hollowness. Offered the prospect of limitless material satisfaction provided by what Harold Wilson described in 1964 as 'the white heat of the technological revolution', a substantial section of the post-war generation bit the hand that fed.

First in America, then in Britain, it became fashionable for the sons and daughters of the middle classes to reject the trappings of wealth, materialism, possessions and profit and adopt a primitivism of style. Their aim was to deconstruct the old reality and construct a new one. This atavism took both urban and rural forms: the urban was aggressive and anarchic and by 1968 had been channelled into direct political action such as that seen at the Chicago Democratic Convention in August of that year; the rural atavism, passive and apolitical, bore direct similarities to Hobbit culture, whether in the troglodytic communes of Taos or the mountain communes of Washington State. In spite of urban poverty, a rich society had created a huge surplus; it was sated. You could live on the surplus and provided you did not think too much about its origins or about overconsumption of the world's resources, you could still claim a philosophy. Steinbeck's shabby hamburgerstands on Route 66 in *The Grapes of Wrath* had thirty years later become air-conditioned diners where meals were often ordered not eaten, or only pecked. You could ride down 66 and dine well every few hours at no expense or just the price of a coffee to sit at an uncleared table.

Britain never saw such surplus as America; there was less fat. For that reason, the alternative society was first and strongest in America; a whole sub-culture could live from the well-stocked trash cans of supermarket parking lots. And for that reason too the cult of Tolkien was first and strongest in America. There an alternative world was possible; there were resources to spare, especially land. The virgin tracts of the United States and Canada made the atavistic pursuit of a pre-industrial way of life feasible. In its purest form this might entail an attempt to establish a commune in the wilderness of Canada or to live in a driftwood log cabin on the Pacific shores of Oregon.

For the first time it became fashionable for young Americans to interest themselves in the last vestige of tribal life in the United States, the red Indians. That the traditions of most tribes had been progressively destroyed by two centuries of white political and cultural imperialism signified little. Denied peyote, offered instead alcohol and, through inherited genetic vulnerability, inevitable alcoholism, the dignity of ethnic tribal life had been perniciously eroded. In its death throes it was embraced in selfish naïvety by handfuls of the young white educated middle class in pursuit of an illusion, tribal life untouched by industrialism and technology.

If in America Middle-earth could seem like a model for an alternative reality, in Britain, with the second highest population density in Europe, Tolkien's world could be most readily perceived as fantasy. Attempts to set up microcosms of Hobbit-like communities centred around rural crafts and simple technology were less grand, more domestic in conception. In fact, many young Londoners shaped the peripheries of their lives to the Middle-earth model in 1966 and 1967 while still continuing their modern industrial way of life. A popular rock music club in the capital was called 'Middle Earth'. Underground magazines like *Hobbit* and *Gandalf's Garden* contained an eccentrically English mix of bucolic whimsy, drug lore, Eastern mysticism and, later, anarchist politics as well as letters signed with such sobriquets as 'Pippin of Notting Hill

Gate' or 'Frodo of Stoke Newington', aliases only partly ironic, for Tolkien had spawned a layer of sub-cultural style that ran deep and for a while possessed a distinctive and fashionable cachet.

In Britain, those who took the atavistic path, denied the voids and wildernesses of North America, had less far to travel and so travelled less far. The United Kingdom's northernmost outpost, the Shetland Islands, enjoyed brief popularity in the pre-oil boom days of the mid-'60s as southern rumour of cheap crofts, local grants, uninhabited islands and aurora borealis sent some north in search of primitivism. With rare exceptions, like the island community of Papa Stour, few lasted out the bleak, black winter at that latitude.

Much further afield, there was Nepal, cheaply accessible from Britain by thumb, bus and train at a time when Iran and Afghanistan were not difficult to cross. The immediate attractions of Nepal were cheap living, Kathmandu's marijuana shop and the Himalayas, but the deeper pull was from its illusory Shangri-la ambience, its offer of ethnic living unbesmirched by the values of western industrialism. Goa and Marrakech too became fashionable destinations of those of the post-war generation in search of the vicarious experience of primitive, tribal culture. The atavistic thirst was quenched, security assured by a return ticket or a misplaced faith in consular benevolence, and the only dangers were disease (hepatitis, typhoid) and the occasional tribesman of Afghanistan or the Atlas who took primitive ethnicism to its logical conclusion and fleeced, sometimes literally, the wealthy tourists.

That the Indian sub-continent in particular at that time drew many from Britain is only partly explained by the colonial connection; they were drawn primarily by the mystique of supposed primitivism and assumed industrial virginity, an understandable attraction for those Westerners who rejected their high tech. consumer society. If the India they found, E. M. Forster's 'mess', was not the India they supposed, the received perception in the West nevertheless remained intact. High-rise blocks in Bombay, bikers in New Delhi, Westernized Indian pop music on transistor radios in Poona did not square with the atavist vision, but enough of pure ethnic quality had survived to satisfy a Tolkien-engendered hunger for primitivism. Travellers' tales returned to the West, invented and embroidered, to enrich and endorse the Tolkienite vision. *The Lord of the Rings* became a traveller's handbook, especially for those who did not travel.

The Lord of the Rings provided the alternative course of a cerebral atavism for those in Britain and America who did not want to stray much beyond the end of the block. This is why paperback sales of the book took off so strongly in 1965 and maintained momentum until 1968: this was the period of atavistic chic, the precursor of Tom Wolfe's radical political chic of the late '60s which saw the end of Tolkien's period of popular cultural relevance. Thereafter, sales of *The Lord of the Rings* were steady; Tolkien's book continued to sell because it had achieved best-seller status but the text had become culturally stale, had inevitably lost that cutting edge of immediacy it had accidentally acquired in the mid-'60s.

Tolkien creates a primitive, atavistic yet safely benevolent world in which good and evil are reassuringly compartmentalized, the bestial is kept at bay, and other worlds are entered without the unsettling effects of parallel, psychological dislocation. Its physical topography is vast, awesome, a central influence on the characteristic rock album design work of artists like Roger Dean in the late '60s and early '70s.[2]

Yet because its psychological topography is cosily familiar the book retains its reference points to sanity throughout. As narcotic literature it is unthreateningly accessible, massaging not mirroring psychotomimetic experience, unlike, for example, the work of William Burroughs. It is no coincidence that *The Lord of the Rings* became a best-seller at the height of middle-class youth drug fashion: it found a ready market in the world's first mass audience to be both truly stoned and truly literate. Little promotion was necessary. As a piece of marketing the timing of paperback publication was immaculate. It provided an appropriate hallucinogenic screenplay in its separation from reality, visually authentic creation of landscape, sense of humour and absurdity and the essential hook of an absorbing narrative as an aid to concentration.

The writers of the '50s whose work was available to be marketed to meet the new popular drug fashion were either, like Aldous Huxley, too dull or, like William Burroughs, too disorientating to give the cerebral comfort required by an essentially soft-centred, potentially mass readership. Huxley's descriptions of the pattern of his trousers in *The Doors of Perception* were visually authentic and clinically precise comments on the visual effects of mescalin use but suggested a retreat into reality rather than an escape from it; and it was too understated to answer the needs of this new readership and lacked the grandeur of vision that Tolkien gave.

William Burroughs had in the '50s attempted and achieved a style that mimicked and mirrored the effects of harder, non-hallucinogenic drugs like methedrine and heroin through cut-out techniques, disintegration and fragmentation of thought, the slowing down and speeding up of perception and the breaking-down of logical sequence, all of which was too disturbingly paranoiac for the new readership who preferred to play with psychosis in a less committed way.

The main attractions of *The Lord of the Rings* for such readers were its blandness of style, its reassuring adherence to narrative expectations nurtured in childhood, its lack of moral ambiguity, its placing of evil and violence in an otherworldly context rather than next door, its safety, its essentially benevolent, anodyne tone. It was not so much its drift from reality that made Tolkien's work so popular at that time as its highly marketable combination of imaginative originality and psychological anaesthetic. As an experience it was neither radical nor disruptive and so provided a secure path for dissenting youth in search of a safe alternative to their own environment.

From being the *recherché* pursuit of an eccentric clique in the late '50s, reading *The Lord of the Rings* had become by 1966 the thing itself for a large section of the young educated middle class in Britain and America, a key experience and a necessary preliminary to most kinds of literary or cultural discourse with peers. Not to have read it meant exclusion from full participation in the contemporary dialogue.

This period of the book's intense sub-cultural relevance was necessarily short-lived; it was rendered ephemeral by the political events of late '67 and early '68. Like any literary work whose popularity depends upon a precise imaginative enactment of transient cultural concerns, a nailing of the *Zeitgeist*,

The Lord of the Rings rapidly became after 1967 a sub-cultural relic preserved in the aspic of the middle-class psyche, a literary anachronism paradoxically assured by its best-seller status of continuing popular success and of endless cultural transference from teacher to pupil, parent to child.

In the years between 1965 and 1968, as sales climbed, *The Lord of the Rings* began to influence the dress and manners of youth sub-culture. The description that Tolkien gives of Hobbits early in the Prologue provided a model, a set of stylistic indicators, for the alternative society's appearance: clothes of vivid primary colours, long hair, bright eyes (an effect, as it happened, of LSD ingestion), mouths given to laughter (ditto), and a general mien of delight.[3] This latter was important for LSD cultists as a myth had grown around the drug's power to open doors not only of perception but also of ecstasy. To take the chemical and not look delighted about it could be read as a sign of psychological weakness; similarly, the many who aped the lifestyle but did not have access to the drug often mimicked what they supposed to be its effects for fear of being culturally out of synch. This attitude penetrated deep into areas of the popular media, where magazine writers and disc-jockeys with middle-class youth audiences acquired this approach to style *de rigueur*.

The Lord of the Rings, then, owes its delayed mass success and popularity to that period of time between 1965 and 1968 when the text coincidentally provided the symbolic and metaphorical expression of the *Zeitgeist* for disaffected Western middle-class youth.

The collective memory of this alternative culture has been absorbed into the mythology of the '60s and has established for it an importance and dominance out of proportion to its short period of ascendancy. For two specific factors soon perverted the shape of this new reality as it had originally been conceived: commercialism and revolutionary politics. These were, in fact, the predictable responses of the right and of the left to the emergence of the alternative society, exposed and vulnerable from the beginning in its apolitical naïvety. From 1966 commercial interests began to move in on the counter-culture and market its many saleable features, not the least of which was *The Lord of the Rings* itself and the associated paraphernalia of wall-posters, badges and Hobbit/hippy dress; revolutionary politics began in late 1967 to harness the disaffection of those in their late teens and early twenties and to acquire widespread student support in both America and Western Europe.

The counter-culture had begun in a spirit of selfless, communal optimism. How far that could be exploited and corrupted was shown by the activities of Charles Manson in the Los Angeles area between 1967 and 1969. By 1968 all had changed, changed utterly. In youth cultural terms 1965–67 had been marked by a rejection of political involvement, a reluctance to engage reality head-on. But events in 1968 made such a position less tenable than it had ever been. The escalation of the Vietnam war affected few in Europe as directly as it did in America but it provided a ready example of imperialism, a cause around which to unite and a lever for politicization not of the proletariat but of young, mainly middle-class university students.

Political activity and direct action became in late 1967 and early 1968 the counterparts of fashionable radical chic. Whereas in '66 and '67 the real world had mirrored hardly at all the mind games of a hedonistic, disengaged youth culture, in 1968 the streets of European and American cities saw the frequent enactments of the newly politicized; reality had necessarily become fashionable again.

The style of Middle-earth had become passé. Those who had a year before aspired to look like Bilbo Baggins now sought political credibility and sub-cultural acceptance by cloning themselves from Ché Guevara; knee-length leather bikers' boots replaced bare feet, paramilitary berets replaced ethnic woolly hats, beards were shaped to imitate two months hard-won growth in the Bolivian jungle instead of the gnome-like outcrops of pubic-type facial hair. Hairstyles too were shorter, sculpted to indicate physical activity and political preparedness and were perceptibly different from the lank, middle-parted bucolic styles of a year earlier. Surplus ex-service greatcoats (many, ironically, from the police), double-breasted, ankle-length, full of Pasternakian revolutionary romantic chic, displaced the rough Afghan coats flown in from Kabul and Herat the previous winter. Harsh aggressive leather, dark and sombre hues, ousted soft, agrarian wools and the bright, kaleidoscopic Hobbit colours of '67; action displaced contemplation, electric blues displaced acoustic folk. The fashionable gaze was no longer open and beatific but forbidding and pugnacious. And the reading: Marx, Engels, Regis Debray and Herbert Marcuse's 1966 work, *The Ethics of Revolution*. Tolkien was back on the shelf.

These were the signs, the surface indicators, of a sharp change in cultural attitude which was effectively to end Tolkien's brief period of corruscating contemporary relevance. For the fashionable mood of early '68 accurately prefigured the events of that year which revealed a new, less benevolent *Zeitgeist* that turned Tolkien's work from the textual embodiment of pop cultural ethic to its archaic memory.

The chain of political events which occurred across the Northern hemisphere in 1968 which directly confronted so many in their late teens and early twenties with unavoidable political choices effectively ended the period of cultural relevance of *The Lord of the Rings*. In America, the escalation of the Vietnam war presented males between 18 and 26 with the lottery of the draft. Related college campus unrest spread to Europe where hitherto the reality of the Vietnam war had been largely ignored. In both Britain and France the urgent need perceived by students for macrocosmic political awareness of what was at stake in the war engendered a parallel quest for an understanding of the political forces shaping the microcosm of the university, college and factory. The two levels of political awareness were perceived to be intrinsically related, the academic and intellectual imperialism of university administrations matching the more overtly political and ideological imperialism of the American involvement in Vietnam. For decades university administrations had survived in an atrophy prolonged by lack of democracy and by student apathy. The years of Tolkien's cultural ascendancy had also been years of fashionable dissociation by students from academic political concerns. The atrophy had been prolonged, but when in 1968 students directed existential questions outwards not inwards, from the myth and fantasy epitomized by Tolkien's work to the political commentaries on their own world by Marx, Engels, Lenin and Marcuse, the pressure for change that had lain dormant erupted.

83

It is difficult to identify the precise point at which the sub-cultural climate ceased to be one in which Tolkien's work could retain contemporary relevance, but the shooting of Ché Guevara by the Bolivian army on 8 October 1967 immediately established his place as the hero of a thousand bed-sit wall-posters which distilled the new *Zeitgeist* to a single laser-sharp image. There were student demonstrations in many cities across the world in protest at the circumstances of his death and Guevara came to epitomize qualities that were to be fashionable in 1968, political commitment, social awareness and a willingness to fight, the very opposite of the passive, apolitical sub-cultural style predominant in the previous two years. In dress and attitude, guerilla chic had been spawned.

Between Guevara's death and the Grosvenor Square, London, demonstration in October 1968 outside the U.S. embassy against American policy in Vietnam there was an international chain of events in different cities which marked the increasingly militant Western sub-culture's confrontation with political reality and which textured its style and attitudes.

1968 was the year of the shooting in Berlin at Easter of German student leader Rudi Dutschke in the head and chest as he left the headquarters of the S.D.S. (German Socialist Students' Federation). There followed four days of street clashes in many German cities between an estimated 50,000 demonstrators and police outside the offices of the right-wing Springer Press, whose anti-S.D.S. campaign was blamed for inciting Dutschke's shooting. In Paris, it was the year of the alliance in May between students of the Sorbonne and car-workers from the Renault plant in Cligny, Paris, which brought similar clashes, street barricades and led by 13 May to a general strike of 10,000,000 French workers. It was the year of the Prague Spring of reform in Czechoslovakia, of the Warsaw Pact forces' invasion in August, of popular passive demonstration in Wenceslas Square and of the self-immolation of student Jan Palach. It was the year of the Chicago Democratic Convention, of the mass anti-Vietnam demonstration there organized by the Youth International Party, the yippies (the '68 politicized model of the '67 hippies), of Mayor Daley's violent police response, and later of the trial of the manacled Chicago Seven. In October in Grosvenor Square marbles rolled under police horse hooves—revolution the English way. It was the year of the street-fighting man, of a radicalism that was not merely chic.

The momentum of events in 1968[4] possessed an inexorability which radically altered the style and attitudes of Western youth and shattered the naïve optimism of '66 and '67. Though the student/youth movement was determinedly anti-élitist, and therefore theoretically leaderless, heroes and victims (Guevara, Dutschke, Palach) created a new mythology more resonant and relevant now than the benign mythologies of Middle-earth so influential in the previous three years. The *Zeitgeist* which had nurtured Tolkien's ascendancy was dead; by the end of 1968 *The Lord of the Rings* was a cultural anachronism.

However, as the Tolkien generation grew older certain residual traits of style remained with them. The citified pseudo-ruralism of the mid-'60s left its legacy after the Middle-earth fad had passed. Domestic crafts and wholefood cooking became popular middle-class family hobbies in the suburbs. The relative value of country cottages in England doubled in the early '70s as aspiring young professionals, divested of their Middle-earth trappings, invested in second homes buried deep in the fantasies of their late adolescence.

The irony of the elevation of *The Lord of the Rings* to bestseller status is that it was its radically imaginative appeal to a transient sub-cultural atavism and a related hallucinogenic hedonism which forced it into mainstream international popularity and academic acceptability. It had been quintessentially apolitical in effect and had matched and conditioned a fashionable eschewal of political thought and action amongst the West's alienated youth between 1965 and 1968, the years which saw paperback sales reach 3,000,000. The sudden ideological, philosophical and political shift which took place in 1968 ended Tolkien's period of influence on Western youth culture.

NOTES

1. Robert Giddings and Elizabeth Holland, *J. R. R. Tolkien: The Shores of Middle-earth* (Junction Books, 1981), Ch. 1.
2. See *The Lord of the Rings*, Vol. 1, Ch. 8, 'Fog on the Barrow-Downs'.
3. See *The Lord of the Rings*, Prologue, 'Concerning Hobbits', paragraph 5.
4. For a detailed account of these events see Richard Neville, *Playpower* (Paladin, 1971).

5

The Shape of the Narrative in *The Lord of the Rings*

by DIANA WYNNE JONES

When I say 'narrative', I do not mean simply the plot. I mean considerably more. Plots and their shapes—the bare outlines of stories—were something I know Tolkien himself was interested in. When I was an undergraduate, I went to a course of lectures he gave on the subject—at least, I think that was the subject, because Tolkien was all but inaudible. He evidently hated lecturing, and I suspect he also hated giving his thoughts away. At any rate, he succeeded in reducing his substantial audience to myself and four others in two weeks. We stuck on, despite his efforts. He worked at it: when it did appear that we might be hearing what he said, it was his custom to turn round and address the blackboard. Dim inklings alone reached me of what he meant, but these were too fascinating to miss. He started with the simplest possible story: a man (prince or woodcutter) going on a journey. He then gave the journey an aim, and we found that the simple picaresque plot had developed into a quest-story. I am not quite sure what happened then, but I know that by the end he was discussing the peculiar adaptation of the quest-story which Chaucer made in his 'Pardoner's Tale'.

As you see, Tolkien did not give away half of what he knew, even about plots, and I suspect he never talked about narrative at all, but it is clear from *The Lord of the Rings* that he knew all about narrative as well. The plot of *The Lord of the Rings* is, on the face of it, exactly the same simple one that he appeared to describe in his lectures: a journey that acquires an aim and develops into a kind of quest. But the bare plot is to any writer no more than the main theme of a sort of symphony which requires other themes added to it and the whole orchestrated into a narrative. To shape a narrative, you have to phase the various incidents and so control their nature that you set up significances, correspondences, foretastes and expectations, until your finished story becomes something else again from its simple outline. Tolkien does this orchestrating supremely well: so much so that, by various narrative sleights-of-hand, he almost reverses the normal flow of a quest-story, or at least makes an adaptation of it every bit as peculiar as the one he described in his lectures, and nobody ever notices. It continues to fool me even now, though I think I can see what he is up to.

The Lord of the Rings is organized in movements, just like a symphony, but with this difference: each movement has an extension, or coda, which reflects partly back on the movement just completed, and partly forwards to what is to come. This coda is highly characteristic of Tolkien's method, and it becomes increasingly important as the narrative proceeds. You always have to watch what happens in these codas. And yet they, and the movements which precede them, in no way interfere with the story, the actual events being described, which appears to march steadily forward and to unfold with the utmost clarity and regularity. This limpid tale of events is one of Tolkien's major achievements, when you consider all the other things he was doing too. However, one thing he was *not* doing was striving to put it all in elegant language. His manner is at all times prolix and a little threadbare. The most he will do is to attempt a rough appropriateness. When he is dealing with hobbits, he is chatty and a little arch: 'If Frodo had really wanted to write a book and had had many ears, he would have learned enough for several chapters in a few minutes' (I, 167). In more awesome places, he uses a hackneyed high style: 'Then his wrath blazed in a consuming flame, but his fear rose like a vast black smoke to choke him' (III, 223). It is symptomatic, I think, that he at all times overworks the word 'suddenly'. To take the most random sample: 'Suddenly he knew in his heart . . .' (I, 225); 'Suddenly the lights went out' (II, 197); 'Suddenly the silence was broken' (III, 127). As I know well enough myself, 'suddenly' is a word hard to avoid in this kind of narrative. For Tolkien, as D. S. Brewer points out (*J. R. R. Tolkien, Scholar and Storyteller, Essays in Memoriam*, ed. Salu and Farrell), was writing a Romance in the old sense of the word. A Romance, unlike a novel, does not aim to draw attention to the way it is written. Tolkien was far more concerned with the matter of his narrative than its manner, and he only exercised his undoubted gift for language in inventing names, particularly names of places—which is again exactly in the tradition of a Romance. I always wish that Tolkien's many imitators would notice how comparatively modest his language is, and not insist on writing their stuff in translationese.

The first movement of the narrative lasts until the flight from Bree. Here, along with the chatty manner, we are in a cosy hobbit world not very far removed from that of fairy tales and nursery rhymes. Hobbits have that prosaic fubsiness one associates with a certain kind of children's story. And they are agreeably greedy and, above all, secure. But there is more to it than that. Throughout this section, Tolkien, like Lewis Carroll before him, is drawing heavily on the landscape round Oxford where he lived. Just as, I am sure, the chessboard view of three counties from White Horse Hill suggested *Alice Through the Looking Glass*, it surely also gave rise to the Shire. But Tolkien took a leaf out of William Morris's book too, *The Well at the World's End*, and drew on the whole Upper Thames Valley. Here there are stuffy willow-choked flats, Wychwood, rivers like the Windrush and the Evenlode, the Rollright Stones, the longbarrow called Wayland's Smithy, ploughland and orchards round Didcot, the Seven Barrows, Thames water meadows, and the austere landscape of the chalk downs. And he used them all: there is even a real place called Buckland. Three other things he did not use here, though they are immensely important in the rest of the book, are the Thames itself; the old prehistoric road called the Ridgeway, which is probably the oldest road in Britain, leading from east to west (like the way to the Grey Havens), sometimes as a cart-track, sometimes as broad as a motorway, and at other times vanishing in a valley;

and finally a strange Oxford phenomenon, whereby the streets of the town are at times filled with a scent of distant flowers, for hours on end, as if one were smelling Heaven somehow. This is in a manner setting a thief to catch a thief, since I lived in Oxford for many years too and tend to use these things as well, but it is not important to know about them. I only draw attention to them to point out this first of Tolkien's narrative sleights-of-hand: by writing of things which were home to him, he contrives to give the reader a sense of home and security too.

But he is about to do something much more complicated than Carroll or Morris. He opens with a party. A burst of fireworks and fun. And here at once he surreptitiously introduces three major themes. The first, and by far the most important for the rest of the book, is the pressure of events which have happened long before the story opens. Later, this pressure comes from the far-off heroic past; but here it is underplayed, deftly, and seems merely to be a hangover from Bilbo's former mad journey. Which of course brought the Ring into Bilbo's possession. The Ring, whatever else it does, always brings the tragic past into the present. But at this stage Gandalf, in a pedagogic way in keeping with the homely tone, simply makes Bilbo give the Ring to Frodo and retire into the past himself.

But make no mistake. Undertones of the heroic and of the chivalry of Medieval Romances are being firmly introduced too, in the other two themes. One of these is the Quest itself. Because of the beguiling domesticity of the Shire and Tolkien's manner at this point, you are lulled into thinking of it in fairy-story terms: the hero journeys to a confrontation and receives supernatural help on the way. Of course the hero wins. And yet it starts with a party, like the best-known of all high Romances, the stories of King Arthur. A Quest nearly always begins with the King feasting in Camelot. Enter a damsel or a churl demanding a boon. In this case Gandalf, and the quest is delayed, but the pattern is there. And you should remember that, though a lot of Quests, like that of Sir Gareth, prove the hero a man, a great many, like Gawain's with the Green Knight or that of the Grail, do no such thing. Furthermore, the title of the most famous collection of

Arthurian Romances, Malory's, is *The Death of Arthur*. In fact, You Have Been Warned—although you need only feel a little uneasy at the moment.

For his third theme, Tolkien also drew on Romances. The poet of *Gawain and the Green Knight* calls King Arthur 'sumquat childgered'—i.e. rather boyish. Froissart too regards this as the most chivalrous aspect of real knights (and so did Kipling later). Sir Percival is traditionally naïve to childishness. And so are the hobbits who set out on their journey. So you have a notion here which at once reinforces the prevailing nursery-tale atmosphere and contradicts it: it is cosy, but it is also heroic.

It seems reasonable to mention these things because it is quite certain that Tolkien had them at his fingertips. The marvel is that he was capable of handling them, just as he did with the Oxford landscape, so that it is not necessary for the reader to know them in order to get the message. The message is a fourth theme, also thoroughly traditional, which these three come together to suggest: people have gone downhill from the heroic days. Now it is ordinary people who have to cope as best they can.

So Bilbo plays his practical joke and vanishes. Frodo lingers, even after Gandalf has reappeared and introduced seriously for the first time the deep notes of the distant past. It is typical of this movement that the history is hobbit-orientated, and concerns Gollum as much as Sauron and Isildur. Frodo, with what we are meant to consider dramatic irony, repudiates Gollum. The lingering ensures that, as Frodo and his companions set off, autumn is coming on, with all that can imply. We are meant to take the point that local changes of season are cosmic in origin, but attention is on the domestic landscape through which the hobbits journey. This is so solidly persuasive that Tolkien is able to introduce the Ringwraiths with the lightest of touches. A few words, and they are spine-chilling. A black figure *sniffing* for you. They are childhood nightmares and gaps in the order of things, just with that.

Then a new theme enters, as the Elves intervene in their remote way. Their songs are of departed glories, which are still, it seems, things to conjure with. It is the past-history theme again, but it has a powerful woodwind nostalgia. It

91

begins—just—to suggest that the coming autumn is a season of Middle-earth, not only of the year. But the scene is still so firmly local, that all you get at this stage is a sense of yearning, both for the past and for the Sea-crossing of the future. The present is detached from the Elves. The story has begun to spread a little in time, and a little in space too.

Anyway, we are briskly back again to the domestic, with the matter of the mushrooms and the adventure-story excitement of the river-crossing and the escape through the Hedge. The hobbits muddle through, until they get into real trouble with the sinister Forest. This too is wonderfully spine-chilling by reason of being only just removed from a real wood. Even Old Man Willow is solidly a real willow tree. And once again they need rescuing, this time by Tom Bombadil. By now, it looks as if the fairy-story pattern, of travellers being saved from their own errors by supernatural intervention, is here to stay.

I find Tom Bombadil supremely irritating myself. I am well aware that he is a chthonic figure seen from, as it were, knee high, and I can see his presence here is important, standing as he does between earth and sky in the first truly open country, but I am always glad when he is dismissed by Elrond. It is a relief to have him distanced with high-sounding names as Iarwain, Forn and Orald. As Bombadil he is perverse and whimsical. He is the quintessence of the nursery story gone wrong, as it does from then on. Tolkien was quite right to put him in, but I wish he hadn't. He was quite right because here, in the haunting country of the Barrows—which was still domestic to Tolkien, though not perhaps to his readers—dead history, with all its wasted heroism and lingering evil, literally comes up and grabs the hobbits. The Barrow Wights, however, are not strictly this: they are spiteful ghosts. All the same, this is where Tolkien does, briefly, confront you with the scale of his narrative. Tom is near eternal. The bones in the Barrows are so old their deeds have been forgotten. The present is represented by the hobbits, apparently neither very noble nor very effectual. Around them the landscape first opens, then closes to lead them to death's door, and from the dead they acquire a knife that will be important later. It is a notable piece of foreshadowing, which ends in their rescue by Tom.

This is really the last time they are rescued in this way.

That comforting pattern, and the movement, ends with their doings at Bree, which is, not insignificantly, a town half of men and half of hobbits. Men are now going to enter into the picture. The nursery tales, despite the cosy inn scene, are done with. And—this is an example of Tolkien's ability to use surreptitious themes from elsewhere—Frodo, like Adam and Eve and all the failures of fairy stories, has come there under a prohibition: not to put on the Ring. Which he proceeds to disobey. The fact that he puts the Ring on while singing a nursery rhyme only underlines the fact that such things are now inappropriate. And the movement ends with the same thing as it began.

The coda to this movement is very short but packed out with adumbrations: a journey of hardship over a desolate landscape, towards a hill topped with fires. While purporting simply to carry on the story, this section does all manner of things. It spreads the narrative considerably in space, and in time too. The past reappears in two forms, first as the petrified trolls, harking back to Bilbo's adventures, and then, far more potently, as the Black Riders. It now becomes clear that the Ring-wraiths are not simply terrifying, but that they can harm the living. That they could win. We should remember here that Bilbo's victory over the trolls had been almost by luck. Frodo is almost not lucky. And, when they race to the Ford and it appears that even an Elf-lord has limited powers, your doubts increase, although you still hope for the supernatural rescue that the main movement has led you to expect. It comes, after a fashion, in the confusion at the Ford. This confusion, considering Tolkien's ability everywhere else to present landscapes and events with total clarity, must be deliberate. It must look forward to the profusion of doubtful events to follow. I do not think it comes off at all, but it does provide a wonderful introit to the ordered peace and measured debate of the next movement.

Rivendell is the Last Homely House of *The Hobbit*. But of course it is no such thing. It is under threat from Mordor. You realize this and cast your mind back, uneasily trying to find somewhere that *is* safe and homely. Bree? Tom Bombadil— no, not even him. And the Ringwraiths were in the Shire too. Even before the debate begins, you become aware that the only defence can be some form of attack. But this is not for Frodo to decide: he has reached his limited objective. The narrative stops short and reassembles itself by means of the debate.

Tolkien performs several remarkable narrative feats here. One is of course the retrospective doubts cast back on the earlier illusion of security. But the one which amazes me most is the fact that the debate is not in the least boring. It could be. Milton, in a similar situation, almost is. But there are so many questions by now raised that need answers, and so many new people to present—Gimli, Legolas, Boromir, Strider in his new role as Aragorn, Elrond revealed as truly half Elf, Gandalf acquiring new stature, and news of Gollum's escape—that I find my attention truly riveted. For the first time, the major themes enter undisguised, and you are made aware not only of the depths of past history, but of the huge spread of the land affected by it. You are shown a divided kingdom now reduced to a few outposts, once again threatened and likely this time to dwindle away. Elves, dwarves, men and hobbits are all likely to go down with it. A solution is propounded: destroy the Ring.

And this is the other amazing feat of narrative: you are told, this early on, exactly what is going to happen. And you are still in doubt that it will. Each of the Fellowship of the Ring says exactly what his intentions are, and yet you do not believe they will do as they say. Each time I read it, I am still pained and shocked when the Fellowship divides later on. I am still in doubt that the Ring will be destroyed, or what good it would do if it was. It seems to me to need some explaining how Tolkien got away with it.

The main answer, I think, is the depth and variety of the history he invokes in the course of this movement. I suppose it is a commonplace that he took over the idea of the inset histories and legends from the Anglo-Saxon poem *Beowulf*, in which each inset vaguely echoes the action in the poem's present and each is progressively more doom-laden, but I am not sure if it is realized how thoroughly Tolkien adapted the notion to his own purposes. *Beowulf* uses the things purely for atmosphere. Tolkien uses his histories that way too, but only secondarily. His primary use for history is as a motive power, pushing his present-day characters into certain actions, to bring about the future. He presents us with triple measure: Elven history, mostly as hints and songs, immeasurably old and indicating the Elves are a dying race; that of men and dwarves, both of whom have more than once flourished heroically and then been decimated by the power of Sauron; and hobbits, who have existence rather than history. All are united by the rings and against the Ring. Thanks to the Elves, there is a huge timespan here, showing a continuous falling-off. Elrond says, 'I have seen three ages in the West of the world, and many defeats, and many fruitless victories' (I, 256). The effect of this, on top of the first movement's suggestion that only ordinary folk are left to cope, is to present the Fellowship, once formed, as a thread-thin company. It is as narrow in numbers and space as the present moment is in time. Against the past weight of failure, its only hope seems to hang together.

If this picks up and amplifies the earlier suggestions in the Shire that the present is small and ordinary, so does the nature of the Quest, now properly revealed. It is to be a negative one, a raid to destroy the enemy's inmost defences. It can only be made by beings so insignificant that the chances of success are minimal. It is destructive. It does not suggest renewal. Or does it? I have heard *The Lord of the Rings* stigmatized as simply a Goodies v. Baddies story. Insofar as this is true, it is of course a very modern story. Romances, fairy tales and even *Beowulf* do not have Baddies the way we do, the way Sauron is. But it is more original than it is modern, now that Tolkien has shown his hand, because it is really about people in time. It concerns the present, fully conscious of the past, injured by it in fact, pressing forward to make the unformed future. And of course the present is very small compared with both: mere instants. Tolkien makes the outcome dubious, if not equivocal, by having his Fellowship set off in winter—a time of ill omen, of traditional heroism, and of hope too, since Spring is to follow—and then by cunningly organizing his narrative in its later stages, so that the issue is continually in doubt, just as the future always is.

The coda to this movement is, very characteristically, the start of the journey. Through more of Tolkien's meticulously visualized country, the Fellowship sets out. There is a strong sense that this is the nitty-gritty, the real stuff, because the landscape is now harsh and strange and because the proper Quest has been determined. In fact, not insignificantly, this is only partly true. This section serves mainly to lead into the next movement, which is a double one, bringing us hard up against endurance of two kinds.

First comes the achievement of the dwarves, heralded by the entry into Moria. The finding and opening of the gate is pure magic. I wish I could have written it. But once they get inside, I am never as impressed as I could wish. True, we have majestic evidence of dwarves' industry, and proof that their legends at least did not lie—and this tacitly reinforces the rest of the histories we have been given—so that when we come upon the long dead dwarves, it should strike us cold as evidence of the latest heroic failure. But I never find it does. I just feel the easy regret one feels on being told someone one didn't know had died. I suspect that Tolkien has here slipped over into the Goodies v. Baddies, adventure-story mode. The Orcs, when they appear, do not have personalities as they do in Volume II. They are just the enemy. And then, sudden and shocking, comes the demise of Gandalf. Tolkien must have meant it to be so. I am sure he wanted to impress us with the fact that there is always the unforseen disaster, and I am sure too that he wanted an ominous foreshadowing of the Lair of Shelob and the Paths of the Dead, but it won't do all the same. Who or what is the sudden Balrog? Up it pops, and down it goes again, taking Gandalf with it. For all that, the sense of loss is real, and leads in admirably to the second part of the movement, the sojourn in Lorien.

Oh good, you think, we are at last going to plumb the mysteries of the Elves! Legolas has been there for some time now, hinting at these mysteries, and yet, since he is one of the Fellowship, kidding you that Elves can be human and approachable. This is not the case. Tolkien lets you see much, but still leaves the Elves almost as mysterious and alien as they were before you saw it. They are genuinely not human. Their concerns seem other, even when they help. The reason seems to be their intense, abiding melancholy. The nostalgia shown earlier by the Elves in the Shire, and then, in a more restrained way, by Elrond, swells here into a huge woodwind theme. The Elves are dwindling, we are told. The dwarves awakened evil and forced many Elves over the Sea. This could be the explanation, but it is not really. You get the real reason by hints, which you pick up mostly subconsciously: the Elves, by reason of their apparent immortality, are widowed from history. They are forced back on their own, which is merely living memory, unimaginably long. Tolkien conveys quietly, without ever quite centring your sights on it, the immense burden immortality would be. He uses women to do it: the Morning Star, Arwen Evening Star, and Galadriel herself. I daresay Women's Lib could make destructive points here, but it is entirely appropriate in a Romance, in which women are traditionally mysterious and a little passive. He is drawing on all the stories of Elf women loving mortal men, and quietly pointing up the concealed consequences: when the lover dies, the immortal woman grieves for ever. Women are generally more often widowed than men. But this stands for the situation of all the Elves. When they enter the temporary brawls of history, they pay for it by having to endure its horrors for ever. So they are forced for the most part to stay withdrawn among their yellow trees, never dying, but never quite coming to maturity either. The yellow trees vividly express their state. Are mallorns the yellow of Spring, or Autumn? Both, but not Summer or Winter. I find them profoundly saddening.

The Elves have wisdom, by a sort of natural compensation, but this can be an equal burden. Galadriel does, in her aloof way, enter history, but she has to do it in full knowledge that she is helping to end the Third Age of the world. You come away from Lothlorien with two pieces of hidden knowledge: a sense of a doomed age, and the fact that every gift exacts its price—sometimes a terrible one.

By now you should be well aware that putting on the Ring exacts its price. This is what happens to end the coda to this movement, just as it ended the coda to the first movement. It has become a pattern now: another stage in the journey, down the Anduin this time, ending in Frodo putting on the Ring again. Because of the pattern, you are half expecting another last-minute rescue. So it comes as a real shock when this does not happen, and the Fellowship breaks up. Lothlorien fools us to some extent, by appearing to awe and tame Boromir—though it is never *said* that it has—and the great river fools us too. The Fellowship appears to be sliding united along its current to a single end. But you always have to watch Tolkien with water. He never uses it unmeaningfully. Pools and lakes mirror stars, and hold hidden things. The previous river crossings have both been crucial. This Anduin has contrasting banks and, moreover, reeks of history. In a way, it *is* history, and the Fellowship is going with its current, to break up in confusion at the falls of Rauros. It is worth pointing out that when Aragorn later uses the same river, he comes *up* it, against the current, changing a course of events that seems inevitable.

The other water is of course the Sea. This has been sounding dimly in our ears throughout the book, but in Lothlorien it begins to thunder. Does it suggest loss, departure and death? Certainly. But since water is always life to Tolkien, it must also be eternity. Eternity, we must not forget, is by its nature both all time and no time at all. It is quite a feat to invoke the Sea so far inland. The effect is to end the movement with two symbols: a line of scattered figures with the ocean at their backs, confronting the ringed Eye of Sauron. The Eye, which also comes out into the open in Lothlorien, is an absolutely spine-chilling expression of evil—the more so because we never see more of the enemy than that. But it is possible to see the Eye, among its various significances, as the eye of the storm, the self-contained here-and-now, which the present has to pass through before it becomes the future.

Volume II inaugurates what might be called the great choral movement. The scene widens enormously and the numbers of both enemies and friends suddenly multiply by hundreds. The scale of the story, which Tolkien has unobtrusively been preparing us for, is now shown to be immense. It also involves a fiendishly difficult piece of double and treble narration. I know from bitter experience how difficult it is, when your narrative divides into two or more and both parts happen simultaneously, to decide which part to tell when. But Tolkien's narrative makes it more difficult still, because Frodo's part of the story is plotted to run counter to Merry and Pippin's, to narrow where theirs expands, to flow uphill as it were from the main course of events, so that not only does their Quest seem bound to fail, but you are in doubt as to whether this is what the narrative is really about.

If Tolkien agonized at all about how to do it, it does not show. He solved it characteristically by adopting a pattern: he will tell the positive side first, and the negative second. So he succeeds, apparently carelessly and prolifically, in flinging a huge double and treble twist of narrative across a huge area of land. He fools us a bit, of course, as usual. He represents the destruction of the Ring throughout as the thing of real importance, whereas it is only half of it. The act of destruction must be accompanied by the act of creation—in this case the mustering of allies to Minas Tirith to found a new Gondor. But he represents that as a desperate rearguard action. Indeed, some of his point is that such desperate defences are unintentionally regenerative. But, from the mere fact of devoting half his narrative to it, he gives away its importance.

First, however, he devotes himself to the Ents, the Riders of Rohan and to Saruman. The first and last of these have been so firmly foreshadowed in earlier parts of the narrative that one receives them almost with recognition, like a theme emerging from the orchestra, or prophecies fulfilled. Rohan, though it has been mentioned, is like a new theme entirely— which is as it should be. Against all three, the power of Mordor is slowly defined as the true great evil. I do not think that it could have been suggested so strongly in any better way. Mordor is never actually present, but always there in the searching Eye.

Orcs, on the other hand, representing Mordor and Isengard, are very much there, in numbers, splendidly solid: 'his aching head was grated by the filthy jowl and hairy ear. . . . Immediately in front were bowed backs and tough thick legs going up and down, up and down, unresting, as if they were made of wire and horn' (II, 55). And I think it a stroke of genius to have the Elvish for Orc be *Yrch*, like an expression of disgust in itself. These Orcs serve the double purpose of presenting the might of Mordor and Isengard and of getting Merry and Pippin to Fangorn—I do like things to pull their weight. Here are the Ents. I remember reading a review of *The Two Towers* when it first came out, in which the reviewer could not take the Ents. Walking trees! He indignantly concluded Tolkien was trying to foist a children's story on him as serious literature. He was not far wrong in a way. Here in Fangorn, Tolkien is echoing the Forest outside the Shire. He is also echoing the childish innocence of the first movement, deliberately and with a difference. Treebeard and his fellows are innocents. I am always impressed by how simply and completely Tolkien expresses this innocence. Like Mordor, Treebeard has eyes.

> These deep eyes were now surveying them, slow and solemn, but very penetrating. They were brown shot with a green light. Often afterwards Pippin tried to describe his first impression of them. 'One felt as if there was an enormous well behind them, filled up with ages of memory and long, slow, steady thinking; but their surface was sparkling with the present. . . .' (II, 66)

As I said, take note when Tolkien talks of water. The well of the past contains truth, but it stops short at the present. In this, it is like the hobbits of the Shire, but unlike the Elves, whose pools reflect stars. The Ents, however, unlike Hobbits, who are pragmatic and capable of growth, are grown up and complete as they are. They are hard to budge towards the future. It is a measure of the seriousness of the situation that the Ents are actually persuaded to move, and even then they only move against the lesser evil of Saruman. They are one of the things which will not survive long in a new Age. You are meant to feel, and you do, that it is a pity: they embody the mature innocence of the Third Age. But you have to look for real help to the Riders of Rohan, the comparative newcomers, who have yet to make history.

Rohan and its grassy plains has been foreshadowed too, in a way, in the Barrow Downs, so that new theme when it emerges seems entirely in keeping. But here, instead of Tom Bombadil between grass and sky, it is Gandalf who suddenly reappears, with something of the same force. This too is not unheralded, both by Galadriel's Mirror and by the previous pattern of the narrative. Gandalf disappears: sooner or later after that, the Ring is used: sooner or later, after that again, Gandalf reappears, a spearhead for the allies, just as the Ringwraiths are for Mordor. Gandalf's coming to Rohan ought to make one certain that Frodo will put on the Ring again in Mordor.

The Rohirrim are purely Anglo-Saxon. Tolkien lifted them

entirely from his study of Old English—even their horses, I suspect, come from the legendary first Saxons in Britain, Hengist and Horsa. They have the Old English heroic culture complete. Tolkien does a delicate job here of differentiating them from Aragorn, who is at once both rougher and more sophisticated, coming as he does from a far older culture. For, as I said, these are a people without a past to whom we should look for the future. If you doubt this, you should contrast the passive roles of the Elf-women with that of Eowyn and the active part she plays, albeit disobediently. But before the Riders can do anything, they have to put their own house in order. Theoden King has to cast off evil counsel and the weight of age, and then to fight in Helm's Deep—all of which involves such bewildering coming and going that I always have twinges of incredulity about the stamina of Shadowfax. I also have twinges of doubt, as I am sure you are intended to, about the reliability of Rohan, despite their nobility. I go very Welsh, and when the men of Minas Tirith later say 'Rohan will not come', I shake my head and mutter about perfidious Albion. Tolkien, as a Welsh scholar, may have had this reaction of mine in mind too. Certainly he is once again performing one of his sleights-of-narrative: for the thing at the back of his mind must certainly have been the way the Saxon King Harold had to march North to fight one invasion force in 1066, before rushing South again to fight the Normans, who were the real threat. Again, there is no need for the reader to know this. It comes over very clearly that the Rohirrim are having difficulty disentangling themselves from their own pressing present. Quite early on, you are asking, Can they do it in time to be of use to the future?

Parallel to this in time at least, Frodo and Sam and the noxious Gollum are creeping towards Mordor. This is the section foreshadowed in the coda to the first movement, but the landscape is now far more luridly depressing. Vividly in tune with the negative nature of their Quest are the marsh pools containing images of dead people. Again, watch Tolkien with water. What is history now? Similarly, the only virtues they can exercise are negative: endurance, and forebearance towards Gollum. Everything is sterile, for all their heroism. Tolkien begins asserting their heroism from here on, and it

101

obviously exists, like the positive love between Frodo and Sam, but the negatives are so overwhelming that you sense impending failure.

Therefore you feel relief as well as surprise when they run into Faramir and his guerrillas. It is like coming out into the sun. Tolkien does wonders of suggestion here: the landscape is meticulously Southern and the ferns are brown with winter, but the herbs Sam uses to cook with are all evergreen, and so is the cedar he makes his fire with. This has to be deliberate. About the same time, the others are meeting the futureless Ents and the pastless Rohirrim: Frodo and Sam meet those who have a long past but also obvious potential for the future. But notice that, when Tolkien typically re-inforces his point with water, that Frodo and Faramir are both behind the waterfall at the time when they spare Gollum in the pool. But at the time you ignore that hint and realize simply that here is hope, and a potent force for good. You discover that Mordor has only yet spread patchily in Ithilien.

Be that as it may, as the others make their successful onslaught on Isengard, Frodo and Sam also attack a tower, by way of Cirith Ungol and Shelob. This section has been heavily foreshadowed in the Barrows and the mines of Moria, with their unavailing heroisms, and the weight of that makes this one more horrible. It is horrible enough on its own. The indecisions of Sam make it worse. And finally, despite Sting, and Galadriel's aid, while the other hobbits triumph in Isengard, Frodo is taken prisoner, an exact reversal of their respective positions at the beginning of the movement. This reversing is part of the deliberate counterplotting of this whole section.

And now we turn to the marvellous city of Minas Tirith, in nearly the final swatch in the plaiting of this huge penulti-mate movement. We already admire the place because of Faramir, with whom, in a brief episode, Tolkien has succeeded in dissipating the impression left by Boromir. It adds to the sense of marvel that Minas Tirith is not degenerate and cynical after all. The city has been kept before us one way or another since the Council of Elrond, so that, along with the surprise when we come to it at last, there is a sense of familiarity, as of a hidden theme related to all the others finally emerging from the orchestra. Something of it has been suggested too in the episode back in the Shire when Fatty Bolger is left alone to deal with the Black Riders, and the hobbits sound their alarm. We are told that the horn 'rent the night like fire on a hilltop. AWAKE!' (I, 188). And again in II when the watchfires of Rohan surround the Orcs. Now the beacon fires spring alight round the city as Pippin rides up with Gandalf. The effect is to give Minas Tirith distinctly Christian associations—and why not, since Tolkien has used everything else in our heritage?—because you think at once of 'Christians awake!' and that bit of a hymn 'How gleam thy watchfires through the night', which not only adds to the stature of the city, but, as we shall see, casts a little Christianity on Frodo and Sam too.

But it would be daft to see Minas Tirith as Jerusalem, bravely fronting evil. It owes far, far more to the doomed city of Atlantis. With it, Tolkien is working another sleight-of-narrative. Atlantis was very old, wonderfully civilized and built in a series of terrace-like rings. And it was inundated, before the dawn of history. By deliberately using and knowing that he was using Atlantis as a model, Tolkien again ensures that the reader gets the message without needing to know: Minas Tirith is doomed. And, as the muster of Mordor proceeds, you cannot see how, even if Rohan comes, that could make much difference.

Rohan is preparing to come. So is Aragorn. In an action heralded in the Barrows, in Moria, and again in Shelob's Lair, Aragorn sets out with his Grey Company to take the Paths of the Dead. Aragorn is of course, as the descendant of the Kings of the North, pre-eminently qualified to summon those faithless dead in there and make them keep their word at last. But this episode, terrifying as it is, repeats such an often-adumbrated scene that it almost carries the weight of an allegory: you can take the failures of the past, much as Tolkien has by now taken most of Western literary heritage, and force them to do at least some good towards the future. Tolkien would deny this. He says irritably in the Foreword to the second edition of *The Lord of the Rings*, 'I think that many confuse "applicability" with "allegory"' (I, 7), and maybe he is right. And watch out.

Strewn all around this section are striking examples of the fey or doomed utterance. Aragorn himself says, 'It will be long, I fear, ere Theoden sits at ease again in Meduseld' (III, 46). Halbarad says in Dimholt, 'This is an evil door, and my death lies beyond it' (III, 59). And in the midst of the battle, the Black Captain himself says, 'No living man may hinder me!' (III, 116). This sort of thing has also been heralded, when Aragorn warns Gandalf against entering Moria. Because of that, we are prone to believe these sayings. Then notice that not one of them comes true in the way it suggests. Theoden is killed and never sits in Meduseld. Halbarad is not killed in the Paths of the Dead, but a long way out on the other side. And the Black Captain is hindered by a hobbit and killed by a girl. Since the bringing about of the future is what this movement is concerned with, we should be troubled.

For, you see, the battle which ought to be final, in which the forces of good throw everything they have at Mordor, is no such thing. It is a magnificent battle though. One of Tolkien's gifts is being able to rise to the largest occasion. I wait with bated breath every time for Rohan to come, or not come, and sing as they slay. But when it is over, the enemy is still working on Denethor and Mordor is not destroyed. So, in a pattern which is now familiar, there is a coda to this huge movement. By now these codas are definitely forming an 'afterwards' and looking to the future. In this one, Faramir and Eowyn find healing and love, and the other protagonists debate, in a way that echoes the Council of Elrond, and like that Council resolve on an act of aggression: they will attack Mordor as a diversion for Frodo. So are we to suppose that this whole movement has been a huge diversion?

Only then does Tolkien take up the story of Frodo and Sam. This is what might be called the slow movement, drear and negative and full of tribulation. Although it is odd that the positive side of the action is compounded of killing and politics, and the negative of love, endurance and courage, this is how it seems to be. Tolkien insists that the first is valueless without the second. Odd, as I said, particularly as the slight Christian tinge given to Minas Tirith definitely reflects on Frodo, who is now displaying what one thinks of as the humbler Christian virtues; and because the careful plotting of this movement, to make it in most ways the antithesis of the preceding one, keeps suggesting, to my mind at least, Clough's poem 'Say not the struggle nought availeth.' The force of that poem is that, even if you are not succeeding in your own locality, someone somewhere else *is*.

Anyway, as one side enters glorious Minas Tirith, Frodo and Sam creep into Mordor, its antithesis; and with them Gollum, a sort of anti-hobbit. This ignoble trio are the only ones likely to succeed. And they fail. Make no mistake, despite their courage, and their wholly admirable affection for one another, and Frodo's near transfiguration, their action is indeed negative. At the last minute, Frodo refuses to throw the Ring into the Cracks of Doom and puts it on instead. Their almost accidental success is due to a negative action both hobbits performed in the past. Frodo, not lovingly, spared Gollum's life. Sam, not understanding Gollum's loneliness in the marshes, threatened him and turned his incipient friendship to hatred. So Gollum bites off Frodo's finger and falls with it and the Ring into the Cracks of Doom.

Now what are we to make of this? I have of course put it far more baldly than Tolkien does, but it is there for everyone to read. I think the explanation is suggested in the very long coda to the entire story which takes up nearly half the last volume. Most writers would have been content to stop with the destruction of Mordor, or at least after the shorter coda of rejoicing and the celebrating of Nine-Fingered Frodo that follows the fall of Mordor. But Tolkien, characteristically, has a whole further movement, which now definitely is 'and afterwards . . .'.

Before we try to make sense of it, let me draw your attention to another aspect of Tolkien's narrative skill: his constant care to have each stage of his story viewed or experienced by one or other of his central characters. He had to split them apart to do it, but it is a great strength of the narrative, and one not often shared by his imitators. Each major event has a firm viewpoint and solid substance. Things are visualized, and because hobbits are present eating and drinking gets done. The overall effect is to show that huge events are composed of small ones, and, as was signalled at the beginning, that ordinary people can get forced to make history—forced by history itself. By this stage of the narrative, however, the idea is being proposed in a different form: even the smallest and most ignoble act can have untold effect. And thank goodness for Gollum.

Well, yes. But remember that Gollum only did for Frodo what the Dead did for Aragorn. And indeed much of this coda-of-codas is concerned with shrinking the scale again, back to the Shire, where the now battle-hardened hobbits make their bit of personal history by dislodging Saruman, and the hobbits of the Shire settle down with a happy sigh to draw quietly aside from the path of history. As Tolkien has been unobtrusively pointing out all along, if it were not for such folk, there would be nothing worth doing heroic things for. But we are being lulled again. We must not forget the Sea, nor the very clear statements that an age of the world is passing. Tolkien was not cheating about that—it proves to have passed—but only suggesting that the next age *could* be an age of Sauron. And remember Sauron was never really precisely *there*, unlike all the other characters. Before we are prepared for it, the woodwind nostalgia theme is swelling again, to drown everything else. Sam is saddened to find his actions not remembered. A mallorn tree grows in the Shire. Frodo is ill and finishes writing his history. And at length it becomes evident that the destruction of the Age entails the passing of Elf rings too, along with Galadriel, and Gandalf, whose nature has been concealed in his name all along. And Frodo too. Frodo has become Elvish, quite literally. By his not-doing, however heroic, he has widowed himself from history, just like the Elves, and must now go off into the Sea like the rest.

Tolkien works his final sleight-of-narrative here. He was perfectly aware of the Germanic custom of ship-burial, in which a dead king was floated out to sea in a ship. Crossing the Sea is represented as a matter full of sadness, and Cirdan the shipwright is given many attributes of a priest, but the passing of Frodo is never represented as other than a permanent voyage. So the ending is heart-rendingly equivocal. You can see it as Frodo moving into eternity, or into history— or not. You can see it as a justification—or not—of the negative side. In fact, we are experiencing the proper mode of Romance which was signalled right from the start. The values of the people who wrote Romances never seem quite the same as our own. This kind of equivocal ending where winning and failing amount to the same, Arthur passes to sleep in a hill, and a gift exacts its price, is exactly what should have been expected. You Were Warned. For good measure, you knew that life never comes round to a happy ending and stops there. There is always afterwards. But such was the skill with which this narrative was shaped that you could not see the pattern, even when it was being constantly put before you.

Yes, there really was nothing about narrative that Tolkien didn't know.

6

The Hasty Stroke Goes Oft Astray: Tolkien and Humour

by DEREK ROBINSON

An audit of the humour in *The Lord of the Rings* is soon done. Not that there is nothing to laugh at, but there is so little of it that the jokes stand out like flowers on a blasted heath: easily seen and quickly counted. What is interesting is examining why Tolkien has been so successful despite being so desperately unfunny, and how he tried—in nervous and gingerly fashion—occasionally to use humour, only to give up almost at once.

For there is no doubt that Tolkien would have liked *The Lord of the Rings* to be funny, not throughout, but in places. The first sentence of the first chapter (a crucial bit of any book, since it sets the tone and often wins or loses the casual browser) contains what P. G. Wodehouse used to call a 'nifty'—something amusing to reward and encourage the reader. Bilbo Baggins announces 'his eleventy-first birthday'. That looks like a firm nudge in the direction of A. A. Milne/Lewis Carroll/maybe T. H. White. One might reasonably expect a fair amount of vigorous and colourful wordplay to come. One doesn't get it. An extraordinary aspect of the book—given Tolkien's great powers as a linguist and his vast knowledge of the roots of English—is the poverty of its wordplay.

Here I'm not talking about Tolkien's vocabulary (which is

more than adequate); nor do I include the business of invented language, which far from being wordplay is a device that tends to distance the reader: when Tolkien has Frodo exclaim *'Aiya elenion ancalima!'* we do not participate because we cannot understand. Wordplay is a game. It seeks to involve the reader in a shared joke, a mutual enjoyment of verbal rule-bending (for instance, puns). Tolkien very rarely bends the rules. He writes a steady, upright, unequivocal prose that scarcely ever takes a chance with the reader. In all of *The Lord of the Rings*, I found only half-a-dozen examples of wordplay, moments when Tolkien permitted his words to have two meanings and briefly trusted us to be as brave as he. Here they are (page numbers are from the Unwin paperback edition):

33. eleventy-first.

77. Gandalf accuses Sam of eavesdropping. 'I don't follow you', Sam replies. 'There ain't no eaves at Bag End. . . .'

363. The hobbits sleep in a tree. Pippin is afraid of rolling off. Sam dismisses this: '. . . the less said, the sooner I'll drop off, if you take my meaning.'

680. Sam orders Sméagol to collect herbs for rabbit stew. Sméagol refuses. Sam growls: 'Sméagol'll get into real true hot water, when this water boils. . . .'

1052. Sam's gaffer dislikes Sam's armour: 'I don't hold with wearing ironmongery. . . .'

1060. When Hobbiton is restored, Bagshot Row is re-named 'New Row', but '. . . it was a purely Bywater joke to refer to it as Sharkey's End.'

Perhaps I have overlooked a few examples, but even so a grand total of a dozen (or even two dozen) items of wordplay in such a long book suggests a cautious temperament. Tolkien, for all his rich language and his athletic syntax, was not an adventurous writer if adventure meant trusting the reader to see more than one meaning.

It's significant that Sam features in four of the six examples. Sam, like his namesake in *Pickwick*, is the closest Tolkien gets to establishing a comic character; and despite what feels like considerable. effort, that is never very close. Take this line (143): 'As far as he could remember, Sam slept through the night in deep content, if logs are contented.' By Tolkien's standards that is a joke, or maybe half a joke; just as when the midges bite them (199) Sam asks: 'What do they live on when they can't get hobbit?' Later, when Sam unexpectedly recites poetry (224) and Frodo jokingly comments on his revealed talents—'First he was a conspirator, now he's a jester. He'll end up 'by becoming a wizard—or a warrior!'—Sam replies 'I hope not, I don't want to be neither!' That final touch of the ungrammatical is as important as the rejection of importance. Sam has been cast as the common man. His job is to establish and maintain a level of ordinariness against which the major characters can be more effectively measured.

That is why Tolkien occasionally lets a sprinkling of humour fall on his shoulders like dandruff. Sam talks to his horse, Bill, as if they are equals; he talks to himself; and when the Company meet the Elves (360) and Legolas tells him 'they say that you breathe so loud that they could shoot you in the dark', Sam not only puts his hand over his mouth but he also—long after it's clear that the Elves will harm nobody— walks behind 'trying not to breathe loudly'. Sam is the comic butt, not very bright, not totally literate, but with a heart of gold, rather like a Hollywood Cockney. He knows his place; he knows how to behave proper.

Consider this, on 672: 'Sam stood up, putting his hands behind his back (as he always did when "speaking poetry")....' Am I alone in squirming a little when I read that? Doesn't it leave a slightly patronizing taste in the mouth? A touch of *de haut en bas*? There are times when I suspect that Tolkien believed the lower orders (like Sam) were funny simply because they were working-class. If only life (and writing) were as easy as that.

When Tolkien loosens his stays and tries to make Sam more colourful, the results are unconvincing. 'You're nowt but a ninnyhammer, Sam Gamgee,' Sam declares (632), 'that's what the Gaffer said to me often enough, it being a word of his.' And when Gollum escapes (741): 'Slinker and Stinker, as I've said before,' said Sam. 'But the nearer they get to the

Enemy's land the more like Stinker Slinker will get.' I have chosen those remarks not because they are typical but because they are, for Tolkien, unusually forceful and slangy. Yet their net effect is to emphasize Sam's immaturity. He never grows up, never escapes his father's influence. 'Stinker Slinker' is schoolboy talk. We laugh *at* Sam as often as *with* him.

None of this would matter very much if it were not for Tolkien's determination to convince us that *The Lord of the Rings is* funny, at least in parts. He wants us to believe that hobbits are very big on humour. Hobbits have 'mouths apt to laughter' (14) and 'laugh they did, and eat, and drink, often and heartily, being fond of simple jests at all times. . . .' Tree-beard calls them 'the laughing-folk' (609) and in truth they are easily amused. When talk in *The Green Dragon* gets around to monsters (57), Ted displays his wit. " 'There's only one dragon in Bywater, and that's Green," he said, getting a general laugh.' And Tolkien rubs it in with his next line: ' "All right," said Sam, laughing with the rest.' It's hard to avoid the conclusion that (a) Tolkien didn't spend much time telling jokes in pubs, and (b) whenever he strayed off the fairway and into the rough he liked to trample down the grass as much as possible.

Which leaves me wondering at all the references to laughter in the book. Are we meant to take them literally? When Goldberry announces that the rain has stopped and the stars are out (146), she says 'Let us now laugh and be glad!' It's a curious invitation. Outside the covers of *The Lord of the Rings*, that sort of remark could be guaranteed to kill the conversation for the foreseeable future; but Tolkien's characters are inclined to treat laughter like a demonstration of sociability. When the hobbits enter Bombadil's house (138) Goldberry welcomes them with the words 'Laugh and be merry!' the way other hostesses might say 'Can I take your coat?' The hobbits don't laugh—what is there to laugh at?—and as the story develops it becomes clear that Tolkien is using *laughter* as a codeword for *reassurance*. Often, when his characters laugh, it's a sign that there is nothing to worry about. Late in the story (789) Pippin asks: 'Are you angry with me, Gandalf? I did the best I could.' The reply: ' "You did indeed!" said Gandalf, laughing suddenly. . . .' This example could be multiplied many times. *The Lord of the Rings* often presents a surface impression of hilarity which on examination turns out to be less an expression of mirth than an antidote to anxiety: the literary equivalent of a dog rolling onto its back to avoid a fight: a shorthand way of saying *Look, we're all pals together, really.*

For Tolkien dislikes bad feeling. There is remarkably little friction in the Company; he rarely allows them to argue and he almost never lets them get into a full-blooded quarrel. All the 'aggro' is saved for the enemy. Frodo and his mates are thoroughly decent, moderate, considerate chaps who don't take liberties with each other. In the whole book I can recall only two occasions of leg-pulling. When they are planning the journey (289) Pippin demands to go, saying 'There must be someone with intelligence in the party.' Gandalf retorts: 'Then you certainly will not be chosen, Peregrin Took!' And on the Stairs of Cirith Ungol (741), when Frodo and Sam are reviewing their quest as if it were an adventure story, Sam speculates whether the appalling Gollum would like to play hero or villain (unfortunately Gollum has sloped off, so his slimy leg remains unpulled).

Without bad feeling it is difficult to generate humour. That may sound like a paradox. It is. Humour promotes friendship but its roots are in conflict. There is no such thing as a completely non-malicious joke: everything that is capable of raising a laugh is also capable of drawing blood. (I speak with some authority on this subject. I once wrote and presented a B.B.C. radio series that featured listeners' comments and complaints, and I rapidly discovered that any and every comedy programme is capable of giving offence to someone. Comic items about dogs offend dog-lovers; sketches involving deafness get condemned by the hard-of-hearing; jokes that mention religion are blasted by the pious; and a gag about a deaf dog that went to church—be it never so funny—gets hammered from all sides. Any comedy producer must reconcile himself to upsetting someone; indeed, if his material fails to upset anyone then it is not funny.) It is in the nature of humour to be aggressive. Humour is possible only when a more or less violent rearrangement of the intellectual scenery takes place, because humour requires a sudden recognition of absurdity. A joke works when the joke-teller leads his listeners by the nose in the wrong direction and then allows them to discover their mistake at the last moment, when they tread on the stair that isn't there, tumble into space, and land, astonishingly, on their feet.

This is beyond Tolkien's ability, and I suspect that it was outside his personal taste, too. By all reports he was quite an amusing man to know but it was never his style publicly to rock the boat, even if he thought the boat was upside-down and would benefit from rocking. (There is some little evidence that he did feel the world was out of sorts and needed reshaping, as I shall show later.)

Whenever anyone of the Company threatens to stray outside the bounds of decent courteous behaviour and indulge in a touch of Bad Taste, Tolkien quickly cuts him short. Gandalf, explaining to Frodo the actions and motives of the Ring (69), tells how the Ring had decided to leave Gollum. That's more than Frodo can swallow. 'What, just in time to meet Bilbo?' he says. 'Wouldn't an Orc have suited it better?' This levity is instantly slapped down by Gandalf. 'This is no laughing matter', he says, and Frodo is squelched. Indeed, there's not much fun in Gandalf at any time. Bilbo has the nerve to fence with him once or twice ('As all your unpleasant advice has been good,' says Bilbo, 'I wonder if this advice is not bad.') but Gandalf never bothers to fence back. He just walks all over Bilbo with his superior knowledge and his unarguable powers. You get the impression that Gandalf doesn't enjoy his work a lot. He worries about it, and he speaks sternly, and if he laughs it is pure stage-effect, like snapping his fingers: a politician's laugh. In contest with Saruman (605) he *seems* to be in his element: ' "Saruman, Saruman!" said Gandalf, still laughing. "Saruman, you missed your path in life. You should have been the king's jester and earned your bread, and stripes too, by mimicking his counsellors." ' But there is no real sting in this confrontation because he knows, and Saruman knows, and we know, that Gandalf holds all the aces. Any time he likes, he can out-magic Saruman and make him shrivel (which he does, shortly thereafter). So Gandalf's sarcasm is not a real weapon. It accomplishes nothing.

If Tolkien can be said to feel comfortable with any form of

humour I suppose it might be sarcasm, and yet all too often the exchanges he puts into the mouths of his characters are neither biting nor effective; by which I mean they don't change anything. When the hobbits stay at *The Pony* and Butterbur distrusts Strider the Ranger, Strider fights back: 'Then who would you take up with?' he asks the hobbits. 'A fat innkeeper who only remembers his own name because people shout it at him all day?' Now that's a good line. The trouble is, it's wasted. Butterbur doesn't matter. And later, when there is genuine conflict between people who *do* matter, the sarcasm is pretty feeble stuff. When Gandalf tells Saruman that, according to Radagast, the Nine have come forth again (276), Saruman's scorn is expressed thus: 'Radagast the Brown! Radagast the Bird-tamer! Radagast the Simple! Radagast the Fool!' With each limp phrase, Saruman diminishes himself. Any primary-school playground could produce better abuse than that.

Not that Gandalf is much more lethal. His response to Butterbur's mistake (281) is 'Ass! Fool!' and when the mistake is shown to be good news: 'May your beer be laid under an enchantment of surpassing excellence for seven years!' Only seven years? For a man who is so at home in the supernatural Gandalf can be sadly pedestrian. Think what another wizard, Merlin in *The Once and Future King*, would have made of that scene. His treatment of Butterbur would have been more cantankerous, more colourful and more extravagant. Butterbur wouldn't have understood half of it, but we, the readers, would have enjoyed a genuine 'nifty'.

Among members of the Company, loyal comradeship is the factor that constantly saps the strength of sarcasm, even when the pressure of events is on and the staunchest comrade would be justified in letting rip occasionally. Boromir wants to leave the Great River before the rocky rapids, and to strike overland (409). Aragorn says no: too much bog and fog; stick to the River. 'But the Enemy holds the eastern bank,' objects Boromir. 'And even if you ... come unmolested to the Tindrock, what will you do then? Leap down the Falls and land in the marshes?'

As taunts go, that doesn't go far; and Aragorn is too much of a gent to be provoked, more's the pity. Although there is much

passion and intense commitment in *The Lord of the Rings*, much
of the Company's behaviour would not be out of place in the
Home Counties. Gimli annoys Éomer (453) so much that
'Éomer's eyes blazed. "I would cut off your head, beard and all,
Master Dwarf, if it stood but a little higher from the ground,"
said Éomer.' Not a very telling thrust: too oblique; lacking in
venom. What's more it invites a retort. If Tolkien had been
prepared to screw the tension tighter, he could have made
Gimli jump onto a rock and say: 'Is that high enough for you,
you fat bag of wind?' But Tolkien rapidly defuses the scene and
soon they're all pals again. Much later, there is a scene where
Gimli is allowed to lose his temper (the reunion on the road to
Isengard: 580) but his oaths are sub-Shakespearean: 'You
rascals, you woolly-footed and wool-pated truants. . . . Hammer
and tongs! I am so torn between rage and joy, that if I do not
burst, it will be a marvel!' And of course Gimli is not really in a
bad temper: it's just the excitement of relief.

Given Tolkien's nervousness over differences of opinion and
his eagerness to make friends and get back to unanimity as
soon as possible, it's not surprising that there are very few
occasions when his characters test their wits and try to score
points off each other. Yet when they do, the effect is briskly
refreshing. Briefly, the story perks up. In Lothlorien (366) the
whole Company are bickering and Gimli is especially obstinate.
Legolas cries: 'A plague on Dwarves and their stiff necks!' A
dozen lines later, Legolas is the stubborn one. 'A plague on the
stiff necks of Elves!' says Aragorn. It's only a touch, a flicker,
but it brings to life the impatience and competitiveness of the
two.

Legolas and Gimli are involved in another piece of banter:
the running joke about their Orc-killing scores. When they
meet on the Road to Isengard (566) Gimli shouts: 'Forty-two,
Master Legolas. Alas! My axe is notched: the forty-second had
an iron collar on. How is it with you?' That little spurt of
boastfulness gives an immediate boost to the story: eternal
modesty can get very wearing. There is another bit of cut-and-
thrust, between Aragorn and Legolas in the chapter *The Riders
of Rohan* (450). Aragorn hears riders coming, and Legolas says,
'Yes, there are one hundred and five. Yellow is their hair, and
bright are their spears. Their leader is very tall.' Aragorn

remarks on his keen eyesight, but Legolas dismisses this: 'The riders are little more than five leagues distant', he says. Five leagues is fifteen miles. Delicious.

Not surprisingly, Tolkien's restraint and caution mean that his rare ventures into humour are often understated in the typically English way. Aragorn, recounting his fight with Gollum in the Dead Marshes (271), says 'He will never love me, I fear'—which, considering Gollum's squalid nature, is a considerable understatement indeed. Again, when the hobbits enter the Mines and nearly stumble into a well, Aragorn says (330): 'One of you might have fallen in and still be wondering when you were going to strike the bottom.' Neither line is a world-beater, but against so many acres of Tolkien's absolute literalness, where almost everything means just what it says, they catch the eye. Similarly, when Sam and Frodo have watched their enemies quarrel, blame, betray, fight and slaughter each other (961), Sam says: 'If this nice friendliness would spread about in Mordor, half our trouble would be over.' What distinguishes that remark is its redeeming cynicism. *The Lord of the Rings* is a very *good* book; indeed a very goody-goody book; and the goodness mounts up until I, for one, thirst for a sliver of redeeming vice, just one little taste of genuine bloody-mindedness. Considering the enormity of the death and destruction in it, there is an astonishing absence of black or gallows humour. I could find just one such line, where we're told (195) that Bill Ferny's pony 'didn't look like dying just yet'. There is more black humour in the Old Testament than there is in *The Lord of the Rings*.

However, to be fair to Tolkien, the book does contain two, perhaps three, comic set-pieces.

The first is Bilbo's birthday party (41–3). The build-up is brisk and rich—gifts and fireworks and feasting—and Bilbo's speech is nicely confused. He welcomes everyone, including the Proudfoots, at which an elderly hobbit shouts 'ProudFEET!', so Bilbo wilfully repeats 'Proud*foot*'. He asks if they're all enjoying themselves and there are cries of *Yes* (and *No*). Some young hobbits get up an impromptu orchestra, 'supposing Uncle Bilbo to have finished (since he had plainly said all that was necessary)'. When Bilbo describes his 144 guests as One Gross and nobody cheers, the scene has the authentic ring of a family reunion about to turn nasty and become interesting. Unfortunately for us, Bilbo then vanishes and we're left unsatisfied. There is a posthumous taste of his sardonic style (49–50) in the collection of presents he has left for friends and relatives: the umbrella for Abelard, the waste-paper basket for Dora, the pen for Milo; but the joke is weakened by having to be explained (Abelard steals umbrellas, Dora writes too many letters, Milo too few, and so on).

The other set-piece (such as it is) occurs in the Houses of Healing (899). It starts with Aragorn trying to get hold of some kingsfoil to help save the injured Faramir. After a delay, the herbmaster enters and says: 'Your lordship asked for *kingsfoil*, as the rustics name it, or *athelas* in the noble tongue, or to those who know somewhat of the Valinorean . . .'. Aragorn tries to hurry him up. The herbmaster begs his pardon but then rambles on, saying nothing at great length, and quoting bad verse for which he apologizes—'It is but a doggrel, I fear, garbled in the memory of old wives'—until Gandalf abruptly sends him packing. It's all reminiscent of *Henry V* where, in Act 1, Scene 2, Henry is twitching with impatience to attack France but has to endure a rambling analysis of his legal rights to the French crown: the man of action baffled by the egghead. In *The Lord of the Rings* it pays off a few pages later (904). Merry wants a smoke but he's lost all his smoking-matter. Aragorn suggests he send for the herbmaster. 'And he will tell you that he did not know that the herb you desire had any virtues, but that it is called *westmans-weed* by the vulgar, and *galenas* by the noble, and other names in other tongues more learned, and after adding a few half-forgotten rhymes that he does not understand, he will regret-fully inform you that there is none in the House. . . .' There is a hint of needle in that passage. Maybe Tolkien was settling an old score. At all events, his tone was unusually tart; and no bad thing, either.

The other possible candidate for consideration as a comic set-piece is Sam's lecture on oliphaunts (672–73), but it's a pretty thin joke. If you go through it and substitute *elephant* for *oliphaunt*, the joke virtually disappears. It's a bit of country-bumpkin semi-literacy, and an obvious retread of A. A. Milne's 'heffelump' joke in *Pooh*.

None of these set-pieces is exactly hilarious. Humour emerges best from character, and Tolkien's characters are fairly one-dimensional. Even his picaresque inventions are never outrageous. Tom Bombadil (135+) is, so he repeatedly tells us, 'a merry fellow'. I was glad to see the back of him. People who refer to themselves in the third person and who sing *Hey dol! merry dol! ring a dong dillo!* are not easy to live with, and Bombadil's merriness seems to consist largely of capering, an exercise of limited comic range.

Similarly Treebeard, the Ent, is a creation who is original rather than interesting. Tolkien treats him like a lumbering great shambles of a man, not very bright and inclined to tell long, sad stories, illustrated with short, sad verse. There is not much fun in Treebeard; he's like the pensioner you meet in the park who tells you, at great length, how the district's gone down in the last twenty years.

What is more of a loss, I feel, is Tolkien's inability to extract any humour from his villains. Wormtongue grovels and Gollum crawls. They are both so squalid and despicable that they stand as little chance of producing a moment of wit as a garden slug does of playing the Palladium. I think Tolkien went too far there. He should have given them a little more strength, more skill, more independence; then they would have been more interesting because more worth beating. As it is, nobody can make good jokes about Gollum; he's too bestial. And Wormtongue isn't bright enough to match his wits with the hobbits. It's not a fair contest.

I said earlier that *The Lord of the Rings* contains a hint of Tolkien's dissatisfaction with the world he lived in. Could it be that he saw his book as a monumental spoof on the way we are all going to the dogs? Gloin says (257):

> It is many years ago that a shadow of disquiet fell upon our people . . . Words began to be whispered in secret: it was said that we were hemmed in a narrow place, and that greater wealth and splendour would be found in a wider world. . . .

Is the whole thing a colossal dig in the ribs, Tolkien's way of telling us that if we go on being so envious and greedy it will all end in tears? I wish I could think so. I wish I could read *The Lord of the Rings* as a sort of reverse *1984*, in which Tolkien looks back because he despises what he sees when he looks forward. The trouble is, Tolkien's message is that there is no message. To my mind, the most curious passage in *The Lord of the Rings* is Sam's speculating with Frodo on the difference between art and life; between adventure stories and real adventures (739). Nobody seeks real adventures, Sam says. 'Folk seem to have been just landed in them, usually—their paths were laid that way. . . .' No, Tolkien doesn't pretend to have any of the answers. If there is a private joke anywhere in the story it comes on page 291. Bilbo, discussing his book, asks Frodo if he's thought of an ending for it. Bilbo suggests: *and they all settled down and lived together happily ever after.* Frodo comments: 'It will do well, if it ever comes to that.' If what ever comes to that? The book, or the world? There is a rare double-edged quality here.

But it is very rare indeed. With Tolkien the style is the man, and his style is almost totally resistant to humour. The natural and simple place for humour is in dialogue. That is where differences of opinion emerge; that is where quirks of personality appear—especially the staples of comedy: impatience, vanity, pretension, greed, hypocrisy, self-delusion. Exposing them through dialogue is one of the major jobs of fiction, because it requires the characters to reveal themselves, thus avoiding the heavy-handed, omniscient dictat of the author as he tells us what to think.

The trouble is that Tolkien is not terribly good at dialogue. He is quite definitely bad at handling lively exchanges where views are challenged or where temperaments clash. He much prefers the orderly decencies of drawing-room conversation, where everyone is allowed to say as much as he likes without fear of interruption. This makes for some mind-numbing speeches. Consider this relatively brief one, by Aragorn (413):

> Fear not! Long have I desired to look upon the likenesses of Isildur and Anárion, my sires of old. Under their shadow Elessar, the Elfstone son of Arathorn of the House of Valandil Isildur's son, heir of Elendil, has nought to dread!

He says all this while steering a small, frail boat down a long, dark chasm in which 'the black waters roared and echoed, and a wind screamed over them.' It's hard to believe that Frodo

119

was not thinking, *For the love of God, stop ranting and watch where you're bloody well going!* But he says nothing. Nobody interrupts anyone in *The Lord of the Rings*.

Well, almost nobody. In all of the 1,077 pages I found seven, perhaps eight places where Tolkien broke a line of dialogue, but in only one of those places does the speaker actually suffer interruption from another person. This occurs while the Warden of the Houses of Healing is telling Lady Éowyn of Faramir's state of health (995). She cuts in and asks Faramir to be brought to her, thus revealing a touch of impatience. All the other breaks are caused by some outside event—a trumpet-call (1,002) or a great clamour (876)—or because the speaker has suddenly remembered something (846) or has run out of words.

Apart from the impetuous Lady Éowyn, nobody in the story butts in because he can't wait for the other person to finish speaking. This, of course, is highly artificial. In life, people interrupt each other all the time. It is the cut-and-thrust of opinion and counter-opinion that makes conversation interesting, and that makes it such a marvellously flexible, fruitful device for the novelist. Tolkien's dialogue is formal and stately, which is why it is almost entirely humourless. Humour is a risky business. The risk is that it requires the mental agility to change one's point-of-view, perhaps several times. Tolkien does not take that risk. Given his self-made rules of dialogue, he cannot take it. Clive James once wrote: '. . . commonsense and a sense of humour are the same things, moving at different speeds. A sense of humour is just commonsense, dancing.' Tolkien's commonsense can't dance.

So what? As long as he cranks out a good thick read, does it matter that humour plays so small a part? I believe it does matter. Humour is not incompatible with picaresque fantasies or with bloody epics—look at *The Once and Future King*, or the *Gormenghast* trilogy, or even *Beowulf*. But humourlessness *is* incompatible with the best story-telling, because humour—far from being a literary additive, a sort of artistic sodium monoglutamate to be sprinkled over the prose—humour is an essential ingredient. (After all, it's found everywhere in human life, even on battlefields, in the terminal wards of hospitals, and inside concentration camps.) Remove humour and you don't make the story more serious; you make it less true. So to the extent that Tolkien cannot handle humour, he is painting with an incomplete palette.

The formality of minuet-type dialogue is not his only inbuilt deterrent to humour. His whole literary style works against it. His habit of constructing statements backwards, as if they gain weight by inversion, is an alienating device. 'Edoras those courts are called,' said Gandalf (529), 'and Meduseld is that golden hall.' It's like listening to a Welsh butler announcing distinguished guests. *The Lord of the Rings* is stiff with these inversions. In its early years, *Time* magazine had the same habit, until Dorothy Parker wrote of it: *Backward run sentences until reels the mind.* Tolkien's endless inversions have that effect on me, made worse by my resentment of their pretentiousness. All too often, when Tolkien hasn't much to say he says it backwards in the hope that it will sound more impressive.

In the same way his choice of archaic words has a dulling and distancing effect. 'Some were laving their hands in basins,' Tolkien says (702). No, they weren't; they were *washing* their hands. Why make us translate? Why say 'yesterevening' (712) or 'swordthain' (835) when what he means is 'last night' and 'swordsman'? I believe that Tolkien felt uneasy whenever his writing strayed in the direction of normalcy. If he thought it was becoming too accessible he stuck in a 'laving' or a 'swordthain', just to keep the reader at a properly respectful distance. This theory is reinforced by a study of Tolkien's use of plebeian speech. He is not at ease with the working class: he makes them talk woodenly, as if he had assembled the phrases from a Glossary of Underworld Slang. Here, for instance, is Gorbag the Orc talking to his mate Shagrat (765):

> . . . if we get a chance, you and me'll slip off and set up somewhere on our own with a few trusty lads, somewhere where there's good loot nice and handy, and no big bosses.

Good loot and big bosses: it's the sort of imagery that goes with broken noses and cauliflower ears and burglars carrying sacks marked SWAG.

Probably the greatest antidote to humour is Tolkien's long-windedness. He goes on too long, about almost everything. Strider's two-page poem (208) is just the worst of many tedious examples, although Bilbo's effort (295) surely takes the prize for vacuous, plonkety-plonk, greetings-card verse:

> I sit beside the fire and think
>   of all that I have seen,
> of meadow-flowers and butterflies
>   in summers that have been.

There are five more stanzas like that (including one that rhymes 'were' with 'hair'), and they go nowhere. The effect on the reader is, as Wodehouse would have said, like that of a sock full of sand on the base of the occiput. Tolkien's long-windedness saps his rare ventures into levity. When Pippin is supposed to be ravenously hungry (791), his discussion with Beregond about the possibility of breakfast goes on so long that it loses all its point: anyone who can talk that much can't be really hungry. Therefore whatever humour lay in his initial eagerness is lost.

There is, too, a kind of imitation-Old-Testament quality in *The Lord of the Rings*. Here's the sort of thing I mean (814):

> And while Théoden went by slow paths in the hills, the Grey Company passed swiftly over the plain, and on the next day in the afternoon they came to Edoras; and there they halted only briefly, ere they passed up the valley, and so came to Dun-harrow. . . .

One can almost hear the vicar's drone. Indeed, at its most extreme, Tolkien's writing has a tombstone ponderousness that invites parody. When Legolas goes on about the Lost Elves (301)—

> Only I hear the stones lament them: *deep they delved us, fair they wrought us, high they builded us; but they are gone.* They are gone . . .

—I'm reminded of Oscar Wilde's remark about how stony-hearted one must be to read the death of Little Nell without laughing. Parts of *The Lord of the Rings* sound like lines rejected from the draft script for *Monty Python and the Holy Grail* because they weren't quite pompous enough. The most Pythonesque passage (298) occurs when the Company starts swapping proverbs:

> 'Faithless is he that says farewell when the road darkens,' said Gimli.

'Maybe,' said Elrond, 'but let him not vow to walk in the
dark, who has not seen the nightfall.'

'Yet sworn word may strengthen quaking heart,' said Gimli.

'Or break it,' said Elrond. . . .

And there, unfortunately, Tolkien stops them. The rustiest
saw of all is uttered much later, by Aragorn (812): 'The hasty
stroke goes oft astray.' Every book is said to contain, somewhere, a line that condemns it; and Aragorn's could be the
one. Tolkien made no hasty strokes, ever. Everything he wrote
is uncontroversial, one-dimensional, monochrome in its attitude. The villains are black, the good guys white—often
literally so. But the writing of fiction is an inescapably hazard-
ous profession, and the harder you concentrate on walking
down the middle of the road, the sillier you look when you trip
over your own feet. Sooner or later Tolkien, with his obsession
for linguistics and his blinkered, literal view of events, was
bound to write something as daft as the immortal line (406):
' "Yrch!" said Legolas, falling into his own tongue.' Thus
humour keeps breaking in, whether the author likes it or not.

You will have guessed by now that I am not the greatest
admirer of Tolkien. Nevertheless, I respect his success. Any
writer who can get such a grip of millions of readers must be
doing something right; and the fact that his spell fails to work
on me is just too bad for me. However, I believe there are
things to be learned from Tolkien's enormous appeal, from his
unswerving seriousness, and from both together.

One conclusion is that he wasn't much good at humour, and
knew it, and wished he were better at it. The extreme caution
with which he tackles any wordplay, the nervousness with
which he approaches comedy, the speed with which he shies
away from any sarcastic confrontation or leg-pulling, the
pedestrian quality of his characters' insults, the virtual
absence of good jokes or even of crisp one-liners—all these
factors suggest a man who was miserably uncomfortable on
the teeter-totter of humour and who jumped off it as soon as he
could. I believe Tolkien was afraid of humour: it was too
volatile an element for him: it might blow up in his face. What
he liked was stability, certainty, centrality. The extraordinary
thing about *The Lord of the Rings* is that, for all its extravagance

123

and its perils, it is really a very safe story; cosy, even. It takes the reader out of the present world of worrying insecurity and places him in an ancient world of reassuring insecurity. What's so reassuring is the knowledge that—no matter how big and black the bogeymen may be—Frodo & Co. will win through in the end. Does anyone seriously think, when Sam finds Frodo stretched out lifeless (758), that he is really dead? We all know better. We all know that Frodo has star billing and you don't kill off your star halfway through the epic. Does anyone seriously believe that Gandalf is gone for ever when he vanishes into the abyss (349)? We all know that Gandalf will be back. Gandalf is the joker that Tolkien plays whenever it looks as if Frodo is beaten. Gandalf can do anything, when he tries. This makes the story very comforting.

Politically, of course, it is simpleminded. Nobody ever thinks to question the way power is acquired or used, apart from routine denunciations of the Enemy's intentions. It is assumed that the Enemy has no plan or purpose except enslavement, exploitation and a permanent diet of woe; just as it is assumed that the Good Guys will govern benevolently because they are not the Enemy. There is actually very little to discuss, let alone to worry about, in *The Lord of the Rings*, and it seems reasonable to conclude that its readers prefer it that way. Humour being notoriously subversive, Tolkien was wise to play the whole yarn as straight as possible, thus eliminating any risk of valued judgement.

Two remarks come to mind when I hold this great bludgeon of a book in my hand. One is the saying of Muriel Spark's Miss Jean Brodie: 'For those who like that sort of thing, that is the sort of thing they like.' The other is a comment by Jonathan Miller: "Wagner is musical Tolkien.' I see what he means. But is Tolkien literary Wagner? I wonder.

7

The Rippingest Yarn of All

by KENNETH McLEISH

Yin and yang

A clue to the essential nature of *The Lord of the Rings* is the almost total absence of femininity. I don't just mean that we hear nothing of Mrs. Gandalf, Merry's girl-friends (he surely wasn't a Brandybuck for nothing) or the home life of our own dear Wormtongue (was Mrs. Grima a shrew—or nagged to shreds?). I don't mean that the few female characters we *do* hear about are cardboard figures from Welsh legend (like the ineffable Arwen (I, 239), who was, if you'll pardon Tolkien's prose, 'so like in form of womanhood to Elrond that Frodo guessed she was one of his close kindred') or knockabout comediennes from the Victorian stage (*The Wooing of Sam and Rosie Gamgee* would surely have rolled 'em in the aisles, an 1880s farce equivalent of the courtship of Eddie and Carrie Grundy from *The Archers*). By absence of femininity I mean the lack of any true gentleness, grace or what the Oxford dictionary calls 'passivity' in the characters, of any vision of behaviour beyond gruff comradeship (or its mirror sycophancy), bully-boy rant (or its mirror fortitude) and, to remind us now and then that our heroes are really just like us, the brushing away of a furtive but manly tear. (There's a lot of that in III, 305ff, as Frodo and Sam prepare to part. ' "I am wounded," he answered, "wounded; it will never heal." ' Henry Irving, eat your heart out.)

Homer's *Iliad*, an epic which *does* include the feminine, hinges

125

on the quarrel between Agamemnon (the masculine principle in nature, or *yang*, personified) and Achilles (the feminine principle, or *yin*) over a captured princess; its climactic battle (between Achilles and another yangy male, Hector) is not only preceded by one of the most moving 'feminine' scenes in literature, the farewell between Hector, Andromache and their baby son (who is terrified by his father's overshadowing helmet-plumes), but is followed by another, in which Priam pitifully pleads with the Greeks for Hector's corpse. Homer's *Odyssey*, the 'quest' narrative to end them all, charts Odysseus' growth not only as he comes to terms with every conceivable variety of female (calculating Calypso, nymphet Nausicaa, Marlene-Dietrich Circe), but more importantly as he realizes that the gentle and pliable qualities in his own nature are strength, not weakness, and as he persuades first his wife Penelope and then his people that because he has changed, has united the warring aspects in his own nature, he is worthy at last to be Penelope's husband and his people's king.

Where is this kind of profundity in *The Lord of the Rings*? Do its characters grow, in yin-and-yang harmonization or in any other way? Boromir, to be sure, learns that he is as greedy for the Ring as anyone else, that he is not the gentil parfit knight he thought himself; Frodo is revealed more and more as 'the outsider' (Camus, and Sartrean existentialism, were much in the air as Tolkien wrote); Gandalf turns from grey to white convincingly enough to pass the strictest window-test. But this is declaration of character, not growth: in each case it reveals only what was latent from the start. Like a preacher, Tolkien first tells us what his moral lessons are going to be, then goes through them painstakingly one by one. The dwarves become more dwarfish, the elves more elvish, the orcs more orc-like, even the hobbits more hobbity. The underlying moral messages are 'Discover your true self, and be true to it', and—less creditably—'Be wary of anyone Not Like Us.' I think only the kindly old Ents avoid such pragmatic chauvinism—and all even they ever want is to be left alone.

Comparing Tolkien with Homer—as Tolkien would have been the first to point out—is pompous and silly. All he claimed to be doing was producing 'mythologies', extending his plunderings of the Red Book, already used in *The Hobbit* (his masterpiece, because it never aspires to allegorical significance, and is therefore superbly self-consistent); he nevertheless pointed out that

> since my children and others of their age, who first heard of the finding of the Ring, have grown older with the years, this book speaks more plainly of those darker things which lurked only on the borders of the earlier tale, but which troubled Middle-Earth in all its history.

It speaks of them all, that is, except—as J. W. Lambert pointed out when he first reviewed the book—except for God and sex. Leaving God aside for the moment, let's consider sex. Is there, somewhere in the morass of material which might have constituted *Silmarillion II* (and still might: *there's* a thought) Tolkien's *Tristan and Isolde*, his solution to the problems of uniting yin and yang? Or was *The Lord of the Rings* intended from the start as no more than an adult *Hobbit*, a fairy-tale for grown-up people?—in which case, like all half-way decent tale-tellers (Bilbo himself states as much), if a particular aspect of experience didn't suit Tolkien's story, he left it out. Fair enough. But for those who claim higher status for *The Lord of the Rings* than that of a simple tale, the absence of sex—to say nothing of its benign transfiguration, love—is a matter to be reckoned with.

Upmarket and down

Grown-ups, writing tales for children (and for other grown-ups): those are the key factors. What other tales might Tolkien himself, or his children, have experienced? What was a chap (or a chap's friend) likely to be reading in the 1900s, or in the 1930s (when Tolkien himself started publishing children's books, and presumably sniffed out the market first)? On what well-established foundations, in short, on what familiar ground, was the edifice of his life's work laid down?

I stress that I'm not talking about things like *Beowulf*, the *Kalevala* or the *Mabinogion*, the material Tolkien and his friends loved reading aloud to each other over mugs of ale. This kind of source-material is well documented elsewhere (and the documents should be known to every self-respecting Tolkien enthusiast. *A propos*, has anyone noticed the links between his work and Hermann Hesse's *Narciss and Goldmund* or *The Glass Bead Game?* Worth looking up.) I'm talking about popular literature, mass fiction, the furniture of the growing mind which we all take for granted as we grow, which helps our growing and which we generally put aside as soon as we've grown.

Curiously, this brings us straight back to God, to that other element crucial to literary stature which is missing from *The Lord of the Rings* (because it consistently confuses the metaphysical with the supernatural). The first inkling comes from the writings of Tolkien's donnish colleague and friend C. S. Lewis. Lewis was much concerned with metaphysics, with the Problem of Good and Evil (the capitals—and the simplification of the issue—are his), and produced a clutch of books (notably *The Screwtape Letters*) depicting the quest of and for the human soul in the form of a kind of Shavian fishing-manual, full of urbane jokes and shallow-profound metaphorical advice—'Whatever you do, don't cast where God is, or you'll foul your line.' He also wrote a legend-cycle for children, the *Narnia* books, which Tolkien heartily disliked and in which Good heroically and interminably battles Bad. But the clue lies less in any of these works than in his three remarkable science-fiction novels for adults, the first of which, *Out of the Silent Planet*, was published in 1938, just before *The Hobbit*. (Like Tolkien, Lewis went on in subsequent books, *Perelandra* and *That Hideous Strength*, to darken and broaden an originally simple theme.)

Out of the Silent Planet starts with a lone walker in a leafy, placid Shire, who can't find a pub and calls instead at a lonely house. Here he meets someone, a 'slender man' (the adjective is fanged) who claims to be a fellow spirit (' "By Jove," said the slender man, "Not Ransome who used to be at Wedenshaw?" '), and takes him for a ride and on a quest on which ultimately the whole future of the race depends. Like Bilbo in *The Hobbit*, Lewis's nudgingly-named Ransome travels with strange companions to very strange places; like Bilbo, he triumphs in the end over terrible evil by a mixture of ruefulness, determination and muddling through; like Bilbo, he is forever changed by his experience.

128

The difference is that Lewis's hero journeys not overland to Misty Mountains and beyond, but through space to Mars. *Out of the Silent Planet*, for all its overtones of Christian redemption and of decency and honesty fighting the fascist beast—overtones which Lewis, like Tolkien later with *The Lord of the Rings*, strenuously and disingenuously disclaimed—is an H. G. Wells science-fiction tale made over for a darker age. The traveller is a middle-class 'loner'; his 'slender' companion is at his least trustworthy when he smiles; mysterious, attractive beings are met *en route*, and reluctantly abandoned; there is an all-important battle and a sad aftermath. This is *Hobbit* country, but it is also the well-charted territory favoured by the literate Edwardian middle class.

Lewis is a far worse writer than Tolkien, chiefly because he lets his moral messages overburden his prose. But whatever its quality, *Out of the Silent Planet* reminds us how much *The Lord of the Rings* also owes to H. G. Wells. One example, in particular, leaps out of Tolkien's narrative. When Frodo, Sam and Gollum finally begin struggling up Mount Doom (III, 193ff), the landscape, in its mixture of desolation, devastation and threat, seems uncannily familiar. It's not the Brecon Beacons, the Peak District or the Scottish Highlands (much too sinister); it's not even modelled on those shattered, barren vistas we all know as a fall-out from twentieth-century war. The impression that you've been there before arises because you *have*, in Wells's *The War of the Worlds*, first published in 1898, and a best-seller for ten years (i.e. all through Tolkien's adolescence). In this book, Martians and earthmen face each other for the final battle on just such scorched, bleak and above all menacing terrain. Wells could have been in the back of Tolkien's mind as he wrote *The Hobbit*, too: the terrifying film of *Things to Come* was issued in 1936, and its reputation would have reached even the most kinematophobic Oxford don, as it occasioned Questions in the House and even Letters to *The Times*. There was a fine film of *The War of the Worlds* in 1953, two years before the publication of *The Return of the King*. Still another Wells story, *The Island of Doctor Moreau* (again hugely popular during Tolkien's adolescence) is about ugly, satanic and pitiable creatures, animal/human hybrids produced by vivisection and genetic manipulation. One of the most striking of them all (the puma-creature) has large, pale eyes, grasping bony hands and hissing speech. . . .

We shall never know if Tolkien consciously imitated (or even remembered) Wells; but clearly the man was around at the crucial time to strike sparks in Tolkien's adolescent mind. So was the masterpiece of another fine writer, Kenneth Grahame, whose *The Wind in the Willows* (first published in 1908, when Tolkien was 16) could be found on every middle-class child's bookshelf for three generations, a superb (if daunting) model for any aspiring writer of children's fantasy. There's no need to rehearse the similarities in detail—the description of Mole's house at the beginning, the gargantuan meals, Toad's Sackville-Bagginsy social pretension, Badger's twinkly-eyed crustiness (so like Gandalf's)—but two sections in particular are close to Tolkien in both spirit and style. The chapter at the end, in which all the nasty creatures from the Wild Wood are routed, is described with the same panache as Tolkien uses for Merry's or Pippin's adventures with the orcs (I'm thinking especially of II, 47ff); and the chapter in *The Wind in the Willows* which I always found baffling as a child, in which the animals hear distant pan-pipes and are transported into a kind of rural trance, an ecstatic revelling in the sounds, smells, feel and psychic peacefulness of nature, is remarkably like what happens to Frodo and his friends when they stay with the Elves (I, 231ff), and is told in that archly suggestive, Dante-Gabriel-Rossetti style—writing about magic trances was once as embarrassing to English authors as discussing sex or metaphysics—which is the hallmark of all Edwardian writing involving nature-mysticism, from the twee mythological rehashings of Andrew Lang to the poems of Walter de la Mare and the plays of Barrie (about whose *Peter Pan* Tolkien wrote in his 1910 diary 'indescribable, but shall never forget it as long as I live').

Wells, Grahame and Barrie: for many of those of us who passed our childhood and adolescence in the 1930s and 1940s, those are potent names. We learned from them that there was a world outside our own, much less comfortable and inhabited by unpredictable and often monstrous mutations of our own kind; we learned that our own world was safe and desirable, and could, if we used ingenuity and courage, be saved from outside threat. (It needs no palantír to see more anti-fascist implications here.) We're not quite in Tolkien territory— dignity and elevation of style are missing—but we're getting close.

Our Sort

The over-simplification of moral issues in Wells, Grahame or Barrie was self-declaring and harmless, and made their work a wholesome tonic for the growing mind: silly enough to see through, but serious enough at least to raise the problems that perplex the young. A far more insidious, and far more sinister, influence comes in another type of children's literature, embodied in Tolkien's boyhood by the public-school sagas of Talbot Baines Reed and the adventure stories of Captain Marryat or G. A. Henty, and in his children's childhood by the messing-about-in-boats yarns of Arthur Ransome on the one hand, and on the other the 'he smiled grimly as the Boche spun out of control to his well-earned doom' tales of Percy F. Westerman and the unspeakable (but readable) Captain W. E. Johns. For adults, exactly the same philosophies were persuasively peddled in the 1910s and 1920s by Sapper, Edgar Wallace, Dornford Yates and their ilk, and in the 1930s and 1940s by what Colin Watson memorably christened the 'snobbery with violence' school of detective fiction whose joint headmistresses were Agatha Christie and the learned but muddle-headed Dorothy L. Sayers.

This literature is dangerous because it takes all ethical or moral problems for granted, as part of a desirable *status quo* which the villains constantly challenge and the heroes constantly reaffirm. Without exception, it hymns the British Imperial certainties of Tolkien's youth, a time when no one— except foreigners like Freud and Marx—seriously 'got in the way of things'. Society, by and large, worked well—and it was sturdily structured on the premise that everyone knew his place. Women's place, for example, was firmly at home, queening it at tea beside the buddleia or scrubbing and scrimping behind the scenes; the few eccentrics who chained themselves to railings or chaired Fabian Society meetings were regarded by everyone else (including the majority of their own sex) as 'unladylike', 'beyond the pale'. The Lower Orders were servile or perky to a man—and the extent of their servility or perkiness depended on their employers' whim. Even within the ruling class there were Those who Decided and Those who Agreed: in real life, the Cabinet formulated policy and the Whips ensured that the House of Commons enacted it; in popular literature every Raffles, Berry or Holmes had a devoted but flea-brained sidekick, and Wimsey, Poirot and their rivals delighted in outsmarting everyone in sight; even in the public-school dorms and studies of *Stalky and Co.* or on Ballantyne's notorious *Coral Island* there were patrol-leader types and the Good Scouts they led.

Outside this charmed circle, as everyone knew (in the way that everyone 'knew' about Timbuctoo), but as only trouble-makers like Wells and Shaw kept pointing out, there was a vast, inarticulate army who maintained the edifice: the factory-workers, labourers, salesmen and shopgirls of country towns. They surfaced every five years (males over 21, at least) to vote at elections; but Parliament was reliably a talking-shop, and real government was carried on discreetly and imperturbably by a civil service as silkily irreplaceable as a first-class family retainer, and by the occasional, essential derring-do of aristo-cratic loners. It was Ruritania, happy and glorious; it was Tolkien's Shire. Only when the inarticulate army of the suburbs became the all-too-visible (and embarrassingly dead) army of the War to End Wars was the Edwardian British twilight seen at last for what it was, the genteel decadence of a once thriving and invincible force.

It is my view that the books of Yates, Sayers and their like—favourite reading, we are assured, of the governing class—dangerously carried this shallow view of affairs, this smug or brainless clinging to the ethical verities of a vanished Victorian era, into the wholly alien decades of the first world war, the Depression and the General Strike—and that *The Lord of the Rings* still perpetuates them in an (even less appro-priate) era of mass democracy on the one hand and the imminent possibility of a nuclear apocalypse on the other. The view—which had once been true—that 'all that sort of thing can be left to Our Betters' or to 'Those Who Know about Such Things' underlies every page of *The Lord of the Rings*, an indication of how far in the establishment past its author's view of affairs was formed, and of how little it had been shaken by Mosley, the Spanish Civil War, the abdication, Chamberlain, by the aristocratic oafs who generalled and air-marshalled Britain through the Phoney War (till Churchill, that visionary ostracized for a dozen years by his own caste, was plummeted into power), and by Dachau, Hiroshima and the closing of the Iron Curtain (all events predating *The Lord of the Rings*, and proving that the world was a bigger and far more dangerous place than placid Oxfordshire, and could never be so scaled-down again).

There are those who claim that all this turmoil *is* reflected in *The Lord of the Rings*, that the message underlying it is that if only humanity would return to a species of hierarchical rural decency (but never religious—God is, as I have said, rigorously excluded from Tolkien's cosmology), all might again be well. There are, Tolkien says somewhere, many people who know nothing of Frodo's and Sam's adventure, but who are able to sleep more easily in their beds because it has taken place. I would suggest two things: first, that carrying a Ring to dump into a volcano against all odds, helped by a representative of every species (a League of Nations with a constitution borrowed from the Icelandic sagas), and rescued at crisis-points by coincidence (Gwaihir the Windlord, yet!), by magic or by blundering-through (the climax on Mount Doom is a glorious, shambolic *mess*, one of the very few places in the whole epic where Tolkien contrives even a twitch of irony at his characters' expense)—I would suggest that this is a very poor allegory for how we should run our century, and second, that it was precisely this Edwardianly cosy view of human affairs in real life that cost Britain its Empire, cost Europe millions upon millions of its young men, and, unless we abandon it right now, will quite possibly cost us this planet and everything on it.

The quality of Tolkien

The other day I drove past a house called Bag End. It wasn't a hole-in-the-ground house, either (though in these nuclear-shelter days, it might well have been): it was an ordinary

133

suburban bungalow. Nor were the people who lived inside, I'm quite sure, three-feet-high creatures with furry feet and a large acquaintanceship of dwarves, Ents and firework-making wizards. But the question I wanted to ask them was, did they wish they *were*? What power in *The Lord of the Rings* makes sane adults, all over the world, want not only to read it but actually to enter into it? Why *does* Frodo, as the lapel-badges once assured us, live? Researchers say that Tolkien's fantasy appeals more to men than to women, more to the young than to the old, more to southerners than to northerners. And the extraordinary thing, to those of us who aren't addicts, is that people make those surveys and say these things *seriously*, as if the books, and the cult they started, really matter. Whenever I criticize Tolkien even mildly in print or on the air, I get a bag of letters earnestly, lengthily, passionately begging me, for my own sake, to reconsider. Have *you*, dear reader, got your pen poised (not to say poisoned) as you read, right now?

For the reasons outlined above (among others) I don't think Tolkien is an epic writer to compare with Homer, and I find his mythopoeic view of life too restricted, too simplistic, to stand up against the moral truths, meticulous observation and metaphysical profundity of the finest novelists (e.g. Balzac, Mann or Proust). The cult that has mushroomed round his imagined world is as dottily devoted, and ultimately as frivolous (because remote from reality) as those endless genealogies of invented races and grammars of made-up languages that stuffed Tolkien's own mind and plump up even his minor work. I think that the vision of society put forward in *The Lord of the Rings* is old-fashioned, wrong-headed and a lethal model for late twentieth-century living, as likely to succeed as the wooden rifles and bean-poles with which Dad's Army once hoped to keep the invading Hun at bay. To put it bluntly, we live in a nasty, dangerous and brutal world, and dressing up in elven-cloaks, baking lembas and writing poems in Entish, though a commendable and delightful game, is a way of avoiding, not finding, the truth of life.

So where does that leave Tolkien? If those of his cultists who take him seriously are dangerously deluded, does that necessarily make him a fool as well? Of course not. The time has come to lay my cards on the table and say that I think Tolkien was one of the finest writers of escapist fantasy in any language and of any time. (Homer, Tolstoy, Dickens, aren't in competition. Their subject was reality.) His verse may be appalling, his prose convoluted and often arch, and his inspiration a magpie's nest of half-remembered instances from every piece of literature he ever read, from *King Lear* to *Noddy in Toyland*. But he hooks you from the first sentence, and drags you gasping and sighing through every spiral of his narrative, leaving you always hungry, always wanting more. The Quest is one of the surest of all fictional plots. It has a clearly marked start and a clearly defined end—and this clarity allows for all manner of diversions, twists and turns *en route*. In Tolkien's landscape every stone and tree has a part to play and a story to tell—indeed trees come to life and *tell* their stories. His world is full of wonders; magic is not special, but particular to everyone. Any author who invents Moria, Rivendell, the Ringwraiths, my own favourites the Ents, Gandalf and Saruman, is a storyteller to reckon with—and when he goes on to detail his fantasy with whole cycles of history, whole geographies, whole languages, how can we not be charmed? Tolkien's world, unlike the real world of infinite possibility in which we live, offers the attractions of completeness: he has anticipated every question and found an answer before you asked.

If your work is a magpie's hoard, what matters for greatness is the use you make of the glittering jewels you find—and this, I suggest, is the main facet of Tolkien's genius. He keeps reminding us of other things, stirring our memory of books, images and ideas we'd long forgotten; but he gives each memory, each allusion, a new twist and so redoubles its power. (Well, not always. The whole Theoden episode is a very faint echo of the hero-sagas from which it derives: try *Beowulf*, or consider what Wagner—whom Tolkien so heartily despised— did with Nordic mythology in *his The Ring*.) The underground sequences are brilliantly brought off, the finest portions of the book; the Balrog, Shelob and above all Gollum are both persuasive delineations of evil and creepily credible as characters; the Ents (though their origin could be unkindly traced to Enid Blyton's *The Faraway Tree* and their siege of Isengard, as recounted by Merry in II, 170ff, to Hesiod's version of the

Earthborn Giants' attack on the Olympian gods) are a spec-
tacular creation, as convincing a metaphor for the force and
dignity of nature as Bombadil is a plastic one. And, most
striking of all, Tolkien's careful blend of tones of voice—he
moves in a paragraph from the down-to-earthness of the
Hobbits (all grumbling bellies and hamster-like alarm) to the
'Lo! how brave the banners blew' alliterative-epic nonsense of
the Rohirrim, the stabbing gutturals of the orcs, the hooming
and homming of the Ents and the hissing duplicity of Gríma
and Sméagol—all this gives the story forward movement,
pace, and that essential ingredient of all good yarns, un-
expectedness: you *have* to turn each page to see what horrors or
delights are lurking there.

So, from the great cycles of saga and from the far less
elevated but no less evocative tales that helped to form his and
our youth, Tolkien assembles a hundred ideas, a thousand
strands of narrative, and weaves them into a single, glowing
tapestry, a work which reveals not only the capacious literary
ragbag that was his mind, but also his genius for organization
and redeployment. He is like a museum curator, with exhibits
from all the world's cultures arranged to give maximum
delight. And if—as I have suggested—a major part of his
collection consists of pages torn from the children's or grown-
ups' escapist adventure-stories of the twentieth century, what
he has written beggars all his sources, and—providing we
never take it as any kind of answer to the world's problems—is
stunningly readable, breathtakingly exciting and morally
unambiguous: in short, the ripping yarn to end them all.

8

Hobbit Verse Versus Tolkien's Poem

by ALAN BOLD

Tolkien's prose is punctuated with poetry; or, more accurately, verse since the casual reader (as opposed to the committed Tolkienite) will probably agree with Sam Gamgee who prefaced his recitation of 'The Stone Troll' with some words of warning: 'It ain't what I call proper poetry, if you understand me: just a bit of nonsense.'[1] For a man who was capable of writing superlative narrative and descriptive prose Tolkien was virtually incapable of understanding the linguistic point of post-medieval poetry. When he wrote verse he thought like a hobbit and was usually unable to transcend the limitations of hobbit verse which reads the way it does because hobbits 'are fond of strange words, and of rhyming and metrical tricks'.[2] Tolkien's usual assumption that poetry was synonymous with rhyme condemned him to the production of assembly-line verse—safety-first stanzas in which the sense is twisted and the syntax inverted to conform to the exigencies of a pre-determined pattern. His verse is generally composed in trans-lationese with the literal meaning taking massive priority over any sympathy with the sensuous qualities of the English language. It is, therefore, instructive to recall that Tolkien did not easily take to poetry. In his Andrew Lang Lecture, 'On Fairy Stories', he spoke of his schooldays:

> I was, for instance, insensitive to poetry, and skipped it if it
> came in tales. Poetry I discovered much later in Latin and

Greek, and especially through being made to try and translate English verse into classical verse.[3]

When Tolkien began, quite literally, to explore an imaginative world of his own making he retained the habits of the translator of verse and bullied the language rather than responding to it. Only in prose, and in his poetic masterpiece *The Homecoming of Beorhtnoth Beorhthelm's Son*, could he relax enough to have the creative time of his life.

In laying down the principles for a programme of modernism, Ezra Pound emphasized the necessity for a close contact between high art and low life. An escape from contemporary reality was, Pound felt, an irresponsible artistic act and he had this to say about a reliance on booklore:

> No good poetry is ever written in a manner twenty years old, for to write in such a manner shows conclusively that the writer thinks from books, convention and *cliché*, and not from life, yet a man feeling the divorce of life and his art may naturally try to resurrect a forgotten mode if he finds in that mode some leaven, or if he thinks he sees in it some element lacking in contemporary art which might unite that art again to its sustenance, life.[4]

Tolkien's career as a poet illustrates the truth of Pound's suppositions for there is an enormous gap between Tolkien's trifling metrical diversions and the one work of real poetry he published. His verse is derivative, his poetry gloriously revives the medieval alliterative mode. Thematically Tolkien was fascinated by the notion of escape, yet his poetic masterpiece refuses to sanction any escape into artistic isolation or rhetoric. By temperament Tolkien was a dreamer of dreams and when he woke up to the reality of writing poetry he proved there was a fine art of anachronism.

Tolkien's view of poetry was formed by his extensive knowledge of Old English literature and his philological enthusiasm for Latin and Greek poetry, for Old Norse sagas, for the Finnish *Kalevala*. As for post-Chaucerian English poetry he barely tolerated it except in the case of idiosyncratic Victorians like Morris and Thompson. As Humphrey Carpenter explains:

> For him English literature ended with Chaucer; or to put it another way, he received all the enjoyment and stimulus that he could possibly require from the great poems of the Old and

Middle English periods, and from the early literature of Iceland.[5]

Though Colin Wilson conjectures that Eliot's *The Waste Land* had an influential impact on Tolkien, there is no evidence that Tolkien understood modern poetry or even took any interest in it. This is important as an area of ignorance surrounding the Tolkien phenomenon which operates as a self-contained artwork uncontaminated by the modernism preached by Pound and practised by Pound, Eliot and Joyce in the 1920s. In 1922—the *annus mirabilis* of modernism when Eliot published *The Waste Land*, Joyce published *Ulysses*, and C. M. Grieve created his alter ego Hugh MacDiarmid—Tolkien was at Leeds working on an edition of *Sir Gawain and the Green Knight*, appearing in print as author of *A Middle English Vocabulary* and working his private mythology into *The Book of Lost Tales*.

Modern poetry passed Tolkien by and left him none the wiser. He had no curiosity for modern poetry and no high opinion of modern poets. He knew Auden as a former student and a champion of *The Lord of the Rings*, and he contributed a poem in Anglo-Saxon to the Winter 1967 issue of *Shenandoah* celebrating Auden's sixtieth birthday. When Robert Graves came to Oxford as Professor of Poetry, Tolkien considered him 'A remarkable creature . . . *but* an Ass.'[6] His most revealing comments on a modern poet appear in a letter written to Christopher Tolkien on 6 October 1944. Tolkien had just met Roy Campbell and was totally taken in by the man's swagger and boastfulness:

> He speaks Spanish fluently (he has been a professional bull-fighter). As you know he then fought through the war on Franco's side, and among other things was in the van of the company that chased the Reds out of Malaga. . . . The [story of his] I most enjoyed was the tale of greasy Epstein (the sculptor) and how he fought him and put him in hospital for a week. However it is not possible to convey an impression of such a rare character, both a soldier and a poet, and a Christian convert. How unlike the Left—the 'corduroy panzers' who fled to America (Auden among them who with his friends got R.C.'s worked 'banned' by the Birmingham T. Council!).[7]

Now Tolkien could not have known that most of Campbell's stories operated in the realm of fantasy and that he neither led an anti-Red offensive nor even defeated Epstein in a punch-up.[8] The point is that Tolkien was willing to take Campbell at face value because he approved of his theological politics and because he enjoyed the thought of an act of violence against a celebrated modernist such as Epstein.

Tolkien's position as an anachronistic survivor from another age was apparent to such mild young men as Kingsley Amis and Philip Larkin when they attended Oxford and studied the spectacle of the Professor of Anglo-Saxon in action. Amis remembered Tolkien as the embodiment of stuffiness:

> All Old English and most Middle English works produced hatred and weariness in everyone who studied them. The former carried the redoubled impediment of having Tolkien, incoherent and often inaudible, lecturing on it. Nobody had a good word to say for *Beowulf*, *The Wanderer*, *The Dream of the Rood*, *The Battle of Maldon*.[9]

Nobody, that is, except Tolkien who not only admired Anglo-Saxon poetry but was able to approach it with the consciousness of a contemporary of the man who wrote *The Battle of Maldon*. Tolkien invariably came across to his students as a medieval voice from the past; Carpenter (p. 138) quotes J. I. M. Stewart's opinion that Tolkien 'could turn a lecture room into a mead hall in which he was the bard and we were the feasting, listening guests' and Auden's statement that Tolkien's reading of *Beowulf* was 'an unforgettable experience . . . The voice was the voice of Gandalf'.

Naturally Tolkien wanted to capture that voice in verse but was (with alliterative exceptions) unable to do so because he could not find a contemporary metrical model that sounded extravagant enough for his purposes. He tried to adapt his medieval muse to the Victorian manner and then realized that the result was invariably hobbit verse—and so he turned to prose. It is, therefore, arguable that Tolkien's prose master-piece, *The Lord of the Rings*, evolved as a result of his inability to adjust to the radical renewal of poetic tradition in the twentieth century. The evidence suggests that he was not even at home with Victorian verse, and since he could not con-template the possibility of being more progressive than the late nineteenth century, he realized that the options open to him were twofold: he could communicate in a plain prose style ornamented with archaisms, purple passages and hobbit verse; or he could reach right back for the medieval mode most suited to his temperament. The first solution seemed most likely to succeed (as it did, indeed, beyond Tolkien's wildest expectations). The second solution came too late and its impact was delayed too long.

Almost every commentator on Tolkien has acknowledged the anachronistic element in his work; Tolkienites argue that *The Lord of the Rings* is timeless, sceptics that it is 'bogus, prolix, and sentimental'.[10] A balance can be established by considering Tolkien's troubled relationship with poetic modes and his final decision to opt out of the imaginative challenge presented by poetry. Technically he was stuck with an essentially anachronistic concept of what kind of linguistic package actually constituted poetry. Thematically, however, he knew exactly what he wanted and had the commonsense to realize that he probably lacked the literary equipment to achieve all his literary ambitions in verse. Still, we have it on Humphrey Carpenter's authority (p. 97) that Tolkien's determination to create an autonomous mythology was partially motivated by

> his desire to express his most profound feelings in poetry, a desire that owed its origin to the inspiration of the T.C.B.S. His first verses had been unremarkable, as immature as the raw idealism of the four young men; but they were the first steps towards the great prose-poem (for though in prose it is a poetic work) that he now began to write.

Tolkienites will, of course, recognize the T.C.B.S. as the group Tolkien adhered to in his days at King Edward's School, Birmingham. The initials denote the Tea Club and Barrovian Society whose members were Tolkien, Christopher Wiseman, R. Q. Gilson and G. B. Smith. Tolkien's contributions to the T.C.B.S. comprised recitations from *Beowulf* and *Sir Gawain and the Green Knight* and, incongruously, his own poetic efforts.

In 1910, when he was 18, Tolkien began to write verse. Retrospectively Tolkien's early verse seems appropriately twee, yet Carpenter notes perceptively that 'Fairy spirits dancing on a woodland carpet seem a strange choice of subject for a rugger-playing youth of 18 who had a strong taste for

141

Grendel and the dragon Fafnir' (p. 55). The poem in question, 'Wood-sunshine', is full of ecstatic exclamation:

> O! come to me! dance for me! Sprites of the wood,
> O! come to me! Sing to me once ere ye fade!

Such sentiments came naturally enough to Tolkien though the idiom he used was derivative. Tolkien's immediate model, so Carpenter tells us (p. 55), was the first part of Francis Thompson's *Sister Songs* (1895) with its 'sprites/Yet unseen', 'elfin swarms' and 'goblin flame'. Evidently Tolkien took to Thompson; he felt a religious bond with his fellow Catholic and had an affinity with the man's mysticism. William Morris appealed to him for another reason. In 1914 Tolkien used his Skeat Prize for English (awarded by Exeter College, Oxford) to buy Morris's poetic epic *Sigurd the Volsung* (1876) and *The House of the Wolfings* (1889). What Tolkien regarded as a valid precedent was Morris's highly ornamental and archaic style, his obsession with the past, and his method of simulating a dense literary texture by mixing poetry and prose in the same romance.

Since he was 4 when Morris died (in 1896) and 15 when Francis Thompson died (in 1907), Tolkien could regard both of them as recent writers quite modern enough for his purposes. Absorbing them stylistically was his concession to the taste of his time, but his imagination was still, fundamentally, stuck in the middle ages, and he was especially fond of the ninth-century Anglian (probably Northumbrian) poet Cynewulf whose four known compositions include the central part of the sequence *Crist* contained in the Exeter Book. Tolkien responded to two lines in particular:

> Eala Earendel engla beorhtast
> ofer middangeard monnum sended

(which Carpenter, p. 72, glosses as meaning 'Hail Earendel, brightest of angels/ above the middle-earth sent unto men.'). In the summer of 1914 Tolkien spent some time in Cornwall absorbing the light and the landscape and, inevitably, the legends. When he returned to Nottinghamshire to stay on his aunt's farm he wrote a poem expanding his favourite lines from Cynewulf into a narrative account of 'The Voyage of

Earendel the Evening Star'. Unlike the Old English source that inspired it, Tolkien's poem uses obvious and internal rhyme as well as a rigid stanzaic pattern:

> Earendel sprang up from the Ocean's cup
>   In the gloom of the mid-world's rim;
> From the door of Night as a ray of light
>   Leapt over the twilight brim,
> And launching his bark like a silver spark
>   From the golden-fading sand
> Down the sunlit breath of Day's fiery death
>   He sped from Westerland.

While Tolkien was absorbing his Cornish experience, Britain declared war on Germany (on 4 August 1914). English poets were quick to respond to the patriotic challenge and Rupert Brooke's five sonnets on war were published in December 1914 in the fourth and final issue of *New Numbers*. Around that time Tolkien travelled to London for a meeting of the T.C.B.S. and emerged from it absolutely determined to be a poet. The evidence was unconvincing. Tolkien wrote 'The Man in the Moon Came Down Too Soon' (subsequently included in *The Adventures of Tom Bombadil*). It is an escape-yarn and tells how the eponymous lunatic, 'on a mad adventure bent', longed to be brought down to earth:

> He'd have seas of blues, and the living hues
>   of forest green and fen;
> And he yearned for the mirth of the populous earth
>   and the sanguine blood of men.
> He coveted song, and laughter long,
>   and viands hot, and wine,
> Eating pearly cakes of light snowflakes
>   and drinking thin moonshine.

What Tolkien offers is a combination of nonsensical matter—including a childish appeal to the appetite—and a nursery manner complete with internal rhymes and many colours. Long before he had a name for them the hobbits in his head were writing such verse.

Another poem of the period, 'Goblin Feet' (published in *Oxford Poetry* in 1915 and subsequently anthologized many times) was written to satisfy Edith Bratt's love of whimsy, so

Tolkien invokes 'fairy lanterns' and 'little pretty flittermice' and exclaims:

> O! I hear the tiny horns
> Of enchanted leprechauns
> And the padding feet of many gnomes a-coming.

In later years Tolkien rejected the negative connotations attached to the term 'escapist' and praised (with reference to the desire to escape death) 'the genuine *escapist*, or (I would say) *fugitive* spirit'.[11] However, there is something inescapably odd in the spectacle of a young man writing such excruciatingly immature verse in 1914, until, that is, we remember Tolkien's anachronistic nature. Some of his friends certainly thought he could make his verse more relevant to the world he, ostensibly, lived in. According to Carpenter (p. 83), G. B. Smith 'recommended Tolkien to look at the new poems by Rupert Brooke. But Tolkien paid little heed. He had already set his own poetic course, and he did not need anyone else to steer him.'

In 1915 Tolkien began work on his first extended project. He had been evolving his own 'nonsense fairy language' (Carpenter, p. 83) and felt it could function as the speech of the elves observed by Earendel during his starry voyage of 1914. Thus Tolkien began work on a *Lay of Earendel*, a sequence of several poems describing the mariner's odyssey from the beginning, before his ship became a star. The first poem, 'The Shores of Faery', was a Tennysonian search after enchantment:

> There are the shores of Faery
> With their moonlit pebbled strand
> Whose foam is silver music
> On the opalescent floor. . . .

The attempt to achieve a decorative texture through superfluity of epithet is misguided; the piling up of self-consciously strange adjectives merely results in an oppressively artificial atmosphere. 'Errantry', first published in *The Oxford Magazine* in 1933 and later collected in *The Adventures of Tom Bombadil*, was described by Tolkien as an early version of the poem beginning 'Earendil was a mariner' (*LR*, p. 250) recited by

Bilbo at Elrond. We know that, with the exceptions of 'Bombadil Goes A-Boating' and 'Cat', all the poems in the 1961 *Bombadil* volume were composed in the 1920s and 1930s (Carpenter, p. 245). 'Errantry' could have been planned as an essential, and candidly cloying, part of *The Lay of Earendel*. The poem certainly displays all the sentimental silliness of the early Tolkien with its relentlessly contrived internal rhyming and its references to the mariner who

> begged a pretty butterfly
> that fluttered by to marry him.

As an indication of the lengths to which the Perfect Tolkienite will go to defend the master, it is worth noting that Randel Helms justifies 'Errantry' as a parody of Charles Williams's *Taliessin Through Logres* (1938) and, astonishingly, as 'a stunningly skilful piece of versification' with 'smooth and lovely rhythms'.[12] Tolkien himself commented tersely: 'It was evidently made by Bilbo' (*Giles/Bombadil*, p. 79).

Tolkien's escapist nature had not yet found a fugitive spirit in poetry. Rather abruptly, though, Tolkien had to rethink his position as a man and a poet. In 1916 the adolescent escapist became a potential fugitive by seeking out challenges and confronting them. On 22 March he married Edith Bratt and when he returned from his honeymoon in Clevedon, Somerset, he found he had failed as a poet for his first collection was rejected by the publishers Sidgwick and Jackson. On 4 June the married man and rejected poet left friends in London in order to face the official enemy in France. His experience of trench warfare at the Somme sickened him:

> Worst of all were the dead men, for corpses lay in every corner, horribly torn by the shells. Those that still had faces stared with dreadful eyes. Beyond the trenches no-man's-land was littered with bloated and decaying bodies. . . . Tolkien never forgot what he called the 'animal horror' of trench warfare. (Carpenter, p. 91)

Eventually it was all too much and Tolkien was sent home suffering from trench fever, a psychosomatic condition to which imaginative men were particularly prone.

While convalescing in 1917 Tolkien began to work on an indigenous English epic which, under the title *The Book of Lost Tales* (later *The Silmarillion*), was to 'possess the tone and

145

quality [of] Britain and the hither parts of Europe [and display] the fair elusive beauty that some call Celtic [and be] fit for the more adult mind of a land long steeped in poetry' (Carpenter, p. 98). By 1923 *The Book of Lost Tales* was almost complete and amounted to, in Carpenter's outline (p. 113), 'the creation of the universe, the fashioning of the Silmarils, and their theft from the blessed realm of Valinor by Morgoth. The cycle . . . was to conclude with the voyage of Earendel's star-ship that had been the first element of the mythology to arise in Tolkien's mind.' Now Tolkien began to present two of the main stories as verse: 'an indication', says Carpenter (p. 114), 'that he still aspired as much towards verse as towards prose.' The first of these tales was the tragic history of Túrin Turambar 'which is fulltold in that lay that is called *Narn i Hîn Húrin*, the Tale of the Children of Húrin, and is the longest of all the lays that speak of those days.'[13]

Initially this was written in alliterative verse that simulates, impressively, the medieval manner:

> He was gloomy-hearted, and glad seldom
> for the sundering sorrow that seared his youth.
> On manhood's threshold he was mighty holden
> in the wielding of weapons; and in weaving song
> he had a minstrel's mastery; but mirth was not in it.

Tolkien has tried to modernize the metre through abstraction and enjambement, but the extract still justifies Carpenter's opinion (p. 170) that 'alliterative verse . . . suited his imagination far more than did modern rhyme-schemes.' Tolkien was able to think through the alliteration, to use it in an inventive rather than purely imitative way. His mind was attuned to the Middle Ages and he only needed a theme that would fully test his alliterative talents.

By the mid-1920s Tolkien had written more than 2,000 lines of the *Children of Húrin*, but it was eventually abandoned as a poetic performance, as was the work Tolkien referred to, in his letters, as the *Story of Beren and Lúthien the Elfmaiden* (or the *Tale of Lúthien Tinúviel and Beren*) and, in *The Silmarillion*, as *The Lay of Leithian*. It was inspired by his great passion for Edith. A year after his wife died in 1971 Tolkien wrote to his son Christopher explaining her inspirational role in the genesis of the poem:

I never called Edith *Lúthien*—but she was the source of the story that in time became the chief part of the Silmarillion. It was first conceived in a small woodland glade filled with hemlocks at Roos in Yorkshire (where I was for a brief time in command of an outpost of the Humber Garrison in 1917, and she was able to live with me for a while). In those days her hair was raven, her skin clear, her eyes brighter than you have seen them, and she could sing—and *dance*. (*Letters*, p. 420)

Expressed as simple epistolary prose the story has a persuasive beauty. In the 1920s it was written up as a long poem in rhyming couplets and by 1926 this composition amounted to more than 4,000 lines. Two extracts from the poem are given in Chapter Nineteen of *The Silmarillion* and the 'Song of Parting' conveys the level of the verse:

> Farewell sweet earth and northern sky,
> for ever blest, since here did lie
> and here with lissom limbs did run
> beneath the Moon, beneath the Sun,
> Lúthien Tinúviel
> more fair than mortal tongue can tell.

And so on—and on and on and on. Tolkien's misgivings about such verse are understandable and it is to his credit that he finally settled for prose in this instance. He wanted to convey an emotional experience yet had not the metrical means to do so in verse. His rhymes are monosyllabic and banal—*run/Sun, world/hurled*—and the rhythm is forced. Above all Tolkien's technical incompetence drives him to the expedient of fracturing the English language in order to fit the flow into couplets. Thus the poem contains a catalogue of clichés ('lissom limbs', 'mortal tongue can tell', etc.). Tolkien was not writing poetry; he was at the mercy of rhyme.

Subsequently Tolkien attempted to break up the monotony of the couplet-format by devising a more varied stanzaic pattern. The result is seen in Aragorn's song at Weathertop (*LR*, pp. 208–9):

> The leaves were long, the grass was green,
>   The hemlock-umbels tall and fair,
> And in the glade a light was seen
>   Of stars in shadows shimmering.

147

> Tinúviel was dancing there
>   To music of a pipe unseen,
> And light of stars was in her hair,
>   And in her raiment glimmering.

The improvement lies in the greater formal freedom and in the alliteration. Tolkien, however, was not able to capture the intensity of the Beren/Lúthien affair in verse, and it is apparent that the prose in the letter written to Christopher is more eloquent than the two bits of verse just quoted.

In the 1930s English literature was being radically revised by one of Tolkien's students. Auden published *Poems* in 1930 and *The Orators* in 1932 and gradually identified Oxford with a school of poetry that took, as its priority, topicality and polemical urgency rather than nostalgia and escapism. Tolkien was not interested in such developments. To him the 1930s was a time to concentrate on his own poetic efforts regardless of what was fashionable in the literary world. September 1930 saw him working on an experiment mixing alliterative metre and rhyme. He felt, perhaps, he had a chance of mastering rhyme by using the congenial alliterative mode. 'The Lay of Aotrou and Itroun' is, in the opinion of Jane Chance Nitzsche, an example of Tolkien's mimetic approach, since she regards it as a parody 'modelled upon the Breton lay of the twelfth to the fourteenth centuries characteristic of northern France but influenced by old Celtic tales'.[14] Aotrou (Breton for Lord) is anxious to duplicate himself and father a child for

> his pride was empty, vain his hoard,
> without an heir to land and sword

and to obtain the heir he is willing to sacrifice his honour and his Itroun (Breton for Lady). Such deception results in the deaths of Aotrou and Itroun which leads Tolkien to this moralistic conclusion:

> Of lord and lady all is said:
> God rest their souls, who now are dead!
> Sad is the note and sad the lay
> but mirth we meet not every day.
> God keep us all in hope and prayer
> from evil rede and from despair,
> by waters blest of Christendom

> to dwell, until at last we come
> to joy of Heaven where is queen
> the maiden Mary pure and clean.

Again the poem is handicapped by the rhyme for, as usual, Tolkien uses monosyllabic and utterly predictable rhymes. Yet there is a hint of grace and the gracenotes are provided by the alliteration. When the poem appeared in print, in *The Welsh Review* of December 1945, Tolkien was deeply concerned with alliteration.

While 'The Lay of Aotrou and Itroun' was taking shape Tolkien also embarked on 'The Fall of Arthur', an alliterative project. It was shown to Professor R. W. Chambers of London University, who, impressed by Tolkien's alliterative technique, pronounced the poem 'great stuff—really heroic, quite apart from its value as showing how the *Beowulf* metre can be used in modern English' (Carpenter, p. 171). Tolkien had, as important working alternatives, alliterative verse as in 'The Fall of Arthur'; and narrative prose as in *The Hobbit* which he began to write around 1930. Even as he was considering the rival stylistic attractions of alliteration and prose he continued to dabble with rhyme.

In 1934 he published, in *The Oxford Magazine*, the poems 'Looney' (an early version of 'The Sea-Bell' in *The Adventures of Tom Bombadil*) and 'The Adventures of Tom Bombadil'. Without prior knowledge of Tolkien's mythological world the Tom Bombadil poem is rather pointless, but Tolkienites know all about the hero's talent for escapism. Tom, the personification of natural vitality, escapes the clutches of Old Man Willow, Badger-brock and Barrow-wight with the expertise of an accomplished escapologist:

> None ever caught old Tom in upland or in dingle,
> walking the forest-paths, or by the Withywindle,
> or out on the lily-pools in boat upon the water.
> But one day Tom, he went and caught the River-daughter,
> in green gown, flowing hair, sitting in the rushes,
> singing old water-songs to birds upon the bushes.

Tolkien's metrical limitations interfere with the execution of the idea. The feminine rhymes are sluggish and the poem drags its trochaic feet. It is not poetry but hobbit verse, and

Tolkien was increasingly able to accommodate it in a specific area of his imagination.

After the success of *The Hobbit* in 1937 Tolkien worked on *The Lord of the Rings* whose composition coincides with the Second World War (approximately, anyway, as Tolkien was busy on the book from 1936 to 1949). Carpenter believes that the 'outbreak of war in September 1939 did not have any immediate major effect on Tolkien's life . . . in general terms his life was much as it had been before the war' (pp. 196–97). Perhaps Tolkien's private and professional life carried on as before but, artistically, he was unusually alert. Towards the end of the war, from 1944 to 1945, Tolkien was engaged on three projects. The first was *The Lord of the Rings* and Tolkien revealed that in 1944 he forced himself 'to tackle the journey of Frodo to Mordor' (*LR*, p. 8). Then, at the end of 1945, he started to write *The Notion Club Papers* in which two members of an Inklings-style literary club set off on a time-journey. The work was abandoned, though Tolkien published part of it (in *Time & Tide* in 1955). 'Imram' (Gaelic for voyage) relates to the last voyage of St. Brendan in 565–73 and closes with the grave reminder that Brendan died 'under a rain-clad sky,/ journeying whence no ship returns;/ and his bones in Ireland lie.' Jane Chance Nitzsche considers 'Imram' as 'an appropriate transition to *The Lord of the Rings*'.[15] With the gift of hindsight it certainly seems so, but there is a possibility that Tolkien could also have moved on to an acceptable alternative to prose, for the deft alliterative touches in 'Imram' encouraged him to produce a poem (albeit a dramatic poem) entirely in the alliterative mode.

The Homecoming of Beorhtnoth Beorhthelm's Son was completed in 1945, though not published until 1953 (in *Essays and Studies*). For Tolkien the alliterative mode was fresh and richly relevant and thus the perfect idiom in which his medieval mind could comment on the horror of war in general and, by implication, modern warfare in particular. In a study of Old English poetry T. A. Shippey supposed that since 'it is impossible to revive a dead tradition by power of imagination alone, a modern's response must, no matter what desiccation it involves, be based on the sobriety of a printed text.'[16] These words could have been written with Tolkien's poem in mind, for *Homecoming* is a powerful postscript to the printed text of *The Battle of Maldon*. Technically *Homecoming* is a virtuosic work that uses the alliterative style with great artistic impact and a profound sense of purpose. As Tolkien says

> [*The Battle of Maldon*] is composed in a free form of the alliterative line, the last surviving fragment of ancient English heroic minstrelsy. In that measure, little if at all freer (though used for dialogue) than the verse of *The Battle of Maldon*, the present modern poem is written.[17]

The Battle of Maldon is a celebration of a military disaster. In 991 the English, under Beorhtnoth, faced the Danes across a ford near Maldon in Essex. When the Vikings asked for access to the strategic ground commanded by the English, Beorhtnoth obliged with catastrophic results for himself and his men. Tolkien comments:

> Beorhtnoth accepted the challenge and allowed them to cross. This act of pride and misplaced chivalry proved fatal. Beorhtnoth was slain and the English routed. . . . *Homecoming* may be said to be an extended comment on lines 89, 90 of the original: '. . . then the earl in his overmastering pride actually yielded ground to the enemy, as he should not have done.' (*Homecoming*, pp. 77–8 and p. 102)

It is Tolkien's contention that Beorhtnoth sacrificed his men on the altar of his own arrogant pursuit of honour. In his poem Tolkien thus deals with the squalid aftermath of the battle when honour is seen to be done to death. Two servants rummage among the dead in order to find Beorhtnoth's body and return it to the monks of Ely (whose patron Beorhtnoth was). The dialogue between Torhthelm (Totta), a minstrel's son, and Tídwald (Tída), a farmer and seasoned warrior, is calculated to bring out the human dimension of warfare. Tolkien's poem is a realistic rebuke to the rhetoric of heroism as can be seen from the following crucial exchange:

> *Torhthelm.* I wish I'd been here,
> not left with the luggage and the lazy thralls,
> cooks and sutlers! By the Cross, Tída,
> I loved him no less than any lord with him;
> and a poor freeman may prove in the end
> more tough when tested than titled earls

who count back their kin to kings ere Woden.
Tídwald. You can talk, Totta! Your time'll come,
and it'll look less easy than lays make it.
Bitter taste has iron, and the bite of swords
is cruel and cold, when you come to it.
Then God guard you, if your glees falter!
When your shield is shivered, between shame and death
is hard choosing. Help me with this one!
There, heave him over—the hound's carcase,
hulking heathen!

Later in the poem Tídwald produces an incisive critique of the selective and entirely aristocratic operation of the heroic tradition in poetry:

Torhthelm. And now from the North need comes again:
wild blows the wind of war to Britain!
Tídwald. And in the neck we catch it, and are nipped as chill
as poor men were then. Let the poets babble,
but perish all pirates! When the poor are robbed
and lose the land they loved and toiled on,
they must die and dung it. No dirge for them,
and their wives and children work in serfdom.

There Tolkien's humanity shines through. He has found his form.

After all Tolkien was well aware of the reality of war and so could speak impressively through the mouth of Tídwald and give voice to his vision of England as a land where romance was tempered with commonsense. Tolkien had lived through the First World War, had seen his sons endure the Second World War and felt that the Last World War was imminent unless men could live without constant human sacrifice. Tolkien uses the medieval mode with the skill of a contemporary, yet brings to bear on the matter of the poem the concern of a man who has known the wastage of warfare and human wreckage seen through the sham of chivalry—or what Tolkien calls 'misplaced chivalry'.

In *Homecoming* manner and matter are inseparable and it is easy to understand why Tolkien was appalled at a radio production of the poem 'which ignored the alliterative metre and delivered the verse as if it were iambic pentameters' (Carpenter, p. 218). At the beginning of this essay Ezra Pound was cited for his conviction that 'a man feeling the divorce of life and his art may naturally try to resurrect a forgotten mode.' Pound himself did that in 'The Seafarer', a superb imitation of the alliterative mode. Tolkien was able to go a stage further and actually write as a medieval poet presented with a timeless theme made suddenly urgent. The finished product demonstrates that no art form is dead as long as there is an artist able to take advantage of it. Tolkien finally became a real poet in 1945 and immortalized the fine art of anachronism. Commonsense prevailed over art, though, and he preferred to persevere with a prose *Lord of the Rings* and so did not take up the challenge of imposing an alliterative epic on his chronological contemporaries.

NOTES

1. J. R. R. Tolkien, *The Lord of the Rings* (London, 1978), p. 223. All references (*LR*) are to the one volume paperback edition. Sam's poem also appears as 'The Stone Troll', the seventh poem in *The Adventures of Tom Bombadil*.
2. J. R. R. Tolkien, *Farmer Giles of Ham. The Adventures of Tom Bombadil* (London, 1975), p. 81. Hereafter *Giles/Bombadil*.
3. J. R. R. Tolkien, *Tree and Leaf* (London, 1964), p. 40.
4. T. S. Eliot (ed.), *Literary Essays of Ezra Pound* (London, 1954), p. 11.
5. Humphrey Carpenter, *J. R. R. Tolkien* (London, 1978), p. 77. All subsequent page references to Carpenter relate to this edition.
6. Humphrey Carpenter (ed.), *Letters of J. R. R. Tolkien* (London, 1981), p. 353.
7. Ibid., p. 96. Hereafter *Letters*.
8. In Peter Alexander's *Roy Campbell: A Critical Biography* (Oxford, 1982), Campbell's self-indulgent exaggeration is discussed as is his tendency to 'distort and conceal the truth' (p. vii).
9. Anthony Thwaite (ed.), *Larkin at Sixty* (London, 1982), pp. 24–5.
10. Catharine R. Stimpson, *J. R. R. Tolkien* (New York, 1969), p. 43.
11. *Tree and Leaf*, p. 59.
12. Randel Helms, *Tolkien's World* (London, 1974), p. 134.
13. J. R. R. Tolkien, *The Silmarillion* (London, 1979), p. 239.
14. Jane Chance Nitzsche, *Tolkien's Art* (London, 1979), p. 75.
15. Ibid., p. 96.
16. T. A. Shippey, *Old English Verse* (London, 1972), p. 12.
17. J. R. R. Tolkien, *Poems and Stories* (London, 1980), p. 80. *The Homecoming of Beorhtnoth Beorhthelm's Son* was first published in *Essays and Studies* in 1953 and reprinted, along with *Tree and Leaf* and *Smith of Wootton Major* (London, 1975). References are to the pagination in *Poems and Stories*.

9

The Structuralist's Guide to Middle-earth

by NICK OTTY

My title refers to Robert Foster's *The Complete Guide to Middle Earth*[1]: 'An A–Z guide', the cover claims, 'to the names and events of the fantasy world of J. R. R. Tolkien, from the *Hobbit* to the *Silmarillion*.' Designed on the same generous scale as *The Lord of the Rings*, Foster's *Guide* fills 441 pages (counting neither the introduction nor the genealogical tables) with the kind of information you would expect from a companion to literature or a *Debrett's Peerage*. But the title of Foster's *Guide* also makes links with the existing tourist guides to real geographical areas: Spain or The Pennines. Foster thus announces at the outset that fusion and confusion of levels of reality which he sees as so essential to successful fantasy. On page viii of his Introduction he goes on to inform us:

> I count myself fortunate to have wandered in the Fairy-realm of Arda for fifteen years now, and while my tongue is certainly not tied, for the sake of my own delight I have learned not to 'ask too many questions, lest the gates should be shut and the keys be lost.'

It is with this fusion and confusion of levels of reality that the structuralists have most strongly taken issue. Deconstruction of the text is precisely aimed at asking too many questions, not that the 'keys be lost', but so that the gates should be opened as wide as possible; so that the narrative impetus no

longer closes off our interest in the 'values' of the text; so that
we may see the text as a construct produced in a certain
context, take from it what we want or need and when appropriate pass on from the text—no longer 'in thrall' to it.

One way of asserting the freedom of the reader to enter the
text and re-see it in this kind of way is to ignore the narrative
level and to seek other points of entry leading to the appreciation of other kinds of coherence in the text. I am not pro-
posing to divide the text into atoms or even what Roland
Barthes calls 'Lexias'[2] but to use the guide format to explode
and undermine the narrative so that we can see more clearly
the elements from which it is constructed. That deconstruction is a possible danger (or from my perspective, benefit)
of the guide format is clear to Mr. Foster. His guide, he
says:

> . . . is intended to be supplementary to the works of Professor
> Tolkien and no more; its value is that it can clarify deep-hidden
> historical facts and draw together scraps of information whose
> relation is easily overlooked, thus aiding the wanderer in Arda
> in his quest for its particular truth.[3]

It will be seen here that there is a collusion in fiction in such
phrases as 'historical facts', and 'scraps of information' for this
quotation is from the preface and is already 'playing' at being
a 'real' guide (Blue/Michelin) for the status of 'historical facts'
in the *Guide to Middle Earth* is surely different from the status of
'historical facts' in the Michelin guide to the Rhone (however
inaccurate and/or infested with bias and ideology the latter
might be). And these pretended references to 'historical facts'
(fictional, and known by every reader to be fictional) are
surrounded as though for the sake of increased verisimilitude
by other 'real' references to 'encouragement' (real) from 'Dick
Plotz' (real(?)) or to 'help' from 'Judy Lynn and Lester del
Rey' (real, real) at 'Ballantyne Books' (Hyper-real and a
division of Random House, Inc.). Even in the preface the
possible problems caused by levels of reality are smoothed
over by the form and format of 'the academic preface' just as
the different levels of reference in *The Lord of the Rings* are
effaced by the narrative flow. 'When matters', says Foster, 'are
unclear in the Text [Foster's capital T], I have tried to remain

silent'[4]—thus agreeing to conceal the contradictions which it
must be our business (for the greater enjoyment of the reader,
let me insist) to expose. It is the respect for the authority of the
Text which Foster here so candidly acknowledges, that makes
the exercise of 'fantasy' or 'escapism' such a distressing one to
my mind. For it is practice in accepting the blandishments of
ideology; practice in self-deception; practice in living bearably
within our current mental and political horizons. 'Human
kind', says T. S. Eliot 'cannot bear very much reality.'[5] I
prefer to remember at times that they cannot live well with too
much unreality either. The willed exploration of poetic scepti-
cism must be dialectically as important to us (and to literature)
as the much celebrated 'willing suspension of disbelief'.[6] And
I quote here from Eliot and Coleridge, not to display erudition,
but in order to remind the reader of the kind of literary magi
who turn out to be used (whether they would have liked it or
not) against enterprises such as deconstructing the text.

To give an impression of the difference between my brief
guide and Foster's complete one, where he has entries under
'Ancient Darkness', 'Ancient Houses', 'Ancient Speech',
'Ancient Tongue', 'Ancient West' and 'Ancient World', I shall
have a single entry under 'Ancientness'. Where he has under
'Eye', 'The Eye of Sauron, the form in which he appeared in
the third age and his emblem, etc. . . .' I have an entry under
'Eyes' in which I attempt a rough outline of the ways in which
the eyes of Gandalf, Saruman, the Nazgul, etc. are made to
work in the narrative.

Ancientness. The whole of *The Lord of the Rings* is powered by
a deep regret for the passing of time. Although in fact
(obviously) the present turns into the past, the regret is
directed at the idea that the past has turned (declined) into
the present. The good bits of the present are the bits that will
turn into the glorified and regretted past. Sheer longevity
confers respectability and even power. So Tom Bombadil who
vies with Treebeard for the title of oldest inhabitant of Middle-
earth, even has power over the Ring itself—he can reverse its
favourite trick and make it disappear. The respect accorded
him is due to his extreme age, though at the Council of Elrond

it is revealed that he is not immortal. Glorfindel, who *is* immortal, declares that he thinks that in the end '. . . if all else is conquered Bombadil will fall, Last as he was First; and then Night will come.'[7] (See **Capital Letters** below.) A corresponding respect is paid to evil if it has been around long enough, like the 'things' Aragorn refers to on the slopes of Caradhras: '. . . things in the world that have little love for those that go on two legs and yet are not in league with Sauron, but have purposes of their own. Some have been in this world longer than he.'[8]

On the other hand, there are references to ancient roots, to heritage. These are transferred from the political philosophy of prescriptive rights and primogeniture. Establishing lineage back a long way establishes that there have been reasons to record that lineage for a long time. This in turn establishes that the significance of inheritance from father to son has also mattered for a long time, which by prescriptive rights also establishes that it is right that the power and/or property so inherited should *now* be vested where it *is* vested.

It is amusing to see the same principle with its accompanying snobbery transferred to the horses of the Rohirrim which are loved because '. . . their race—as that of their masters—is descended from the free days of old.'[9] What horse, I would ask, is *not* descended from the ur-horses? And no more horses than men are not descended from the original horses and men. What is actually being darkly suggested is that some inferior stock—not-quite-horse-blood, not-quite-human-genes—has leaked into the lineage. Or perhaps that the modern horse breeder (and human match-makers too) can no longer spot a good filly or stallion. (See also under **Race** below.)

Capital Letters. It is worth alerting oneself to the way capitals are used in *The Lord of the Rings* to elevate otherwise quite simple words. This may not be entirely innocent of repercussions since Foster has been infected by the practice where he refers to the book as 'the Text'. See also my quote from Glorfindel (above under **Ancientness**). Since this example is in direct speech it might entertain the reader to imagine Glorfindel *pronouncing* the capitals in 'Last', 'First' and 'Night'.

Cats of Queen Berúthiel, The. Aragorn says of Gandalf in the caves of Moria, 'He is surer of finding his way home in a blind night than the cats of Queen Berúthiel.'[10] This is the only mention of Berúthiel or her cats in the entire literature of the world except for the following blindingly illuminating entry in Foster's *Guide* (under B, not C or Q): 'Berúthiel (S: bereth "queen" + iel "female") [*sic*] Queen whose cats were proverbial for their ability to find their way home.'[11] Tolkien enthusiasts see the Cats as an example of the astonishing detail with which Tolkien invents his alternative world. To me they are an example of the way that world is supported by a series of loops which close off the reader within the fantasy. Aragorn makes a reference. The usual function of reference is to invite comparison from elsewhere—history, philosophy, folk-lore, etc. None of the company questions the reference, so it must be presumed that they understand it. The broad meaning can in any case be grasped. Cats can see in dim light. Cats can find their way home. Since Aragorn is talking about Gandalf, the reference is not going to have a twist, e.g. that the cats were memorable for being blind, fat and idle and getting hopelessly lost. So in following out the reference we may almost find ourselves inventing the tale of Queen Berúthiel for ourselves. The feeling is that a reference has been made, but at the last moment the reader's mind loops back and is recruited by the author as a co-imaginer of the inside of the world of the book.

Although this particular example is justified because the reference is made by Aragorn for the benefit of his companions, and therefore in 'realist' terms he can only make reference to things within Arda, it is the loop structure to which I wish to draw attention. It is a recurrent feature of the fiction. (See under **Paradox** below.)

Proverbs, with their folksy way of making general truths out of references to particular concrete items—'a stitch in time . . .', 'spare the rod . . .', 'spoils the broth . . .', etc.—have on occasion lured Tolkien very near the disaster of self-parody: 'Need brooks no delay, yet late is better than never', says Eomer; 'The wolf that one hears is worse than the orc that one fears', says Boromir. But when it works—while the reader seeks in his or her imagination for those shadowy cats—the device is a powerful forger of empathy (q.v.).

158

Empathy. As Robert Foster has noted, fantasy depends on never climbing out of the world of the work. The author must therefore forge an empathic bond between reader and text which will trap his enquiries, prevent him asking those 'too many questions' which might force the reader to acknowledge the textuality of the text and break from somnambulism in fairy realms.

Tolkien is a master of a number of devices for attaining this end. One is a strong narrative line with what is known in the American T.V. trade as 'Top-spin' at the end of every episode. The reader is drawn into the next chapter by an unresolved enigma at the end of the previous one. Examples at random are: 'Who is the old man? Why did the horses not return?' (*Two Towers*, Ch. II); 'What happened to the orcs beneath the trees after the battle at Helm's Deep?' (*Two Towers*, Ch. VII (this one is never resolved in spite of some dark hints from Gandalf and Gimli about crushing and strangling, so the reader is again recruited in the empathy-forging role of co-author); 'What does Gandalf mean when he says "The Darkness [capital D] has begun. There will be no dawn"?' (*The Return of the King*, Ch. I). But every chapter is ended in this way, except the last, of course.

Also of use in the forging of empathy are those paradoxical loops of reference which curl enquiry back into the text. (See **Paradox** below.)

Nostalgia too (q.v.) by the social strategy 'You and I know things are not what they used to be . . .' gets the reader cosily beside the author. This has links, of course, with the snobbery of ancientness, for to snub the approach is to risk label of *parvenu*.

An undefined and unexplored but constantly labelled evil permits by its very vagueness the insertion of the reader's own pet hates and fears. Mordor becomes whatever we deplore. (In the '60s I saw the word painted on motorway bridges, council flats and office blocks.) The following is an example of how this works.

At the cross-roads above Osgiliath on the road to Minas Morgul, Frodo finds an old statue, '. . . a huge sitting figure, still and solemn as the great stone kings of Argonath'. Huge, still, solemn and great: therefore, good. And what's more, if you can remember the reference 300 pages earlier, the stone kings are 'good' too, Isildur and Anarion by name. If you don't make the connection, the linguistic structure of the name 'Argonath' will keep you on the right lines and the reference will still work on the same principle as the cats of Queen Berúthiel.

> The years had gnawed it [the statue] and violent hands had maimed it. Its head was gone, and in its place was set in mockery a rough-hewn stone, rudely painted by savage hands in likeness of a grinning face with one large red eye in the midst of its forehead. Upon its knees and mighty chair and all about the pedestal, were idle scrawls mixed with the foul symbols that the maggot folk of Mordor used.[12]

The reader is worked on strongly by the list—violent, maimed, mockery, rough, rudely, savage, grinning, idle, scrawls, foul, and maggot—impelled to reject. But the concrete detail, the shape of the stone, the meaning of the writing, the appearance and significance of the symbols to the 'scrawlers', all this must be supplied by the reader for him or her self from their own personal garbage can of all they personally reject. Judgement is provoked but no object of judgement is presented and this is an index of fantasy's terror of criticism. Whatever its therapeutic value in making life more bearable for the reader, fantasy certainly offers plenty of practice in keeping the mind closed.

Evil. *The Lord of the Rings*, like Dracula and the occult writings of Dennis Wheatley, is Manichean in its basic structure of values. I mean this strictly in that there are many references to the co-eternity of the principles of good and evil, though the secondary meaning of 'possessed by a puritanical horror of sex', is also present in *The Lord of the Rings* (see **Women** below): 'Always', says Gandalf, 'after a defeat and a respite the Shadow takes another shape and grows again.'[13]

There are problems with this in the human frame of reference, for there can be no truck with or understanding or limiting of this absolute evil. The conflict is irreducible and eternal. To ask questions about what Sauron and Co. are working *for* is mental treason, almost tantamount to moving onto their side. Such questions, if pressed, crack up the whole dynamic of the fiction and even of Arda itself. All good things will go if Sauron wins. But so too will all the things that offer (no doubt violent, rough, savage, grinning, idle and foul) pleasures to the maggot folk of Mordor.

Aragorn, who within the structure of values is unassailably good, says: 'Good and ill have not changed since yesteryear; nor are they one thing among Elves and Dwarves and another amongst men.'[14] But how are good and evil amongst the orcs and the wolves, the trolls and the maggots? What is wrong with maggots?

When Frodo flees from Boromir and puts on the ring at Amon Hen he feels himself caught at the focus of this eternal struggle: 'The two powers strove in him. For a moment, perfectly balanced between their piercing points, he writhed, tormented.'[15]

It is a wonderful and crazy model. The energy created by the difference between the two powers keeps the sky from collapsing on the earth. And this is carried over into the material relations of those who, and even of the things which, belong to either side, so that Smeagol/Gollum is unable to bear the touch of Elfin ropes or to eat Elfin food.

Furthermore the points between which Frodo writhed are like the tips of the cones of two identically structured hierarchies. It is better to be a good wizard than a good hobbit; and the fallen wizard, Saruman, is correspondingly more terrible than the fallen hobbit, Smeagol. Orcs are Sauron's equivalent of Elves, Trolls or Ents, we are told. To highlight further the identity of structure, consider this account of how Saruman altered Isengard under the influence of Sauron.

> . . . for all those arts and subtle devices for which he forsook his former wisdom, and which he fondly imagined were his own, came but from Mordor; so that what he made was naught, only a little copy, a child's model or a slave's flattery, of that vast fortress, armoury, prison, furnace of the great power, Barad dur the Dark Tower, which suffered no rival, and laughed at flattery, biding its time, secure in its pride and its immeasurable strength.[16]

Imagine Saruman as a medieval ruler converted to good from evil ways. A historian might have written:

161

> . . . for all those arts and skills for which he forsook his evil ways and which he knew were not his own, came in troth from Heaven; so that all he made was but a copy, a child's model, a suppliant's attempt at that vast city, palace, castle, source of power and glory, Jerusalem the bright citadel, which suffers no rival, is unmoved by flattery, biding its time secure in its majesty and its unmeasurable strength.

If we alter the words which have been part of the literary and tautological elaboration of the definition of evil, we find ourselves transposed, with no sense of unease, into the upper reaches of the hierarchy of good. (See under **Eyes** below for a similar example concerning Sauron himself.)

One has also to ask what it is that motivates the inhabitants of Mordor to get out of bed in the morning. There is a serious contradiction here.

> Another dreadful day of fear and toil had come to Mordor; and the night-guards were summoned to their dungeons and deep halls, and the day-guards, evil-eyed and fell, were marching to their posts. Steel gleamed dimly on the battlements.[17]

From this description it sounds as though the inhabitants would welcome liberation. But within the moral values of the book, these wretched of Middle-earth, the terrified and oppressed, merit nothing but destruction, to be hewn by swords, pierced by arrows, crushed and rent by Ents or consumed by the fire and brimstone of the apocalypse when Mount Doom explodes.

Let us look, finally, at a rough checklist of the prejudices gathered together to mark the evil. They include:

(1) Industrial landscapes: Wigan or Sheffield in the 1930s. (See also under **Industrialization** below.)
(2) Marshes, moors, thorns, rocks.
(3) Gunpowder. (Saruman at Helm's Deep.)
(4) Foreign languages. (See under **Language** below.)
(5) Blackness, darkness. (See also under **Race** below.)
(6) Southernness. (Even the best horses come from the North.)
(7) Easternness. (The undying lands are to the West.)
(8) Unloved animals: wolf, octopus, spider, bat, snakes, even pterodactyls, or whatever it is that the airborne Nazgul ride.

(9) The letter K.

(10) Crookedness.

(11) The letter Z—particularly when combined with G. (See **Language** below.)

Thus evil is never described, merely marked. There are no concrete or operational assertions which could make it clear why we should eschew evil. I think we should remember that what is good for bats is good for bats, however *we* may shudder at their insectivore, nocturnal habits and their leathern wings.

Eyes. When Bilbo is reluctant to part with the ring,

> 'Gandalf's eyes flashed. "It will be my turn to get angry soon," he said, "If you say that again, I shall. Then you will see Gandalf the Grey uncloaked." He took a step towards the Hobbit, and he seemed to grow tall and menacing; his shadow filled the room.'[18]

When Sam Gamgee challenges Strider/Aragorn in the Inn at Bree, Strider 'Stood up, and seemed to grow taller. In his eyes gleamed a light keen and commanding.' Ordinary Hobbits do not light up in this way. They do not have the soul-power. But on the other hand we have Saruman greeting Gandalf at Orthanc: '"So you have come Gandalf", he said to me gravely; but in his eyes there seemed to be a white light, as if a cold laughter was in his heart.' And again, when Boromir is about to attempt to seize the ring from Frodo, Frodo catches 'The strange gleam in Boromir's eyes, yet his face was still kind and friendly.' So while we seem to be urged to lock eye-ball to eye-ball if we seek to understand our fellow creatures (they're all doing it on every page with gestures straight from *Ivan the Terrible*), yet activity in there, behind the eyes, is only evidence of extra-ordinariness.

These eyes are part of the furniture (or rather anatomy) of Coleridge's supernatural poems where they signify transcendent knowledge. The 'flashing eyes and floating hair' of the poet in *Khubla Khan*, the mesmeric 'glittering eye' of the *Ancient Mariner*, and the strangely transformable reptile eyes of Geraldine in *Christabel*, all speak of knowledge beyond the ordinary, beyond the market-town, common-sense of Hobbiton. The eyes are windows on that other world where the 'real' battles for good will take place. And not everyone is privileged

163

to be chilled and terrified by these glimpses from 'beyond'. Back in the shire the Hobbits have no idea of the battle that has been won on their behalf. They would need to be as virtuous, courageous or percipient as Sam Gamgee at least before they could understand.

Now in Coleridge the flashing eyes are always ambivalent—the reader is left with the task of evaluating them, but in *The Lord of the Rings* while the flashing occurs equally on either side of the good/evil line, that line is always clearly indicated. The reader is never in any doubt. The light in Aragorn's eyes is 'keen and commanding', while the eyes of the ring-wraiths are 'keen and merciless' and they are dressed in black and so on.

Sauron himself is known as 'The Eye'. The more clearly he is described, the more the descriptions resemble the mystics' accounts of the divine presence: 'The Eye: that horrible growing sense of a hostile will that strove to pierce all shadows of cloud and earth and flesh and to see you.'[19] Rewrite, changing three words: 'God; that terrible growing sense of a loving will that . . .'.

Good. Entirely derivable by inversion of Evil (q.v.). Checklist:
  (1) Green grass in ordered lawns, but without cutting.
  (2) Trees, well managed, but only by Ents.
  (3) Music, of a faintly bardic character.
  (4) English and Elvish (Gaelic).
  (5) Whiteness, silver, gold and light.
  (6) Northernness.
  (7) The west.
  (8) Loved and respected animals. Horses, Eagles, Elephants (only just!).
  (9) The vowels except U.
  (10) Litheness.
  (11) Th (Ah Elbereth Gilthoniel, etc.).

Hierarchy. Both J. R. R. Tolkien and C. S. Lewis were great medieval scholars. The only justification for the divisions between good and evil in *The Lord of the Rings*, as in the *Narnia* books of Lewis, lies in a last gasp attempt to revive the great chain of being, which, I understand, lies at the heart of medieval Christian philosophy and values. So there are no bad Elves, though I presume, on the Lucifer principle, that a bad Elf is not a logical impossibility. There is one renegade Wizard: Saruman. The men are divided (see Boromir and Denethor), though we don't meet many of the bad ones. The Nazgul are men. Hobbits, as the scouring of the Shire reveals, are capable of being led astray; the only really wicked one, however, is Smeagol. There are absolutely no good Trolls, Orcs, Nazguls, so their wholesale destruction poses no moral dilemma. They are imagined as scapegoats. One might argue that this is better than having real scapegoats. But to suggest that a part of the pleasure of escaping into the fantasy world is the relief of being able to indulge in the blameless and total condemnation of scapegoats built in there for the purpose is to admit some (small?) element of danger in the genre. I would suggest we need to cultivate a securely critical rejection of that motion of the mind if we are ever to live in a community which does not continually fall into the shame of the recent reporting of the Falklands war (Nuke the Argies, etc.). When we are invited by the fiction to flesh out these scapegoats in our imagining, we should note where our imaginations run . . . (Huns? Jews? Blacks? Whites? Reds? Capitalists?)[20]

At the other end of the hierarchies, the loftiness of the Elves needs a closer look. In one way it is a matter of social class—a re-awakening of the genetically carried differentials of theocratic feudalism (part of the medieval chain of being; they all wear the trappings of Romantic/pre-Raphaelite/Medieval Lords and Ladies fair). According to this way of seeing things Frodo, 'a jewel among Hobbits', is like one of those Bottoms or gravediggers that Shakespearean royalty are prepared to patronize from time to time.

For the baseness of the Orcs etc., see under **Race** below.

Industrialization. If we consider the economic base of Middle-earth we might just be being churlish I suppose. But the values of the fiction are rooted in and reflect back upon the economic history of England and our reactions to it. In other words this is perhaps one of the places where recognizably concrete description enables us to engage with the values of the work. The Shire, for example, is an unreal agricultural community of gentle work-shy landowners with plenty of time to smoke and dream in their burrows. How the plenty of food in which they take such delight is grown, harvested, marketed, transported, etc. is never even hinted at. Almost the only workers mentioned are gardeners. (See under **Servants** below.) Conversely Mordor is Wigan or Sheffield in the 1930s with no relief of canal or allotment. There *all* is mysterious energy controlled from far away, slag heaps, endless labour and no production of anything.

Sam's vision in the mirror of Galadriel supplies us with a glimpse of the Shire being taken over by the influence of Mordor, which makes it suddenly much more recognizable as a corner of rural England being encroached on by the industrial revolution.

> 'Hi!' cried Sam in an outraged voice. 'There's Ted Sandiman a-cutting down trees as he shouldn't. They didn't ought to be felled: it's that avenue beyond the mill that shades the road to Bywater. I wish I could get at Ted, and I'd fell *him*!'
>
> But now Sam noticed that the Old Mill had vanished and a large red-brick building was being put up where it had stood. Lots of folk were busily at work. There was a tall red chimney nearby. Black smoke seemed to cloud the surface of the Mirror.
>
> 'There's some devilry at work in the Shire,' he said.[21]

So too when Saruman manages to get some high explosives into his attack on Helm's Deep, Aragorn cries 'Some devilry of Saruman's' who according to Treebeard has a mind of 'metal and wheels'.

Where the description of evil is concrete, industry and technology are evil.

Languages. Manichean dualism, parting all 'creation' into good and evil must in representations of that creation offer signals which permit the judgement to flow easily on one side or the other of the divide. The flow of the heart into veneration or execration must never be baffled for long. The invented languages of *The Lord of the Rings* operate on Xenophobic lines to provide such signals. (Just as in John Buchan and in thousands of War Comics and films, German is 'guttural';

'gutturalness' involves force, pressure against resistance; gutturalness is harsh and low; harsh and low is evil; Germans are evil; 'Der Schwarzestein ist in der Siegeskrone', etc.)

English, in *The Lord of the Rings* is neutral, though when spoken with passion by Saruman or Boromir (pressure, resistance) or when it is whispered hissingly by Smeagol or Wormtongue (harsh and low) it is shifted towards the Black Speech. Consider:

> Ash nazg durbatuluk
> Ash nazg gimbatul
> Ash nazg thrakutuluk
> Agh burzum-ishi krimpatul.

When Gandalf recited this at the Council of Elrond, his voice became 'Menacing, powerful, harsh as stone. A shadow seemed to pass over the high sun, and the porch for a moment grew dark. All trembled and the Elves stopped their ears.'[22] Yet when he runs through the little poem a moment later in the English translation:

> One ring to rule them all,
> One ring to find them,
> One ring to bring them all
> And in the Darkness bind them

it has no effect at all. This is surely a great indictment of the English compared with the Black Speech as far as poetic range is concerned. (See also under **Songs** below.) But where does the Black Speech gets its power? Apart from the learned origins of the languages of Middle Earth (outlined in *The Shores of Middle Earth*[23]) the languages affect the ignorant reader by means of the 'portmanteau' word, invented by Lewis Carroll and used particularly in 'Jabberwocky'. So, going through the ring inscription we can find the following: ash, dur (hard), bat, batul (battle), uk (hook, lock), batuluk (battle-hook), grim, krimp, (crimp, cramp). And less obviously: thak (thwack), Agh (aarrgghh! in horror comics) and nazg (snag, nags, gnash).

I think the aesthetic Elf-identifying English reader is also expected to tremble at 'unnatural' combinations of letters such as 'AZG', perhaps on the grounds that they are harsh, intrinsically ugly or difficult to pronounce. Just how far this is to do with seeing rather than hearing may be judged by listening to the same *sounds* in, for example, 'He *has grown*.' a statement which one can imagine innocent Hobbit aunties and uncles using all over the Shire without invoking the slightest shadow.

Z seems to be especially wicked.

Names. Really a sub-section of **Language** (above) so: Glorfindel (glory, find, dell (pastoral landscape)), Galadriel (Glad, Galahad, ariel, real and rill (pastoral landscape)). But: Gorbag (gore bag), Shagrat (strange sexual practices(?), hairy rat, aquatic bird rat), Sauron (Sour one(!)).

Nostalgia. The longing for a pre-lapsarian past and the feeling that we do not belong in the world as at present constituted are related but not identical. The first may be an inducement to nostalgic and/or Millenial fantasies. The second may lead us to reflections on the present state of the world and how that might be altered to make it more humanly attuned.

In *The Lord of the Rings* the Hobbits look back to better days in the Shire, but the narrator looks back to those better days when there were still Hobbits around. The Elves, humans and Hobbits look back to time when the Elves walked freely all over Middle-earth, but the narrator looks back to a time when it was still possible to meet an Elf at all. The Ents regret the disappearance of the Entwives (see also under **Women** below), but the narrator intimates that the Ents themselves will vanish at the end of the third age. To this double perspective of nostalgia is added the third level of the reader looking back to the time when the narrator was still able to know about Hobbits, Elves and Ents.

Within the narrative itself, that is within its own time structure, the most powerfully affecting part in terms of empathy is the end from Chapter VI of *The Return of the King*, 'Many Partings', when we join each member as he departs, looking back on the terrible goodness of the quest and facing the fact that nothing else will ever be quite so good. Right at the end of the book Sam sees Frodo and Gandalf off to the Undying Lands and returns from the Grey Havens with Merry and Pippin.

> At last the three companions turned away, and never again
> looking back they rode slowly homewards; and they spoke no
> word to each other until they came back to the Shire, but each
> had great comfort of his friends on the long grey road.[24]

Although they never look back, they ride 'homewards', i.e.
'back' to the Shire. They appear to have taken a firm, manly
resolve to hanker no more after Frodo and the fellowship, but
their silence speaks of deep, sad (they are in need of comfort)
thought on all that has passed.

Nostalgia is a trap because it only admits of longing in
relation to time. Clear understanding leading to action is not a
possibility. Bathed in the delights of the imagined, censored or
invented past the nostalgic fantasy can only spare a pitying
smile for the present, the material and the un-censored. The
future for nostalgia is mostly a dreary continuation of the
decline from the good past, though in some versions there is a
millenial future when time folds into a circle and the lost Eden
turns up again as the future Paradise.

In *The Lord of the Rings* this trap is formed like a maze whose
corridors are paradoxes (q.v.).

Paradoxes. The paradoxes of narration in *The Lord of the Rings*
form loops which bend the tired mind of the enquiring reader
back into the fantasy, so that attempts to historicize, localize,
in a word realize the fantastic in the sense of establishing its
relationship to the real, tend to be frustrated. Example 1: the
Hobbit Meriadoc unwisely asks of Strider/Aragorn 'How far is
Rivendel?' and, lost in alliteration, he gazes around '. . . wearily.
The world looked wild and wide from Weathertop.'[25]

Such practical questions are a threat to fantasy, since they
tend to evoke practical answers such as 'about five miles'; such
banality might, as the saying goes, bring us down to earth. But
Strider is equal to this threat (as to so many others). 'I don't
know', he says, 'if the Road has ever been measured in miles
beyond the Forsaken Inn, a day's journey east of Bree.' The
Forsaken Inn is like one of the cats of Queen Berúthiel; since
no one ever goes there, this is the only reference to it in the
entire work, and no one can work out why it is that, though
Strider implies that someone *has* measured in miles the

distance between Bree and the Inn, Strider keeps the actual figure to himself. Such a figure would give us a base line on which to work when attempting to follow the rest of his answer to the bewildered Meriadoc.

> 'Some,' he goes on, 'say it is so far, some otherwise. It is a strange road, and folk are glad to reach their journey's end, whether the time is long or short. But I know how long it would take me on my own feet with fair weather and no ill fortune: twelve days from here to the Ford of Bruinen, where the road crosses the Loudwater that runs out of Rivendell. We have at least a fortnight's journey before us for I do not think we shall be able to use the road.'

In a single seemingly wise and knowledgeable answer distance is transmuted into time, weather, fortune and the subjective response to traversing it and the reader can set no co-ordinates of his own judgement on the wide wildness of the world.

Example 2: Sam and Frodo are musing on Life and Art on the Stairs of Cirith Ungol. Their speculations develop a veritable set of Russian dolls around the idea of who is the narrator of the tale. 'I don't like any thing here,' says Frodo, 'but so our path is laid.'[26] Sam develops a comparison between their situation and the situation of characters in 'the old tales and songs.' 'Their paths were laid,' he says and adds, 'I wonder what sort of a tale we've fallen into?' Frodo pontificates then on the nature of classic realist fiction. He and Sam don't know their futures and that's the best way with tales. 'You [reader/listener] may know or guess what kind of a tale it is, happy-ending or sad-ending [only two kinds], but the people in it don't know and you don't want them to know.' Sam then sets their own tale into the context of the (fictional-historical) old tales, and looks forward in imagination to the (fictional) future when 'they' will tell the 'tale of Frodo and the Ring'. By page 986, Sam, musing on the slopes of the exploding Mount Doom, has given the work a more informative and imposing title: 'Do you think they'll say: now comes the story of the Nine-fingered Frodo and the Ring of Doom?' And the circularity of the sequence is closed off on page 990, when a minstrel of Gondor stands forth in the field of Cormallen and says: 'Now listen to my lay. For I will sing to you of Frodo of the Nine Fingers and the Ring of Doom.' This minstrel is, and at the same time is not, Tolkien himself, and there is the further implication that the whole tale is itself 'laid' by Iluvatar, the all-father within the fiction, and by providence or God outside it as the biggest Russian doll of them all.

I have found it helpful to think of this in terms of a formal diagram:

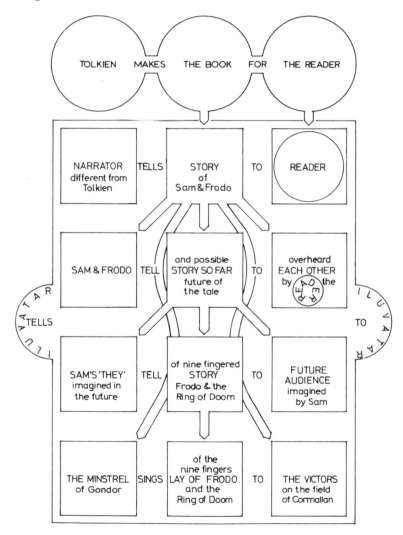

The diagram represents six narrative transactions. The top one with the participants in circles is a 'real' transaction taking place between Tolkien and the reader by means of the book. The others are in a sense increasingly fictional: narratives *within* the narrative. Although the (real) reader is necessarily involved in all of these transactions, as we move through them he or she becomes more and more deeply embedded in the world of the fiction, until the reader vanishes and becomes 'one with' Sam's imagined future audience or the victors at Cormallen. All the transactions within the oblong frame are moreover represented as the subject matter of a sixth transaction in which Iluvatar tells a tale, presumably to himself. By analogy there is yet another suggestion that the whole lot, including the first 'real' transaction are all part of a tale told by Tolkien's (Christian) God. The effect is like being trapped inside one of those visual paradoxes in which the label on a tin of soup shows a can of soup with a label on it which shows a can of soup with a label on it which . . . etc.

Paternalism. The politics of Middle-earth are openly paternalistic (in so far as it is possible to be 'open' about paternalism). This is as it should be in a Manichean, patriarchal creation where values are enshrined in a chain of being.

So at the Council of Elrond, Aragorn reveals his paternal and selfless concern for all the lesser folk of Middle-earth (like a Tory cabinet minister, or a Platonic Guardian, or a mole-hunter in a John le Carré novel). He has for many years been hunting the servants of the enemy, travelling rough and incognito, a king in disguise.

> 'Yet,' he says, 'We would not have it otherwise. If simple folk are free from care and fear, simple they will be, and we must be secret to keep them so. That has been the task of my kindred, while the years have lengthened and the grass has grown.'[27]

The complexities of the middle sentence would certainly baffle the mind of a simple Hobbit; they will help to keep Aragorn's intentions 'secret'. I see a logical framework: if—then—and.

If simple folk are free from care and fear. . . .

Then they will be simple—i.e. remain simple(?)

And we (who are not simple) must be secret to keep them so—i.e. simple.

If this means anything at all it might be revealed by the test of inversion. Thus:

If simple folk are NOT free from care and fear. . . .

Then they will not be (remain) simple. . . . (They will become complex, clever, sophisticated, intelligent, devious, all of which, by implication, must be guarded against by Aragorn and the other Rangers.)

And we, (who are not simple) (i.e. who are already complex, clever, sophisticated, intelligent) must be secret (i.e. devious) to keep them simple.

With Aragorn at the D.E.S. we could make dramatic cuts in the education budget; but then I fear he would be right behind any increase in defence expenditure!

In any case paternalism is only good on the right side. When Boromir, Saruman and Denethor propose in various ways to use the ring paternalistically for the good of Middle-earth, they are all shown to be guilty of self-deception (at best) and, providentially, come to a variety of sticky ends.

Race. After the death of Boromir, Aragorn describes some of Saruman's Goblin soldiers. These are so evil that in time they will be slain by the Ents without a flicker of remorse or pity. They can also be hewn in bits by Gimli or shot by the arrows of Legolas in a kind of bloodthirsty competition. They are 'hideous' and 'the land must groan under their hated feet' and so on. When we get one of those few detailed glimpses which let us know in what this hatefulness and hideousness consists, we find that they are 'swart'[28] and 'slant-eyed',[29] i.e. both black and oriental.

Furthermore there are some curiously contradictory judgements concerning cross-breeding between 'races'. It is evidently acceptable for Aragorn to wed Arwen, an Elf, who thereby renounced her own immortality. But Treebeard is shocked to his roots at the idea that there has been any blending of the 'races of Orcs and Men'. That, he says, 'Would be a black [of course] evil.'[30]

Servants. At the end of Bilbo's farewell party 'Gardeners came by arrangement, and removed in wheelbarrows those who had inadvertently remained behind.'[31] Presumably these gardeners were not invited to the party, or if they were, then the 'arrangement' included the injunction that they were not to get so carried away themselves that they forgot to carry the young gentlemen away when the party was over. The gardener is the most acceptable of servants: even more acceptable than the Oxford college 'scout', who sees the young, undergraduate gentleman through many a jolly jape and scrape and then, if the young gentleman is successful, sees him through the strain of all his intellectual quests from graduate to professor. The idyllic face of the class war. Samwise Gamgee is a gardener turned scout.

Songs. There is a neat trick with the songs. Criticism is usually displaced because the reader is presented with an inferior translation from the Elvish or Entish or the Black Speech. The songs that are in English are rough Hobbit drinking songs, acknowledged to be of little poetic worth. Even Bilbo's story of Eärendil, though it gets some condescending praise from the Elves, is clearly small beer compared to the Elvish songs we *don't* get to hear. Then, too, since they are songs our imagination has to supply the music whose absence can always be held responsible for any deficiencies in the words. Ah! but how sweet those unheard songs are!

> . . . the clear voice of the minstrel rose like silver and gold, and all men were hushed. And he sang to them, now in the Elven-tongue, now in the speech of the West, until their hearts, wounded with sweet words, overflowed, and their joy was like swords, and they passed in thought out to regions where pain and delight flow together and tears are the very wine of blessedness.(!)

Time is a great generator of paradoxes (q.v.) in *The Lord of the Rings*. Time, great stretches of it, is essential to the generation of nostalgia and to the values of ancientness. But if it gets too precise in its description, it can historicize power relationships and demystify the workings of prescriptive rights. As with

174

space in the 'How far is Rivendel' paradox, so with time the narrator is full of devices for trapping the reader's attempts to be clear.

Consider the sentence: 'It was not yet forgotten that there had been a time when there was much coming and going between the Shire and Bree.'[32] In that sentence I detect four times operative within the fiction plus two more possibly pedantic ones, but ones which nevertheless affect the reader's experience of the fiction:

(A) The time when there was much coming and going between the Shire and Bree. A substantial period seems to be implied and it was (from the context of values surrounding Bree, the Shire and the dangers of travel) a 'good' time.

(B) The time of the journey of Frodo. A time when A had not been forgotten. This too was a good time in the limited sense that what in the narrator's 'now' (time D, below) is only known to the narrator and specially clued-up readers, was then known by every Tom, Dick and Hobbit.

(C) Forgetting time, in which most people, the vulgar, forgot A and so could not understand about B. C is a 'bad' time.

(D) Narrator's time, when A, B, and C could only be known by the cognoscenti. The reader, wishing to stand beside the narrator among the cognoscenti, fleshes out the references to fictional periods of time with historical non-inventions as shadowy as the cats of Queen Berúthiel.

For the sake of completeness I would add:

(E) Tolkien's time when he wrote the sentence, and which moves further and further away from

(F) Reader's time when we read it.

Look at page 14 of the prologue for an even richer mess of time relations. The safest posture for the reader is to nod along as though he/she understood.

War is celebrated in *The Lord of the Rings*. There is none of the ambivalence about war to be found in Homer or Shakespeare. It may be grim, but it is necessary; 'good' cannot prevail over 'evil' without the recurrent purging of war. The experience of the War of the Ring ennobles Frodo, Merry, Pippin and Sam, so that they are fit to purge the Shire at the end of the tale.[33]

Women. It cannot escape the reader that the world of *The Lord of the Rings* is almost entirely male. The female Hobbits are either scolds or helpmeets of the most humble kind. The female Elves are devotional exemplars to be called on in emergency like the Virgin Mary. Amongst the humans Eowyn does get involved as a shield maiden disguised as a man and actually kills the Nazgul Lord. But she is an exception and is driven by her passion for Aragorn; otherwise the human women are healers and nurses in Gondor.

How do these folk reproduce? Elves presumably don't have to, because being immortal they would quickly fill up the whole of Arda. So Arwen renounces her immortality for love of Aragorn. The Hobbits do it (see Sam Gamgee's Elanor) but the best of them remain chaste bachelors; Bilbo and Frodo never suffer the slightest twinge of desire, apparently. When Sam returns from the Grey Havens one feels that little Elanor is a poor substitute for a trip to the Undying Lands. The Ents would like to do it and Treebeard voices their frustration at several centuries of enforced celibacy: 'You never see any Ents around there [the Shire] do you?' he asked. 'Well not Ents, *Entwives*, I should really say.' But the Entwives are gone and the Ents are doomed to extinction. There is only one female in the entire book who is unashamedly interested in reproduction; who has spread her broods far and wide 'from Ephel Duath to the Eastern hills, to Dol Guldur and the fastnesses of Mirkwood'.[34] I refer, of course, to Shelob, the great bloated spider monster who inhabits the tunnels under Ephel Duath.[35]

Into this figure Tolkien has poured all the attributes of the female that are so prudishly scoured from Galadriel, Arwen, Eowyn and even Rose Cotton. These attributes are of course described with a Manichean (in the narrower sense) loathing and disgust. The spider is a symbol of the predatory (i.e. sexually active) female; she eats her mates. It follows by transposition that her attempts to eat Frodo and Sam are also attempts upon their Hobbit virginities. . . . She lives in a stinking hole, and the stench is eventually traced to her 'pale and luminous belly'.[36] She has legs, lots of them (enough to lend a pair to most of the legless damsels we've met in Middle-earth), and the legs have hairs which stick out like steel spines.

Her death is appropriately encompassed as the result of her

attempted female rape of Sam. Read from this point of view, the account is almost embarassingly explicit:

> She yielded to the stroke, and then heaved up the great bag of her belly high above Sam's head. Poison frothed and bubbled from the wound. Now splaying her legs she drove her huge bulk down on him again.

But Sam is holding his elfin-blade upwards:

> ... and so Shelob, with the driving force of her own cruel will ... thrust herself upon a bitter spike. Deep, deep it pricked, as Sam was crushed slowly to the ground.
>
> No such anguish had Shelob ever known, or dreamed of knowing, in all her long world of wickedness. Not the doughtiest soldier of old Gondor, nor the most savage Orc entrapped had ever thus endured her. . . .[37]

Z. Ah! poor wicked damned crooked Z.

NOTES

1. Robert Foster, *The Complete Guide to Middle-earth* (London: Allen & Unwin, 1978).
2. See Roland Barthes, *S/Z* (London: Jonathan Cape, 1975).
3. Foster, op. cit., *Preface*, p. viii.
4. Foster, op. cit., p. viii.
5. T. S. Eliot, *Burnt Norton*.
6. S. T. Coleridge, *Biographia Literaria*, Ch. 14.
7. J. R. R. Tolkien, *The Lord of the Rings* (London: Allen & Unwin, 1978). References are to the one volume paperback edition.
8. Ibid., p. 306.
9. Ibid., p. 280.
10. Ibid., p. 329.
11. Foster, op. cit., p. 45.
12. *The Lord of the Rings*, op. cit., p. 729.
13. Ibid., p. 64.
14. Ibid., p. 459.
15. Ibid., p. 420.
16. Ibid., p. 579.
17. Ibid., p. 663.
18. Ibid., p. 275.
19. Ibid., p. 656.
20. In a recent speech (March 1983) President Reagan called the U.S.S.R. a

focus of evil, and asserted that Christ was the divine protector of the U.S.A. 'America is great', he said, 'because America is good.'

21. *The Lord of the Rings*, op. cit., p. 271.
22. Ibid., p. 271.
23. Robert Giddings and Elizabeth Holland, *J. R. R. Tolkien: The Shores of Middle-earth* (London: Junction Books, 1981), pp. 158–63.
24. *The Lord of the Rings*, op. cit., p. 1069.
25. Ibid., p. 204.
26. Ibid., p. 739.
27. Ibid., p. 266.
28. Ibid., p. 434.
29. Ibid., p. 446.
30. Ibid., p. 495.
31. Ibid., p. 49.
32. Ibid., p. 166.
33. In 1983 this model seems to match the foreign policy of both Downing Street and the White House. The 'Empire of Evil' that President Reagan sees in Russia is, like Mordor, an appropriate object for total destruction. *The Lord of the Rings* feeds the Western ideologies of Cold War, and whatever ideologies are promulgated on the other side, the fact that they are materialistic might limit their extension to a universal frame for the justified war.
34. *The Lord of the Rings*, op. cit., p. 750.
35. I am indebted to the work of Ms. Jane Davidson for this perspective on Shelob, though the details of this version of it must be my own responsibility.
36. *The Lord of the Rings*, op. cit., p. 752.
37. Ibid., p. 756.

10

No Sex Please—We're Hobbits: The Construction of Female Sexuality in *The Lord of the Rings*

by BRENDA PARTRIDGE

The claim that *The Lord of the Rings* contains no sex must be strongly refuted; it is there, though it is closely interwoven with and often masked by the various other themes and symbolism. A close analysis of the male relationships and the female characterization reveals much about Tolkien's attitude to sexuality and the role of women.

To understand these relationships and the characters in *The Lord of the Rings* we need to know the background of Tolkien's own relationships. The group of writers and academics with whom Tolkien associated at the University of Oxford, the Inklings, is particularly important. A study of the group is completely and sympathetically documented in Humphrey Carpenter's book *The Inklings* (1978).[1] The group met frequently and regularly to discuss their own writing and other literary and academic matters. Characteristically of the British male of a particular socio-economic class, marked forever by school life in an exclusively male school (often boarding school), the group tried to carry into adult life the club clannishness its members had enjoyed at school. Carpenter attempts to locate

179

the qualities which held the Inklings together and gave them their very strong sense of group identity. He dismisses Christianity, the occult, literary areas of interest and opposition to modernism because of too great a diversification of interests and beliefs, and finally comes down on the idea of friendliness as the cement and seal which held the Inklings together.

The friendship was, of course, exclusively male. Although marriage of Oxford dons was by this time quite common, in the main university life was still dominated by males. Academics worked in their colleges and in general had their meals there. Wives and families were at home in the suburbs. But there is more to it than that. It is the attitude expressed by Lewis, Tolkien and the leading members of The Inklings which claims attention. Lewis was very outspoken about it. It was an article of his faith that full intimacy with another man was impossible unless women were totally excluded. 'A friend dead is to be mourned,' he wrote in his diary 1922, 'a friend married is to be guarded against, both equally lost.'[2] Believing women's minds were not meant for logic or for great art it was his view that women had little to say that was worth listening to. 'Then men have learned to live among ideas,' he wrote in *The Four Loves* (1960):

> they know what discussion, proof and illustration mean. A woman who has had merely school lessons and has abandoned soon after marriage whatever type of culture 'they' gave her— whose reading is the Women's Magazines and whose general conversation is almost wholly narrative—cannot really enter such a circle. . . . If the men are ruthless, she sits bored and silent through a conversation which means nothing to her. If they are better bred, of course, they try to bring her in. Things are explained to her: people try to sublimate her irrelevant and blundering observations into some kind of sense. But the efforts soon fail, and for manners' sake, what might have been a real discussion, is deliberately diluted and peters out in gossip, anecdotes and jokes.[3]

Although Carpenter points out that Tolkien was capable of sympathizing over the plight of a clever woman trapped by marriage into an intellectually empty life,[4] it is clear that he held an equally dismissive view of female intellect; in 1941 he wrote:

> How quickly an intelligent woman can be taught, grasp the
> teacher's ideas, see his point—and how (with some exceptions)
> they can go no further, when they leave his hand, or when they
> cease to take a personal interest in him. It is their gift to be
> receptive, stimulated, fertilized (in many other matters than the
> physical) by the male.[5]

In his relationship with his wife, Edith, documented in
Humphry Carpenter's biography of Tolkien, a substantial
part of the difficulties in the relationship stems from Tolkien's
refusal to admit Edith into his circle of male friends.

> He perceived that his need of male friendship was not entirely
> compatible with married life. But he believed that this was one
> of the sad facts of a fallen world: and on the whole he thought
> that a man had a right to male pleasures, and should if
> necessary insist on them.[6]

The importance of Tolkien's male friendships, particularly
with Lewis, has a significant bearing on *The Lord of the Rings*.
Although by Lewis's own admission Tolkien was not one of his
main, close friends,[7] Lewis was, as far as Tolkien was concerned, a very important friend. The friendship was at its most
intense in the early days but was disturbed by the appearance
of Charles Williams. Tolkien came to resent the close relationship which developed between Williams and Lewis. The
friendship was also seriously rocked by Lewis's marriage, in
his sixties, to Joy Davidman. Tolkien, as a Roman Catholic,
had deep objections to Lewis's marrying a divorcee, but,
Carpenter points out:

> . . . there was, perhaps, some other and deeper reason why he
> resented it. His friend Robert Murray noticed that when he
> talked about Lewis and the marriage it seemed almost as if he
> felt that some deep tie of friendship had been betrayed by it.[8]

That there may have been an erotic element in the relationship is hard to determine. Although always publicly denied
previously, there is considerable and irrefutable evidence of
Lewis's sexual ambiguity.[9] In *The Allegory of Love*, which he
published in 1936, he argued that in the Middle Ages hetero-
sexual romantic love played but a small part in art as in life,
and that social harmony was motivated by the love of man for
man—'the mutual love of warriors who die together . . . the

affection between vassal and lord . . .'. Significantly he compares this to 'a small boy's feelings for some hero in the sixth form . . .'.[10] There is also considerable evidence of deep homosexual feelings (and a latent sadism) between Lewis and his friend in Belfast, Arthur Greeves, revealed in Lewis's letters examined by Walter Hooper (*They Stand Together: The Letters of C. S. Lewis to Arthur Greeves 1914–1963*).

And understanding of Lewis's ambiguous sexuality and latent sadism gives dimension to the seemingly chance remark about Tolkien soon after they first met. Lewis described him as 'a smooth, pale, fluent little chap . . . thinks all literature is written for the amusement of *men* between thirty and forty. . . . No harm in him: only needs a smack or so.'[11]

To determine from biographical and autobiographical material if Tolkien's feelings for Lewis were in any way sexual is more difficult. Mr. and Mrs. Tolkien began to sleep in different rooms at the same time that Tolkien's friendship with Lewis seemed to be at its height. Tolkien kept a diary in one of his own secret languages. His jealousy explodes when Williams comes on to the scene. He is distressed when Lewis marries. He only begins to keep a diary after C. S. Lewis died in 1963. He was quite specific about the reasons for the cooling of the friendship:

> We were separated first by the sudden apparition of Charles Williams, and then by his marriage. But we owed a great debt to the other, and that tie, with the deep affection that it begot, remained.[12]

It would not be sensible to push this evidence any further than it will easily go in an attempt to understand the undercurrents in the relationships which existed between Tolkien, Lewis and Williams. However it does provide a new perspective in the examination of *The Lord of the Rings* and explains the relationships of the sexes in the book summarized very aptly by Edwin Muir:

> . . . all the characters are boys masquerading as adult heroes. The hobbits . . . are ordinary boys, the fully human heroes have reached the fifth form; but hardly one of them knows anything about women, except by hearsay. Even the elves and dwarves and the ents are boys irretrievably, and will never come to puberty.[13]

This comment of Muir's succinctly sums up the relationship of the sexes in *The Lord of the Rings*. In ascertaining Tolkien's attitude to women the most obvious factor is the lack of female characters. Mirroring Tolkien's friendships it is a very exclusive male world. The women that do appear are conceived along very traditional lines either as the idealized goddess figure or as the romantic heroine. The interaction between the male characters and the female is for the most part stilted and distant. The relationships between the males on the other hand is often intensely close and supportive. It is the lack of magical powers and the general helplessness of the hobbits that promotes their friendship with the great Gandalf and in fact throughout their travels invites a protective care from all the human and elfin rulers they meet en route. Most are male and this together with the hobbits' small size makes the protection appear almost paternal. Tom Bombadil is the first to rescue them. Feeding and housing the hobbits and later teaching them about ancient history and the glories of nature he combines the Nature deity[14] with the role of Wise Man, tutor and father figure, as do Gandalf, Strider, Treebeard and the kings and their sons who similarly supply the hobbits with material necessities, protection and advice.

Size and lack of magical power are two reasons provided to account for this care and protection of the hobbits, a third is the feudalistic basis of the relationships. Echoing the feudal society of the ancient Norse myths and the medieval tales of chivalry, the hobbits, like the rest of the warriors, play the role of vassal to the various kings. Pippin swears an oath of fealty to Dethenor[15] and, despite Dethenor's madness, serves him loyally, saving Faramir from the funeral pyre lit mistakenly by Dethenor in the depths of his despair. Merry, too, swears allegiance to Theoden[16] and though he breaks his word by refusing to obey the king's command not to ride into battle with the Rohirrim, he is forgiven and the two are reconciled as the king lies dying:

> Merry could not speak, but wept anew, 'Forgive me, lord,' he said at last 'if I broke your command, and yet have done no more in your service than to weep at our parting.'
> The old king smiled. 'Grieve not! It is forgiven. Great heart will not be denied. Live now in blessedness; and when you sit in peace with your pipe, think of me. For never now shall I sit with

you in Meduseld, as I promised, or listen to your herb-lore.' He closed his eyes and Merry bowed beside him.[17]

As we have seen in Lewis's metaphor idealizing love between men as the deep bonds between warriors, it is obvious that one attraction of the ancient myths, particularly the Norse myths, albeit a subconscious attraction for Tolkien and Lewis, is their portraying of male intimacy, physical as well as mental, in a context which is socially acceptable. That is, war provides a context in which men can be acceptably intimate because they are at the same time being seen to live up to the socially desirable stereotype image of the aggressive male. Similarly aggression on a smaller scale in games, particularly rugby, is another means of promoting socially acceptable physical contact between males.

Frodo and Sam

War and its stimulation of male intimacy on the battlefield appears in *The Lord of the Rings* in another context more modern than its chivalric counterpart. Tolkien wrote that his characterization of Sam Gamgee was based on his admiration for the ordinary soldier, in particular the batman of his First World War experience. The system of batman, 'a servant who was detailed to look after his kit and care for him much in the manner of the Oxford Scout',[18] again reveals a desire for intimacy and devotion between men. Bearing this in mind the description of the relationship between Frodo and Sam offers interesting study. Sam's desire to be with Frodo at the beginning is portrayed as stemming from the love and loyalty of a servant for his master, and Sam is indeed the faithful batman prepared to lessen the load of Frodo's pack.

> 'I am sure you have given me all the heaviest stuff,' said Frodo. 'I pity snails, and all that carry their homes on their backs.'
> 'I could take a lot more yet, sir. My packet is quite light,' said Sam stoutly and untruthfully. . . .[19]

Sam's loyalty later provokes Frodo's exasperated affection and gratitude in 'The Breaking of the Fellowship'. His displeasure is described in the patronizing overtones of an officer chastising a disobedient soldier who is endangering the mission through a foolhardy loyalty.

> 'Coming, Mr. Frodo! Coming!' called Sam, and flung himself from the bank, clutching at the departing boat. He missed it by a yard. With a cry and a splash he fell face downward into deep swift water. Gurgling he went under, and the River closed over his curly head.
>
> An exclamation of dismay came from the empty boat. A paddle and the boat put about. Frodo was just in time to grasp Sam by the hair as he came up, bubbling and struggling. Fear was staring his round brown eyes.
>
> 'Up you come, Sam my lad!' said Frodo. 'Now take my hand!'
>
> 'Save me, Mr. Frodo!' gasped Sam. 'I'm drownded, I can't see your hand.'
>
> 'Here it is. Don't pinch, lad! I won't let you go. Tread water and don't flounder, or you'll upset the boat. There now, get hold of the side and let me use the paddle!' . . .[20]

As Sam stubbornly refuses to leave Frodo, however, Frodo reverts from the superior officer to the simple man glad to have companionship. 'Frodo actually laughed. A sudden warmth and gladness touched his heart.'[21]

From then on, as they alone together face peril after peril, their relationship develops an intensely intimate bond. This bond is described in a variety of terms, invoking and combining several different and important images: the bond of officer and batman, Christ and his devotee, and it is also a caring and very physical bond between two men.

When Frodo is first wounded it is Sam that insists the company halts to give him rest. During Frodo's convalescence Sam remains constantly at his side day and night as Gandalf tells Frodo,[22] and when Sam comes in to greet the recovering and conscious Frodo there is the first sign of a physical side to his affection for Frodo, though Sam is embarrassed.

> At that moment there was a knock on the door, and Sam came in. He ran to Frodo and took his left hand, awkwardly and shyly. He stroked it gently and then he blushed and turned hastily away.
>
> 'Hullo Sam!' said Frodo.
>
> 'It's warm!' said Sam. 'Meaning your hand, Mr. Frodo. It has felt so cold through the long nights. . . .'[23]

185

Much later when the pair are making their way with Gollum through the marshes, sinking into despair, Sam voices his fears about their lack of food. Pessimistically Frodo advises him that he need not worry for they are not likely to need food:

> 'I don't know how long we shall take to finish,' said Frodo. 'We were miserably delayed in the hills. But Samwise Gamgee, my dear hobbit—indeed, Sam my dearest hobbit, friend of friends—I do not think we need give thought to what comes after that. To *do the job* as you put it—what hope is there that we ever shall? And if we do, who knows what will come of that? If the One goes into the Fire, and we are at hand? I ask you, Sam, are we ever likely to need bread again? I think not. If we can nurse our limbs to bring us to Mount Doom, that is all we can do. More than I can, I begin to feel.'
>
> Sam nodded silently. He took his master's hand and bent over it. He did not kiss it, though his tears fell on it. Then he turned away, drew his sleeve over his nose, and got up, and stamped about, trying to whistle. . . .[24]

Their fortunes do take a turn for the better later and they manage to rustle up a feast of stewed rabbit. Frodo, on finishing the meal, sleeps and then, as later, when Frodo lies apparently dead from Shelob's poison, Sam looks upon his face. Once more it is the disciple looking at his saviour, but it is also a lover or very close friend gazing upon the face of his beloved:

> And for a moment he lifted up the Phial and looked down at his master, and the light burned gently now with the soft radiance of the evening-star in summer, and in that light Frodo's face was fair of hue again, pale but beautiful with an elvish beauty, as of one who has long passed the shadows.

The final, full yielding of Frodo's body to Sam's arms comes in the scene of the whipping of Frodo. Again the physical relationship of the pair is contained within and subconsciously masked by the religious overtones (Christ's torture and the loving tending of his body by Mary Magdalene).

> He was naked, lying as if in a swoon on a heap of filthy rags: his arm was flung up, shielding his head, across his side there ran an ugly whip-weal.
>
> 'Frodo! Mr. Frodo, my dear!' cried Sam, tears almost blinding him. 'It's Sam, I've come!' He half lifted his master and hugged him to his breast. Frodo opened his eyes.

> 'Am I still dreaming!' he muttered. 'But the other dreams were horrible.'
>
> 'You're not dreaming at all, Master,' said Sam. 'It's real. It's me. I've come.'
>
> 'I can hardly believe it,' said Frodo, clutching him. 'There was an orc with a whip, and then it turns into Sam! Then I wasn't dreaming after all when I heard that singing down below, and I tried to answer? Was it you?'
>
> 'It was indeed, Mr. Frodo. I'd given up hope, almost. I couldn't find you.'
>
> 'Well, you have now, Sam, dear Sam,' said Frodo, and he lay back in Sam's gentle arms, closing his eyes, like a child at rest when night-fears are driven away by some loved voice or hand.[27]

The union becomes complete, the relationship now consummated develops with no further hesitancy as the two are engaged in the remainder of their battle to destroy the ring and struggle to return to their friends. Finally, Frodo, in the role of saviour, successful but ultimately destroyed in the attempt, leaves Sam and the others to journey towards death. Sam remains and marries—the only function of the marriage lies in Tolkien's habitual tidying up of loose ends; Sam's children will grow up and flourish in the new world. The marriage also ensures that Sam, bereft of Frodo, will not be completely alone though the companionship it provides will never reach the depths of passion and spiritual intensity of the relationship of Sam and Frodo.

Shelob

The physical intimacy and beauty of Frodo's and Sam's coupling is in direct contrast with another very intense relationship in the book: the fierce and protracted struggle with Shelob, the one female monster in *The Lord of the Rings*. As Robert Giddings and Elizabeth Holland have already pointed out in their book, *J. R. R. Tolkien: The Shores of Middle-earth*, Tolkien's characterization of Shelob derives strongly from several mythical sources, Sigurd's killing of the dragon, Fafnir, Theseus and the Minotaur, the spider, Ariadne, and Milton's Sin in *Paradise Lost*.[28] Like Milton, Tolkien is following a tradition in portraying woman as a threat, with implied sexual overtones. Pandora's box let loose all the evils of the world. Eve's succumbing to the serpent produced a similar effect. Circe and the Sirens lured men to their death. Male fear of the power of women's sexual attraction is revealed in the constant connection with black magic, the witch and her familiar, the cat. Shelob herself is compared to a cat in the way she is fed food by Sauron.[29]

The cat itself is often used as an image of a woman, to imply a prescribed ideal of woman's sexuality as graceful, sensual and aloof. These traditional images of wicked and fallen women, due perhaps to the strength of their sexual power, often appear more cunning and devious than their male counterparts. The male figures tend to present a more open threat which is basically that of stronger physical power, the most obvious example is the giant.

The threat of Shelob obviously lies, in part, in her size and strength. Her power is very great indeed. She has existed from the beginning of time, she remains unconquered and whilst we get some sensation of the evil of Sauron with his 'dreadful Eye that sought to look in them' he remains invisible, his minions do the dirty work. Shelob as a presence is far more vivid and vile:

> There agelong she had dwelt, an evil thing in spider-form, even such as once of old had lived in the Land of Elves in the West that is now under the Sea, such as Beren fought in the Mountains of Terror in Doriath, and so came to Luthien upon the green-sward amid the hemlocks in the moonlight long ago. How Shelob came there, flying from ruin, no tale tells, for out of the Dark Years few tales have come. But still she was there, who was there before Sauron, and before the first stone of Barad-dur, and she served none but herself, drinking the blood of Elves and then, bloated and grown fat with endless brooding on her feasts, weaving webs of shadow, for all living things were her food, and her vomit darkness. Far and wide her lesser broods, bastards of the miserable mates, her own offspring, that she slew, spread from glen to glen, from the Ephel Duoth to the eastern hills, to Dol Guldur and the fastnesses of Mirkwood. But none could rival her, Shelob the Great, last child of Ungoliant to trouble the unhappy world.[30]

There are noticeable underlying sexual overtones in the reference to her spawning broods of monsters, reminiscent of Milton's Sin. The symbolism of the description of Shelob's lair also presents a sexual interpretation. The battle takes place underground and this setting derives partly from ancient underground mythologies and as Robert Giddings and Elizabeth Holland point out: 'Those who see myth itself as an expression of man's psychology . . . develop the idea of the cave representing the womb to which we all long to return.'[31] Shelob's lair, reached by entering a hole and journeying along tunnels, may also be seen to represent the female sexual orifice. At the entrance Frodo and Sam have to force themselves through the bushy, clutching growths (the pubic hair). 'As they thrust forward they felt things brush against their heads or against their hands, long tentacles, or hanging growths perhaps.'[32] These growths turn out to be cobwebs which enmesh the victim but Frodo, with the obvious phallic symbolism of the sword, pierces the web.

> Then Frodo stepped up to the great grey net, and hewed it with a wide sweeping stroke, drawing the bitter edge swiftly across a ladder of close-strung cords, and at once springing away. The blue-gleaming blade shore through them like a scythe through grass, and they leaped and writhed and then hung loose. A great rent was made. Stroke after stroke he dealt, until at last all the web within his reach was shattered, and the upper portion blew and swayed like a loose veil in the incoming wind.[33]

The diction used to describe the tearing of the web, 'rent' and 'veil', is traditionally associated with the tearing of the hymen.

Frodo's and Sam's swords, however, despite their Elven magical powers, which usually stand them in good stead, are not adequate on their own to combat Shelob. They require superhuman aid in the form of Galadriel's phial. Galadriel's phial indeed represents good versus evil using conventional light versus darkness imagery, but it also represents a phallus more potent than their swords. When Frodo falters as he tries to out-menace Shelob, the temporary diminishing of the phial's powers is described not in light and dark terms but in sexual terms.

> Frodo and Sam, horror stricken began slowly to back away, their own gaze held by the dreadful stare of those baleful eyes, but as they backed so the eyes advanced. Frodo's hand wavered, and slowly the Phial *drooped*.[34]

189

Despite the phial's powers, Frodo as a man is ultimately overpowed by the female Shelob; paralysed by her venom he lies helpless waiting to be sacrificed at her will. He is rescued only through the valiant struggle of his male companion, Sam.

> No onslaught more fierce was ever seen in the savage world of beasts, where some desperate small creature armed with little teeth alone, will spring upon a tower of horn and hide that stands above its fallen mate.[35]

The description of Sam's battle with Shelob is not only a life and death struggle of man and monster, good against evil but also represents a violent sexual struggle between man and woman. Shelob's 'soft squelching body' is a metaphor for the female genitals swollen and moist in sexual arousal. 'Great horns she had, and behind her short stalk-like neck was her huge swollen body, a vast bloated bag, swaying between her legs.'[36] Her impenetrable skin hangs in folds like the layers of the labia.

> Knobbled and pitted with corruption was her age-old hide but ever thickened from within with layer on layer of evil growth. The blade scored it with a dreadful gash, but those hideous folds could not be pierced by any strength of men, not though Elf or Dwarf should forge the steel or the hand of Beren or of Torin wield it.[37]

So Sam valiantly stabs at the monster, pitifully helpless as she rears over him.

> Now the miserable creature was right under her, for the moment out of the reach of her sting and of her claws. Her vast belly was above him with its putrid light, and the stench of it almost smote him down. Still his fury held for one more blow, and before she could sink upon him, smothering him and all his little impudence of courage, he slashed the bright elven-blade across her with desperate strength.

The male organ puny compared with the vast, evil smelling mass of the female is described in euphemistic sexual terms as his 'little impudence'.

It is not surprising that Sam seeks reassurance from the superhuman, symbolic male organ. '. . . and he fumbled in his breast with his left hand, and found what he sought: cold and hard and solid it seemed to his touch. . . .'[39]

190

And so Sam and Shelob interlocked climax in an orgasm with the male phallus thrusting hard inflicting great pain and a deadly blow deep into the female sexual organ.

> . . . She yielded to the stroke, and then heaved up the great bag of her belly high above Sam's head. Poison frothed and bubbled from the wound. Now splaying her legs she drove her huge bulk down on him again. Too soon. For Sam still stood upon his feet, and dropping his own sword, with both hands he held the elven blade point upwards, fending off that ghastly roof; and so Shelob, with strength greater than any warrior's hand, thrust herself upon a bitter spike. Deep, deep it pricked as Sam was crushed slowly to the ground.[40]

In the aftermath of the climax as the erection subsides the male, though victor, is again seen as frail and overwhelmed by the female's bulk.

Shelob then crawls away in agony as Sam in a final gesture holds up the phial, once more asserting male supremacy, brandishing the phallus, male symbol of power.

> As if his indomitable spirit had set its potency in motion, the glass blazed suddenly like a white torch in his hand. It flamed like a star that leaping from the firmament sears the dark air with intolerable light. No such terror out of heaven had ever burned in Shelob's face before. The beams of it entered into her wounded head and scored it with unbearable pain, and the dreadful infection of light spread from eye to eye. She fell back beating the air with her forelegs, her sight blasted by inner lightnings, her mind in agony. Then turning her marred head away, she rolled aside and began to crawl, claw by claw, towards the opening in the dark cliff behind.[41]

The imagery portraying this gesture appears at first sight to be more overtly religious, representing the Christian victory over paganism. However, as we have seen before, in *The Lord of the Rings* sexual implications are shrouded in religious symbolism, just as they are in Milton's *Paradise Lost*. The phial is phallus-shaped, the female linked with sexuality is seen as evil, paganism. Once again Tolkien interprets myth in such a way as to reveal his inner fear or abhorrence of female sexuality, but his attitude is reinforced by the prejudices inherent in the religious symbolism itself.

J. R. R. Tolkien: This Far Land

Eowyn, Goldberry and Galadriel

In comparison with the intimacy of the portrayal of the male characters and their relationships the female characterization shows a distinct lack of knowledge of women, relying heavily on mythical literature for inspiration and incorporating many of Tolkien's aforementioned prejudices against women.

Eowyn unlike Goldberry and Galadriel is mortal and reveals possible weaknesses and whims that the others as ideal deities do not. Much of her characterization stems from courtly romance, her fate in many ways paralleling that of Elaine in Tennyson's *Idylls of The King*.[42] However an extra dimension to the character, one which comes closer to revealing a more sympathetic view of women, may be seen in her dissatisfaction with her position as a woman. She is left to rule the kingdom when her father and Eomer go to war,[43] but she is not satisfied with this and, disguising herself as a warrior, rides with the Rohirrim into battle. Here perhaps we do see a certain sympathy for the plight of a clever woman trapped by marriage as previously mentioned. However, any understanding of a woman's dissatisfaction with an unfulfilling career is cast aside by Tolkien, who ultimately lays the blame not on poor career prospects and intellectual frustration but on unrequited love. Eowyn's desire for action stems from her despair that Aragorn can not return her love. Tolkien's solution is marriage, to Faramir, and this marriage is Tolkien's own invention. There is no such reward for Tennyson's Elaine who dies of grief alone.[44]

A picture of 'married bliss' has appeared much earlier in *The Lord of the Rings* in the description of Tom Bombadil's and Goldberry's marriage. Goldberry combines the courtly ideal of the woman on a pedestal, a rare beauty to be worshipped from afar, with a more down-to-earth ideal of woman as domestic servant. The courtly ideal may be seen in the portrayal of Goldberry as a goddess-like figure as elf-queen and daughter of the River; like other mythical goddesses she is at once distant and on a higher plane, a figure-head providing inspiration:

> The hobbits looked at her in wonder; and she looked at each of them and smiled. 'Fair lady Goldberry!' said Frodo at last, feeling his heart moved with a joy that he did not understand. He

192

stood as he had at times stood enchanted by fair elven-voices; but the spell that was now laid upon him was different: less keen and lofty was the delight, but deeper and nearer to mortal heart; marvellous and yet not strange.[45]

But paradoxically, because she in part derives from the goddess of fertility, Goldberry, playing the role of earth-mother, appears less distant as a wife carrying out her domestic duties. Ideal goddess and earth-mother, she not only carries out her tasks of cleaning and providing food and comfort without complaining but also manages to maintain her figure and beauty without effort, her hands perhaps not saved by the possession of a washing-machine so much as by elven magical powers. As a spirit of the River she is able to turn rainy weather to her advantage to do the washing and autumn-cleaning.[46]

Robert Giddings and Elizabeth Holland point out that much of the inspiration for Tom Bombadil and Goldberry as spirits of the earth and river lies in MacDonald's story *The Golden Key*.[47] A little girl, Tangle, running away from three bears is entrapped by a tree and rescued by a magical creature (an air-fish) who leads her to a cottage. There a beautiful woman, called Grand-mother, bathes her and feeds her with essence of the fish's spirit. As a result she is able to understand the language of animals. This story is linked with classical and other mythology 'Like Pan, Tom Bombadil is the symbol of fecundity, the very life-force itself.'[48] However, there is a distinct variation on the MacDonald story and other mythology which promotes a female deification of the life force, in Tolkien's portrayal of Goldberry and Tom Bombadil. For it is he as husband who is attributed with and imparts knowledge of the secrets of nature. Goldberry, following the ideal stereotype of submissive and retiring wife, withdraws from the room to sleep or busies herself with domestic chores when Bombadil is engaged in discourse with fellow males, the hobbits.[49]

Galadriel, in comparison, remains much more a goddess figure and is seen to have a very great deal of power and wisdom. The mythical and literary figures that her charac-terization derives from are described in detail in *J. R. R. Tolkien: The Shores of Middle-earth*.[50] Retaining elements of ancient fertility goddess (supplies seeds to promote growth of

193

vegetation in the new world), she appears to be a combination of Venus-Aphrodite and the Virgin Mary, whose role is emphasized in Catholic doctrine. She is linked, in the name of 'Llothlorien' with the lily which is the symbol of purity used particularly by Roman Catholics.[51] And indeed she appears to be the guiding force and inspiration rather than her husband, Celeborn. Having shown Frodo and Sam their fate in her mirror, when tested in turn by Frodo for possible desire to retain the Ring for personal aggrandizement, she shows herself to be a truly formidable power.[52] Above all, it is her gifts that enable Frodo and Sam to overcome the perils of Mordor and restore the lands ravaged by the evil of Sauron.

Her insight and wisdom seem to derive much from the wise and powerful ideal of the Catholic idolization of the Virgin Mary. However, Tolkien also places a strong emphasis on her physical beauty. 'Frodo ate and drank little, heeding only the beauty of the Lady and her voice.'[53]

Gimli, also overwhelmed by her beauty, requests only a strand of her hair[54] and, openly weeping as they depart, Galadriel's last words still resounding in their ears, declares: 'I have looked the last upon that which was fairest.' . . . 'Henceforward I will call nothing fair, unless it be her gift. . . .'[55] The idealization and romanticism of his portrait of Galadriel retains echoes of Tolkien's sentimental description of his wife,[56] though this romantic idealization did not make up for the fact that he tended to ignore his wife as an intellectual companion. And indeed the ancient, Norse and Christian mythologies in which he was immersed reinforced Tolkien's refusal (and that of countless generations) to accept the full and active participation of women in every area of life. For they present an idealized female deity who, though wise and inspirational, is still in many ways remote and passive:[57] still the lady on the pedestal who inspires the knight, the figurehead on the ship, the painted lady on the fuselage of fighter planes. As a deity she retains her beauty and does not age—a hard ideal for any real woman to live up to; and though she is the source of inspiration, it is the male heroes that play the active role in setting the world to right.

Tolkien's deep involvement with his male friends to the exclusion of women has strongly influenced the male and female portraits in *The Lord of the Rings*. His drawing upon mythology and courtly romance as major sources for his material has reinforced the prejudices in Tolkien's own ideas, because the prejudices are inherent in the conventions and symbolism of literary and religious tradition. Such tradition itself reveals deep-rooted contradictions which reflect conscious and subconscious conflicting attitudes to sexuality and the definition of the economic and political role of men and women in society.

NOTES

1. Humphrey Carpenter, *The Inklings: C. S. Lewis, J. R. R. Tolkien, Charles Williams and their Friends* (London: Allen & Unwin, 1978).
2. *The Inklings*, p. 164.
3. Ibid., p. 165.
4. Ibid., p. 169.
5. Ibid., p. 169.
6. Humphrey Carpenter, *J. R. R. Tolkien: A Biography* (London: Allen & Unwin, 1977), p. 156.
7. *The Inklings*, p. 32.
8. Ibid., p. 242.
9. The matter was interestingly raised by Godfrey Smith in the *Sunday Times* in December 1981 and he devoted several precious column inches to it. Former female students at Oxford wrote in and contributed personal anecdote and case history to account for what Godfrey Smith termed his 'unmannerly' and churlish treatment of female students. Other readers wrote in referring him to other evidence of Lewis's unorthodox sexuality. See below.
10. Quoted in *The Inklings*, op. cit., p. 167. The letters which passed between C. S. Lewis and his friend in Belfast, Arthur Greeves, provide evidence of sadism and involve the idea of inflicting pain upon the female. But others are clearly homosexual in interest and at times involve paederasty. See *They Stand Together: The Letters of C. S. Lewis to Arthur Greeves 1914–1963*, ed. Walter Hooper (London: Collins, 1979), pp. 159, 160, 165, 166, 170–71 and 188 and 174–214, 180 and 224. An item in *The Guardian* Diary ('Spankerama', 28 January 1982) on the sexual associations of whipping brought an interesting correspondence, including a letter from Jad Adams who wrote to point out that it was a fascinating reflection on the 'way our public school culture has permeated the world that the sexual perversion involving caning and spanking is referred to in New York sex parlours as "English"' (*The Guardian*, 1 February 1982). See Ian Gibson, *The English Vice: Beating, Sex and Shame in Victorian England and After*

J. R. R. Tolkien: This Far Land

(London: Duckworth, 1979), especially pp. 48 and following.

11. *The Inklings*, op. cit., pp. 22–3.
12. Ibid., p. 252.
13. Quoted in *The Inklings*, op. cit., p. 223.
14. Robert Giddings and Elizabeth Holland, *J. R. R. Tolkien: The Shores of Middle-earth* (London: Junction Books, 1981), p. 44.
15. J. R. R. Tolkien, *The Lord of the Rings* (London: Allen & Unwin, 1975), p. 786.
16. Ibid., p. 831.
17. Ibid., p. 876.
18. Humphrey Carpenter, *J. R. R. Tolkien: A Biography*, op. cit., p. 81.
19. *The Lord of the Rings*, op. cit., p. 83.
20. Ibid., p. 426.
21. Ibid., p. 437.
22. Ibid., p. 235.
23. Ibid., p. 241.
24. Ibid., p. 649.
25. Ibid., p. 678.
26. Ibid., p. 741.
27. Ibid., p. 944.
28. Giddings and Holland, op. cit., p. 118.
29. 'And Orcs, they were useful slaves, but he had them in plenty. If now and again Shelob caught them to stay her appetite, she was welcome: he could spare them. And sometimes as a man may cast a dainty to his cat (*his cat*, he calls her, but she owns him not) . . .' *The Lord of the Rings*, op. cit., p. 751.
30. Ibid., p. 755.
31. Ibid., p. 220.
32. Ibid., p. 745.
33. Ibid., p. 749.
34. Ibid., p. 748.
35. Ibid., p. 748.
36. Ibid., p. 752.
37. Ibid., p. 755.
38. ibid., p. 755.
39. Ibid., p. 756.
40. Ibid., p. 756.
41. Ibid., p. 757.
42. Giddings and Holland, op. cit., p. 89.
43. *The Lord of the Rings*, op. cit., p. 546.
44. Giddings and Holland, op. cit., p. 90. Aragorn's and Arwen's betrothal in fact seems somewhat superfluous and is attached as an appendix (1170). Tolkien is perhaps tidying up loose ends or, more likely, attempting to follow epic tradition. The hero, after performing his feats, marries, has children, and lives happily ever after—order is established through the continuity of the line. Throughout the rest of the book, however, there seems a reluctance on Tolkien's part to have Aragorn associated with the love of a woman in his role as saviour.

45. *The Lord of the Rings*, op. cit., p. 138.
46. Ibid., p. 144.
47. Giddings and Holland, op. cit., p. 39.
48. Ibid., p. 44.
49. *The Lord of the Rings*, op. cit., pp. 140 and 144.
50. Giddings and Holland, op. cit., p. 75.
51. Ibid., p. 75.
52. *The Lord of the Rings*, op. cit., p. 385.
53. Ibid., p. 393.
54. Ibid., p. 396.
55. Ibid., pp. 398–99.
56. Description of Edith dancing in the woods early in their marriage: 'Her hair was raven, her skin clear, her eyes bright, and she would sing and dance'—Humphrey Carpenter, *J. R. R. Tolkien—A Biography*, op. cit., p. 97.
57. Tolkien's reliance on myth to portray women characters with its two dimensional stereotyping itself reveals a lack of knowledge and wariness of women. Paradoxically a more human and less distant dimension of Galadriel is presented in the awe and embarrassment of many of Frodo's companions. Gimli's infatuation has been already noted; Sam also reveals puerile shyness when the Lady presents him with a gift, *The Lord of the Rings*, op. cit., p. 396: 'Sam went red to the ears and muttered something inaudible, as he clutched the box . . .'

Notes on Contributors

ALAN BOLD was born in 1943 in Edinburgh. He has published many books of poetry, including *To Find the New, The State of the Nation* and *This Fine Day* as well as a selection in *Penguin Modern Poets 15*. His *In This Corner: Selected Poems 1963–83* represents his best work over the past two decades. He has edited *The Penguin Book of Socialist Verse, The Martial Muse: Seven Centuries of War Poetry,* the *Cambridge Book of English Verse 1939–75, Making Love: The Picador Book of Erotic Verse, The Bawdy Beautiful: The Sphere Book of Improper Verse, Mounts of Venus: The Picador Book of Erotic Prose* and *Drink To Me Only: The Prose (and Cons) of Drinking.* He has also written critical books on *Thom Gunn and Ted Hughes, George Mackay Brown, The Ballad, Modern Scottish Literature* and *MacDiarmid: The Terrible Crystal.* He has exhibited his Illuminated Poems (pictures combining an original poetic manuscript with an illustrative composition) in venues as varied as Boston University and the National Library of Scotland.

ROBERT GIDDINGS was born in Worcester in 1935 and educated at the universities of Bristol and Keele. He was Lecturer in English and Communication Studies at the City of Bath Technical College 1964–82, and was Fulbright Exchange Professor, St. Louis, Missouri, from 1975–76, and Tutor, The Open University, 1971–81. He is now Senior Lecturer in English and Media Studies at Dorset Institute of Higher Education. His publications include *The Tradition of Smollett* (1967), *You Should See Me in Pyjamas* (1981) and (with Elizabeth Holland) *J. R. R. Tolkien: The Shores of Middle-earth.* He edited *The Changing World of Charles Dickens* in the Vision/Barnes and Noble Critical Studies Series, and has contributed to *Music and Musicians, New Statesman, Tribune, Sunday Times, Vancouver Sun, Music and Letters, New Society, Dickens Studies Newsletter,* and has written and broadcast for the B.B.C. and I.T.V.

FRED INGLIS was educated at the University of Cambridge and is now Reader in Education at the University of Bristol and shortly

199

J. R. R. Tolkien: This Far Land

Visiting Fellow at the Humanities Research Centre, Australian National University at Canberra. His various publications include *Images of Power, Imagination and Ideology*, *The Name of the Game: Sport and Industrial Society* and *The Promise of Happiness: Value and Meaning in Children's Fiction*.

DIANA WYNNE JONES writes books for children, mostly fantasy and usually funny. This was a thing she decided to do at the age of 8. She was put off for many years, because for twelve years after that she lived in a village full of things—like self-confessed witches and a man who went mad at full moon—that seemed too improbable to set down. So she read English at Oxford, married a medievalist, and lived in Oxford for nineteen years. Her three sons taught her to overcome her early disadvantages. Her first children's book was published in 1973, and she has had fifteen others published in various countries. In 1978 she won the *Guardian* Award for Children's Books. She now lives in Bristol.

ROGER KING was born in 1943, in Maidstone in Kent. He is a man of Kent rather than a Kentish man. He read English at King's College, Cambridge 1962–65 and his Ph.D. thesis, on Popular Fiction and Social Change, was supervised by Richard Hoggart and Stuart Hall. He has taught English and Sociology at the Polytechnic of the South Bank since 1968. He contributed *Drink and Drunkenness in 'Crossroads' and 'Coronation Street'* in the collection *Images of Alcohol* edited by J. Cooke and M. Lewinson, and has contributed to *Twentieth Century Views*. He is married with two children and lives in Lewisham. He is now writing a novel about hop-picking.

KENNETH MCLEISH was born in 1940. He writes reviews and criticism for journals as diverse as *The Listener*, *The Literary Review* and *Country Life*, and his voice is regularly heard on Radios 3 and 4. His television work includes *The Serpent Son* (a version, with Frederic Raphael, of Aeschylus' *Oresteia*), and he is the author or editor of several dozen books, including *The Theatre of Aristophanes* and (with Brian Redhead) *The Anti-Booklist*. His most recent books are *Children of the Gods* (the complete myths and legends of the ancient Greeks) and *The Penguin Guide to the Arts in the Twentieth Century* (due out in 1984). He is currently working on a collection of British folk-myths and legends.

JANET MENZIES works for *Kentish Times* newspapers and lives in Kent. She is a graduate of Cambridge University where she read

Notes on Contributors

Anglo-Saxon, Norse and Celtic, and English. While she was at Cambridge the *Journal of Beckett Studies* published her article 'Beckett's Bicycles'. After Cambridge, she joined the *Daily Telegraph*, where she worked on the book page reviewing. Her freelance writing has included articles for the *Evening Standard* on various aspects of London life.

NICK OTTY was born in Aberdeen in 1938. He went to Gordonstoun School and, after National Service in the Royal Medical Corps String Orchestra, he read English at Jesus College, Cambridge, where he first became really confused about the purposes of the English education system. This confusion was deepened by a year's teaching in a Swiss private school (where he first read *The Lord of the Rings* in 1962) and by a further two years in a London 'crammer'. It was not until his re-education was taken in hand by the pupils of a Bristol comprehensive school that the puzzlement began to lessen. His interest in structuralism followed from his attempts to penetrate the ideologies of education, and he gratefully acknowledges the help he has received from the works of Ivan Illych, Paolo Freire, Augusto Boal and Roland Barthes. He now teaches literature and drama on the B.A. Humanities course at Bristol Polytechnic, where he finds structuralist perspectives increasingly important to his work.

BRENDA PARTRIDGE was born in Amersham, Buckinghamshire, in 1952 and educated at Chesham Preparatory School, Dr. Challoners, and Aylesbury and Amersham Colleges of Further Education. She read English literature at the University of East Anglia, her main areas of interest being Shakespeare, fringe theatre, the Romantic poets (with emphasis on William Blake) and sexuality in literature. Having completed an Education course at the University of Bath, she now teaches English full-time at the City of Bath Technical College. Her main research interests are in the literature of feminism and the female role. So far her studies have been concerned with sexuality, female characterization and attitudes to women expressed in the works of male writers. In this sphere, as well as analysing Tolkien, she has also further researched the works of Milton, Hardy, Lawrence and Blake. Future studies will include feminism of literary genres and female writers.

DEREK ROBINSON is an author and broadcaster. His first novel, *Goshawk Squadron*, was shortlisted for the Booker Prize the year that V. S. Naipaul won it for regular attendance. *Goshawk* was a kind of anti-Biggles: it reversed the myth of chivalry in the Royal Flying

Corps and was predictably reviled by some (not all) survivors of that Corps. Other novels have played off the mythology of war; for example, *Kramer's War* described the delicate balance between co-operation and collaboration during the German occupation of Jersey. It has been sternly boycotted by the island's booksellers, a decision that most of them took before they read it. Robinson's latest novel, *Piece of Cake*, is about the Battle of Britain. It is due to be published in the autumn of 1983. He was educated at Cotham Grammar School, Bristol, and Downing College, Cambridge (the latter on public assistance), but learned to write in advertising agencies in London and New York. His pastimes are rugby, squash and trout-fishing, and he broadcasts on Radios 2, 3 and 4.

NIGEL WALMSLEY was born in London in 1949. He was a student at Leeds University from 1967 until 1970, during which time he spent a while in Prague in the aftermath of the Russian invasion. In 1970 and 1971 he travelled widely in the United States and Canada and worked in a Pittsburgh sewage pipe factory. On returning to England he spent a year at Southampton University. For the last ten years his home has been in Bristol where he lives with his wife and two children. Since 1975 he has taught English at Bath Technical College. He wrote articles for the first four editions of *The New Tolkien Newsletter*.

Index

Index

Index

Milne, A. A., 108, 117
Milton, John, 187–88, 191
Monty Python and the Holy Grail, 122
Moorcock, Michael, 9
Morris, William, 27, 35, 89, 90, 142
Mosley, Oswald, 133
Muir, Edwin, 182–83
Munro, H. H. (Saki): *When William Came*, 15, 131
Murray, Robert, 181

McDiarmid, Hugh, 139
MacDonald, George, 193

Nash, John and Paul, 33
Nepal, 78
New Delhi, 78
Nietzsche, Friedrich Wilhelm, 37
Nitzsche, Jane Chance, 148, 150

Old Testament, 116, 122
Orwell, George: *1984*, 118
O.U., 52, 53
Oxford, 11
Oxfordshire, 39, 91, 133

Pantagruel, 33
Panza, Sancha, 33
Pardoner's Tale, 87
Parker, Dorothy, 121
Perceval, 91
Peter the Painter, 15
Pound, Ezra, 138, 139, 152–53
Proust, Marcel, 134

Ransome, Arthur, 131
Reagan, Ronald, 18
Reed, Talbot Baines, 131
Reith, John, 33
Robbins Committee, 53
Rock music, 49ff., 53ff.
Rossini, Gioacchino Antonio, 20
Ruskin, John, 27
Russell, Bertrand, 16

Salcombe Regis, 31
Sartre, Jean Paul, 126
Sayers, Dorothy L., 131, 132
Schiller, Johann Christoph Friedrich von, 36
Scrutiny, 26ff.
Sesame, 53
Shakespeare, William: *Henry V*, 117; *King Lear*, 135

Shaw, George Bernard, 132
Sheffield, 162
Shetland Islands, 78
Shippey, T. A., 150
Sinclair Spectrum, 53
Skiddaw, 33
Smith, Adam, 34
Spanish Civil War, 133
Spark, Muriel, 124
Star Wars, 18, 32, 70
Steinbeck, John, 76
Stewart, J. I. M., 140
Sylvester, Victor, 33

Tennyson, Alfred Lord, 11, 28, 192
Thompson, Denys, 26–7
Thompson, E. P., 18, 40
Thompson, Francis, 142
Three Little Pigs, 47ff.
Time Magazine, 121
Times, The, 73
Tiptree Jam, 31
Tolkien, Christopher, 139
Tolkien, J. R. R.: *The Adventures of Tom Bombadil*, 143, 144ff., 149; *The Book of Lost Tales*, 139, 145ff.; *The Children of Hurin*, 146; *The Hobbit*, 42, 57ff., 126ff., 128ff., 149, 150; *The Homecoming of Beorhtnoth Beorhthelm's Son*, 138, 150ff.; *The Lay of Earendel*, 144; *The Lord of the Rings*, passim; *A Middle English Vocabulary*, 139; *On Fairy Stories*, 137ff.; *The Silmarillion*, 146ff.; *Tree and Leaf*, 42ff.
Tolstoy, Alexei Nikolayevich, 135
Tottenham Affair, 15
Toyah, 70

Verdi, Guiseppe, 37
Vietnam War, 82ff.
Villon, François, 33

Wagner, Richard, 33, 37, 124, 135
Wallace, Edgar, 131
Wanderer, The, 140
Watson, Colin: *Snobbery With Violence*, 131
Waugh, Evelyn, 19–20
Wells, H. G., 129ff., 132
Westerman, Percy F., 131
Wheatley, Dennis, 160
White, T. H., 108, 120
Whittington, Dick, 43
Wigan, 166
Wilde, Oscar, 122

205

Index